Lonely Planet

BEST BIKE RIDES

NEW ZEALAND

BEST DAY TRIPS ON TWO WHEELS

CRAIG MCLACHLAN, BRETT ATKINSON, ROSIE FEA,
RICHARD RYALL AND EILEEN SCHWAB

Contents

DOWNLOADABLE DIGITAL RIDE MAPS

Download GPX or KML files of the rides in this book so you can take the route with you on your ride.

*Cape
Reinga* *North
Cape*

*Bay of
Islands*

Kaitāia Kerikeri
  Russell
Opononi Kaikohe
Dargaville Whangārei

Wellsford *Aotea/
Great Barrier
Island*

*Kaipara
Harbour* *Hauraki
Gulf*
Helensville Coromandel Town
Auckland Whitianga
Pukekohe Thames

Tauranga *Bay of
Plenty* Hicks
Bay
Raglan Whakatāne Ruatoria
Hamilton Opōtiki Tokomaru Bay
Waitomo Rotorua Tolaga Bay
Caves Gisborne
Whanganui *Lake
Taupō* Taupō
New *National
Plymouth Park* *Tongariro
National Park* Wairoa
Opunake Stratford *Mt
Ruapehu* Napier *Hawke
Bay*
Hāwera Hastings
Whanganui Palmerston
North Dannevirke
Woodville

*Kahurangi
National
Park* Takaka *Golden
Bay* *Marlborough
Sounds*
Motueka Lower Upper
Karamea Richmond Nelson Picton Hutt Hutt
WELLINGTON
Westport Blenheim St Arnaud
Murchison *Cook
Strait* *Cape
Palliser*
Punakaiki Reefton
Greymouth Kaikōura
Hokitika Arthur's
Pass
Whataroa *Pegasus
Bay*
Mt Hutt Christchurch
*Aoraki/
Mt Cook* Methven Akaroa *Banks
Peninsula*
Haast *Lake
Tekapo* Ashburton
Jackson *Lake
Pukaki*
Bay/Okahu Temuka
*Milford
Sound* *Lake
Wanaka* Timaru
Glenorchy Wānaka Waimate
Cromwell Oamaru
Queenstown
*Lake
Te Anau* *Lake
Wakatipu* Alexandra
*Fiordland
National Park* Manapōuri Palmerston
*Lake
Manapōuri* Lumsden Dunedin *Otago
Peninsula*
Winton Gore Milton
Invercargill Balclutha
Bluff
Foveaux Strait *The
Catlins*

*Stewart
Island
(Rakiura)* Oban

*SOUTH
PACIFIC
OCEAN*

*TASMAN
SEA*

*SOUTH
PACIFIC
OCEAN*

N 0 ———— 200 km
  0 ———— 100 miles

Welcome to New Zealand

Aotearoa New Zealand is biking barking mad! Off-road bike trails crisscross this island nation, one of the most remote and pristine environments on the planet. There are 23 Great Rides, as well as Tour Aotearoa, a recognised 3000km bike-packing route the length of the country. During the pandemic, while those in other countries queued for daily necessities, in Aotearoa they lined up to buy imported e-bikes to explore their own backyard, while restricted from travelling overseas.

It's not all about biking massive distances, though. We've come up with a biking bucket list for the 'casual cyclist', the visitor who wants to hop on a rental bike and explore on two wheels for a day, or just a few hours. You don't have to be a hardcore cyclist to tackle these rides – just have a bit of enthusiasm to get out there and enjoy Aotearoa at your own pace.

Te Rewa Rewa Bridge (p71), New Plymouth

My Perfect Bike Ride

Craig McLachlan

AROUND FRANKTON ARM

P174

Hard to go past the Frankton Track & Kelvin Peninsula Trails (p000) ride in my hometown of Queenstown. Just down the road from home, it features stunning alpine scenery and reminds me of why I first moved here. The Remarkables, Lake Wakatipu, Queenstown Gardens, Frankton Beach, the Kawarau River and the Kelvin Peninsula Sculpture Trail all feature on this spectacular ride, while Altitude Brewery is perfectly positioned for a Mischievous Kea IPA on the ride home.

Brett Atkinson

HAURAKI RAIL TRAIL

P28

One of New Zealand's best day rides is also one of its most scenic. The Hauraki Rail Trail through the Karangahake Gorge is an easy day trip from Auckland, great cafes in Paeroa provide excellent pre-ride sustenance, and there's even a long tunnel emerging to views of the rocky canyons of the Ohinemuri River. Opportunities to add to the day's experience include an optional train ride and brilliant short walks exploring the region's gold-mining history.

UWE ARANAS/SHUTTERSTOCK ©

Skyline Gondola (p176), Queenstown

ROBERT LAU/GETTY IMAGES ©

Remutaka Rail Trail (p98)

Eileen Schwab

REMUTAKA RAIL TRAIL

P98

The Remutaka Cycle Trail is my go-to escape. I love to kick it off with a ferry from the city across Wellington Harbour, then connect to the mellow Hutt River Trail, the Remutaka Rail Trail through the forested hills and tunnels, quiet backcountry roads, and the coastal track. The wild coastline is perfect for a night under the stars – ruggedly beautiful, it feels far more remote than you might expect so close to the capital.

Rosie Fea

AROUND FRANKTON ARM

P174

Growing up on the Kelvin Peninsula means this trail holds sentimental value for me, as well as being a fantastic path to peddle and plod along by foot. Almost every corner and vantage point brings up some kind of memory, and the familiar neighbourly hellos of repeat offenders on the track over the years make it feel like an extension of home. It's the first stop on my 'proud-local' list for friends to experience when they come to town.

Richard Ryall

AORAKI/ MT COOK EXPLORER

P142

Having been a guide for bike tours on the Alps to Ocean Cycle Trail from Aoraki Mt Cook to the ocean at Oamaru for several years, shadowing and supporting my clients, I can't help but choose this as a top ride. The smiling faces of the clients at the end of each challenging day tells a story of the sheer variety of the scenery you pass through on this incredible journey that is "mostly" downhill.

Our Picks

BEST CITY ROUTES

Aotearoa New Zealand's population sits at 5.1 million, with about a third of Kiwis living in urban Auckland. The country is bigger in area than the UK, but with only around one-fourteenth the population. Our picks here are urban escapes, as Kiwis know them. Even from downtown Auckland, you can hop on your bike and be relaxing on a stunning city beach only 15 minutes later.

TOP TIP

Make sure to keep to the left on urban trails, especially if you're not the only rider out there.

KIRA VOLKOV/SHUTTERSTOCK ©

Tāmaki Drive, Auckland

Cruise the harbourside bays, stopping at beaches and cafes along the way.

P24

Otago Harbour Loop, Dunedin

Bike the paved cycle trail around Otago Harbour and ride the Port to Port ferry.

P204

Christchurch to the Beach

Cycle friendly paths from the central city to the sea and surf.

P138

Hutt River Trail

Connect coastal cafes, urban parks and riverside markets from this riverside trail.

P88

New Plymouth Coastal Trail

Like one big sprawling art installation, with nature at its best.

P70

SKYIMAGES/GETTY IMAGES ©

Left: New Plymouth Coastal Trail (p70)

Right: Spencer Park Beach, Christchurch (p138)

TOP TIP

Ask for a lock with your rental bike so you can drop into a cafe or museum along the way.

TOP TIP

There's quirky outdoor art all over Aotearoa, so treat each urban ride like a little treasure hunt.

TOP TIP

Don't forget your swimming gear and a towel when riding around the coast, especially up north.

TOP TIP

Pack a picnic lunch, but watch out for thieving seabirds who have seen it all before.

Our Picks

BEST SEASIDE RIDES

TOP TIP
Seals, sea lions and other marine life can be spotted in some unusual places around the coast.

One of the last places on earth to be reached by humans, Aotearoa is an underpopulated set of remote islands in the South Pacific. It stands to reason that there's going to be some magnificent coastal scenery – quite how magnificent is difficult to overstate. This is a place that has to be seen to be believed, so get on your bike and check out the beaches and rugged coastlines.

Kaikōura Trail
Coastal riding north and south of Kaikōura township in the shadow of the mountains.

P156

Pencarrow Coast Road
Rugged coastline overlooking Cook Strait; visit lakes, beaches and lighthouses.

P84

Kaikōura Trail (p156)

Mistletoe Bay to Anakiwa
Gorgeous Marlborough Sounds views on the renowned Queen Charlotte Track.

P124

Greymouth to Kumara
The wild West Coast with driftwood-strewn seascapes and pounding surf at your side.

P150

Nelson to Māpua
Swim at white-sand beaches and ride the cycle ferry from Rabbit Island to Māpua.

P116

Nelson to Māpua (p116), part of the Great Taste Trail

Our Picks

BEST RIDES FOR MOUNTAIN SCENERY

These remote islands are where the Pacific and Australian tectonic plates collide, producing a 600km string of high mountains along the spine of the South Island and active volcanoes on and off the coast of the North Island. There's not a lot of flat land out there. While you won't be climbing mountains on these rides, they run through valleys, around lakes and alongside rivers, and alpine views abound.

TOP TIP

Check the weather forecast before you go, as mountain weather can be particularly erratic.

TDWAY/SHUTTERSTOCK ©

 Wānaka Loop Trail

Enjoy the lake, mountains and Clutha River from Wānaka.

P190

 Around Frankton Arm

Explore Queenstown and the Frankton arm of Lake Whakatipu.

P174

 Aoraki/Mt Cook Explore

Glorious ice-blue glaciers groaning and tumbling down from the high peaks.

P142

 Te Anau Lake2Lake

Links Lake Te Anau and Lake Manapōuri below the peaks of Fiordland.

P210

 Remutaka Rail Trail

Some climbing is involved, but it rewards with views over the forested hills.

P98

JANICE CHEN/SHUTTERSTOCK ©

Left: Wānaka Loop Trail (p190)

Right: Lake Pukaki, Aoraki/Mt Cook Explorer (p142)

TOP TIP

Keep your eyes on the trail, even if surrounding mountain views are totally mesmerising!

TOP TIP

It can snow even in midsummer in the mountains of the South Island, especially if a cold southerly is blowing.

Our Picks

BEST RIVERSIDE RIDES

Did we mention the rivers? There are gorgeous rivers, and many in the South Island are a spectacular turquoise colour due to being fed by snow- and glacial-melt water. Abundant mountains usually means abundant rainfall and plenty of lakes, and there are some amazing off-road bike trails that have been constructed alongside the myriad of rivers flowing out to Aotearoa's various coasts.

TOP TIP

Autumn produces magnificent golden colours on many riverside rides as the willow trees love growing near water.

Hauraki Rail Trail

A shaded trail and a thrilling tunnel in the heart of Coromandel's gold-mining country.

P28

Arrow River & Gibbston Wineries

Lots of bridges and wineries on this ride from Arrowtown.

P184

Havelock North to Clifton

Follow the Tukituki River overlooking orchards and vineyards.

P104

Clyde Rail & River Loop

Railway history and Clutha River trails from 'old town' Clyde.

P200

Aratiatia Loop in Taupō

Feel the mighty thrum of Huka Falls and Aratiatia Rapids from up close.

P66

NICKICHEN/SHUTTERSTOCK ©

Hauraki Rail Trail (p28)

Our Picks

BEST OFF-THE-BEATEN-TRACK RIDES

It may be hard to believe, but there are beaten paths in Aotearoa, though it's not really that hard to get off them. A number of off-road bike trails have been constructed here that make previously inaccessible spots reachable on two wheels. Some of these rides may feel like ventures of exploration where, depending on the season, you may not meet another rider for much of the day.

TOP TIP

Take what you'll need in terms of food and refreshments, because there may not be much out there.

 1

Twin Coast Cycle Trail (Kaikohe to Horeke)

Explore forests, switchbacks and rural riverbanks.

P46

2

Walter Peak Explorer

A mini-adventure on the far side of Lake Whakatipu from Queenstown.

P180

Great Lake Trail (p74)

GUAXININ/SHUTTERSTOCK ©

 3

Omarama to Benmore Dam

A rugged remote gorge through backcountry revealed by a new trail.

P162

 4

Great Lake Trail

Take in the volcanoes of Tongariro National Park over the waters of Lake Taupō.

P74

 5

Water Ride

Explore the backblocks of Napier, winding through wetlands with a spot of bird-watching.

P94

When to Go

The warmer months of October to April are the best for biking, especially in the South Island.

September to November is spring and Aotearoa will be warming up. Newborn lambs will be frolicking on the farms, but a cold southerly can still produce snow, particularly in the south. Summer officially kicks off in December and along with January, Kiwi kids are off school and families are travelling the country. February is a good time to hit the road as summer weather is settled and most Kiwis are back working and studying. March and April see temperatures start to cool off, producing amazing autumn colours, especially in the south. May and June are cold, and while winter-sports enthusiasts love the snow season, most cyclists will be preparing their bikes for spring.

Sheep, Lake Wānaka (p190)

Weather Watch (Auckland)

JANUARY	FEBRUARY	MARCH	APRIL	MAY	JUNE
Avg daytime max: **24°C** Days of rainfall: **6**	Avg daytime max: **24°C** Days of rainfall: **6**	Avg daytime max: **23°C** Days of rainfall: **6**	Average daytime max: **20°C**. Days of rainfall: **8**	Avg daytime max: **18°C** Days of rainfall: **12**	Avg daytime max: **15°C** Days of rainfall: **12**

Greymouth (p150)

Accommodation

Book ahead, particularly in the NZ summer school-holiday period of December and January, when prices are at a premium. Shoulder seasons in spring and autumn may produce some bargains, but book early to get these.

COLDER IN THE SOUTH

Temperatures are generally cooler the further south you go. If there's a southerly blowing, wrap up tight, as winds from the Antarctic and southern seas can produce snow, especially at altitude, at any time of the year. The north has much milder winters.

UNPREDICTABLE WEATHER

Crowded House put it best when they sang 'Four Seasons in One Day'. Aotearoa is a couple of narrow islands in a big sea with a maritime climate, so its weather is highly unpredictable, occasionally extreme and can change in the blink of an eye.

BIG EVENTS FOR EVERYONE

Pasifika Festival This is the one not to be missed in Auckland if you love Pacific culture. Food, music, dance and crafts highlight the vibrancy of Pacific Island peoples. **March**

Te Matatini This is the pinnacle event for Māori performing arts. It's held once every two years in a different city around Aotearoa, drawing thousands of visitors. Everyone is welcome. **February**

Lake Taupō Cycle Challenge Join thousands of others pedalling around Aotearoa New Zealand's largest lake. Choose your event and get on your bike. **November**

Wānaka A&P Show The agricultural and pastoral shows down near the lake in Wānaka have been running for more than 80 years. From sheep-shearing and wood-chopping to attractive farm animals – there's lots of family fun. **March**

JULY	AUGUST	SEPTEMBER	OCTOBER	NOVEMBER	DECEMBER
Avg daytime max: **14°C** Days of rainfall: **15**	Avg daytime max: **15°C** Days of rainfall: **12**	Avg daytime max: **16°C**. Days of rainfall: **10**	Avg daytime max: **18°C** Days of rainfall: **10**	Avg daytime max: **20°C** Days of rainfall: **7**	Avg daytime max: **22°C** Days of rainfall: **8**

Get Prepared for New Zealand

Useful things to load in your bag, your ears and your brain

Get Ready for Your Day Ride

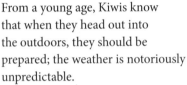

From a young age, Kiwis know that when they head out into the outdoors, they should be prepared; the weather is notoriously unpredictable.

Cycle helmet Compulsory in Aotearoa; usually included in your bike hire.

Comfortable backpack Nothing bigger than a daypack.

Food & snacks Take more than enough, especially if you don't know what's available where you're going.

Water Always set out with sufficient liquids.

Sensible cycling clothes
Have several layers suitable to the conditions.

Rainwear Be prepared, even if the weather forecast predicts fine weather.

Suitable shoes Keep in mind that you may not always be pedalling on your bike.

Cycling gloves Recommended, especially for longer rides.

Sunscreen, sunglasses & sunhat Essential, as Aotearoa's sun is strong. A cap under your bike helmet is a good option.

Mobile phone A fully charged phone is highly recommended, even if coverage is spotty.

Spares & tools Especially if heading somewhere remote and inaccessible, with poor mobile-phone coverage.

First-aid kit A good move if you're heading into rough or remote areas.

Map or navigational aids Be prepared; do your homework before you go and take a map.

Torch, headlamp or bike lights If there are tunnels on your ride or you may be out late.

WATCH

Boy
(*Taika Waititi; 2010*) The Kiwi sense of humour is on full display; written and directed by Taika Waititi.

Once Were Warriors
(*Lee Tamahori; 1994*) Acclaimed adaption of Alan Duff's novel about a struggling urban Māori family.

Whale Rider
(*Niki Caro; 2002*) Brilliant film of Witi Ihimaera's novel about a Māori girl who wants to become chief of her tribe.

Flight of the Conchords
(*HBO; 2007–09*) Hilarious comedy following a Kiwi two-man band surviving in New York.

Mountain-biking, Queenstown

LISTEN

Loyal
(Dave Dobbyn; 1988)
Along with 'Bliss' and
'Welcome Home',
Dobbyn sings the
ultimate Kiwi nostalgic
classics.

**Based on a True
Story**
(Fat Freddy's Drop;
2005) Seven-piece
Wellington band
renowned for its live
performances.

Polysaturated
(Nesian Mystik; 2002)
Award-winning Kiwi
hip-hop/R&B group
with Māori and
Polynesian influences.

Beautiful Collision
(Bic Runga; 2002)
Stunning album by
esteemed and much-
loved Kiwi singer/
songwriter.

Riding Safely

Stick to your limits Ride the right trail for your ability.

Do your homework Research your ride so you know what to expect and that you have sufficient fitness and experience.

Take the right gear Make sure you, your bike and your other gear is up to the specific ride you head out on.

Check the weather forecast

Carry more than sufficient gear for the likely conditions; be prepared to stop if the weather goes bad.

Check track conditions Get advice from the rental outlet before heading out.

Be seen Wear high-vis or brightly coloured clothing.

Time your ride Give yourself plenty of time to be back by dark or when the bike-rental shop closes.

Take care of everyone in your group Not everyone has the same level of fitness and ability. Don't push kids too hard.

Be aware Watch and listen for other bikers, walkers and runners on shared-use trails.

Ride predictably Keep to the left, ride in a straight line and signal your intentions clearly and early.

Cycle safely Ride to the conditions and follow the road rules.

READ

The Bone People
(Keri Hulme; 1985) The
first Kiwi novel and first
debut novel to win the
esteemed Booker Prize
for fiction.

The Luminaries
(Eleanor Catton; 2013)
Second Kiwi winner
of the Booker Prize,
Catton's novel is set on
the wild West Coast
of 1866.

**Bulibasha: King of
the Gypsies**
(Witi Ihimaera; 1994) A
wonderful insight into
small-town Māori life
on the East Coast.

CHAMELEONSEYE/SHUTTERSTOCK ©

Okahu Bay, Auckland

Auckland & the North

Explore

Auckland & the North

Providing evidence that the top of the North Island deserves recognition as a biking destination alongside other more renowned parts of New Zealand, this region combining Northland, Auckland, Hauraki and Waikato includes a journey along the country's longest river, and the two-day overnight adventure of crossing all the way from the east coast to the west coast. History, Māori culture and river scenery all combine on these two-wheeled experiences, while Auckland's coastal and cosmopolitan vibe can be discovered on an easy ride along Tāmaki Drive, or on a (slightly) more challenging exploration of the vineyards, restaurants and beaches of Waiheke Island.

Paihia

One of New Zealand's most popular resort towns, Paihia is the traveller-friendly hub for exploring the Bay of Islands. Shopping – including supermarkets – and hotel and motel accommodation is gathered around Marsden Rd, and good bars and restaurants combine with boat-trip departures along Paihia's wharf. Passenger ferries also cross the harbour to Russell, New Zealand's first capital from 1840 to 1841, and now a sleepy seaside village featuring British and French colonial history. At nearby Waitangi, New Zealand's founding document is showcased at the Waitangi Treaty Grounds, and there's more two-wheeled action at the Waitangi Mountain Bike Park.

Auckland

Built on a narrow isthmus framed by two harbours, Auckland is New Zealand's biggest and most cosmopolitan city, and also the country's economic and commercial capital. Beyond exploring Tāmaki Drive and the waterfront, catch a ferry to Waiheke Island for wine-tasting and vineyard dining, admire urban views from atop Auckland's famed volcanic cones, or venture to the rugged west coast for clifftop walking and rugged surf beaches. Recommended areas to stay in include downtown for access to Tāmaki Drive and the Ferry Building, and the heritage inner-city suburbs of Ponsonby and Mt Eden, both packed with good B&Bs, cafes and restaurants.

WHEN TO GO

All these rides can be ridden year-round, with New Zealand's spring and summer being the best times to experience them (from October to April). Rain can occur year-round too, so be prepared with good wet-weather clothing if needed. Accommodation in the Bay of Islands is in high demand across Christmas, New Year and Easter, and also during school holidays.

Hamilton

Located inland away from the spectacle and excitement of the coast, New Zealand's fourth-largest city sometimes gets a hard time from the rest of the country, but a decent-sized population of 180,000 and a university means it's a well-equipped and vibrant urban centre. Centrally located supermarkets near the CBD include Pak 'n Save and Countdown, and accommodation along Victoria St is recommended if you're overnighting on a two-day journey down the Te Awa River Ride. Check out Hood St for Hamilton's most exciting nightlife, and cross the river to the Hamilton East precinct for good cafes and a global selection of restaurants.

Paeroa

Beyond its history in producing Lemon & Paeroa, one of New Zealand's most popular effervescent drinks, Paeroa is now a popular stop for road trippers exploring the town's antique and vintage-clothing shops. Countdown supermarket is a good spot for pre-ride drinks and snacks, while a diverse range of eating establishments from sushi to Thai and Indian flavours mean travellers won't go hungry. For excellent accommodation, stay at one of the Refinery's cottages. The Paeroa Maritime Museum, 2km north of town, includes details of Captain James Cook's explorations of the nearby Waihou River in 1769. River cruises are also available.

TRANSPORT

Travelling independently around New Zealand, either in a rental car or a campervan, is most convenient. From the country's main international hub of Auckland, InterCity operate buses to Hamilton, and also to Paihia in the Bay of Islands. Both Waihi and Paeroa are stops on InterCity services linking Auckland to Tauranga. Local shuttle operators can provide transport to/from trailheads.

 WHERE TO STAY

Paihia in the Bay of Islands is packed with good motels, with Admiral's View Lodge combining excellent views and secure bike storage. Heritage accommodation popular with Twin Coast Cycle Trail riders includes the Left Bank in Kaikohe and Horeke's Riverhead Villa.

In Auckland, the centrally located Hotel Britomart showcases savvy design features focused on sustainability; it's close to the city's waterfront and Ferry Building.

Located in the Karangahake Gorge near Waihi, Falls Retreat has comfortable cottages and an excellent on-site restaurant. For a relaxing stay after completing the Te Awa trail, overnight at Lake Karapiro's Conach House B&B.

 WHAT'S ON

Auckland Anniversary Weekend

(regatta.org.nz) The last weekend in January features the yachts and boats of the Anniversary Regatta, best observed from Tāmaki Drive and Bastion Point.

Pasifika

(aucklandnz.com/pasifika) Held in March, this annual festival celebrates the food, music and culture of Auckland's Pacific Island communities.

Hamilton Arts Festival

(hamiltonartsfestival.co.nz) Ten days from late February to early March featuring music, art and culture. Many events are held in the Hamilton Gardens.

Resources

Twin Coast Cycle Trail (*twincoastcycletrail.kiwi.nz*) Maps, bike hire and information.

Northland Inc (*northlandnz. com*) Regional tourism website.

Auckland Tāmaki Makaurau (*aucklandnz.com*) Auckland's official tourism website.

Te Awa River Ride (*te-awa. org.nz*) Maps, trail descriptions and local operators.

Hamilton & Waikato (*wai katonz.com*) Official tourism information.

01

Tāmaki Drive

DURATION	DIFFICULTY	DISTANCE	START/END
1–2hr	Easy	11km	Wynyard Quarter/St Heliers

TERRAIN	Paved cycle paths

©EMAGNETIC/SHUTTERSTOCK

Mission Bay

One of Auckland's most leisurely bike rides is also one of its most spectacular. Beginning in the revitalised harbourside precinct of the Wynyard Quarter, this easygoing coastal adventure hops between the city's most popular urban beaches. It's paved all the way, all sections are safely separated from traffic, and en route there are views across the harbour to the islands of the Hauraki Gulf and a few of the volcanic cones characterising Auckland's unique cityscape. Don't bother packing any on-the-road snacks, because excellent coffee, beer and ice cream are all on offer along the way.

Bike Hire

Rent a Lime e-bike in the Wynyard Quarter and catch the TāmakiLink bus back from St Heliers. E-bikes for a return 22km journey can be hired from Power to the Pedal.

Starting Point

Catch a bus to downtown Auckland's Britomart Transport Centre and walk 1km via Viaduct Harbour to the Wynyard Quarter. The convenient CityLink bus stops in the Wynyard Quarter.

01 Developed for the 2011 Rugby World Cup, the Wynyard Quarter is a harbourfront precinct with good bars, cafes and restaurants. There's an excellent children's playground, and throughout summer, the nearby Silo Park area hosts family-friendly outdoor movies. Fishing boats and visiting superyachts sometimes jostle for wharf space, and views from Te Karanga Plaza include the soaring 328m profile of Auckland's Sky Tower.

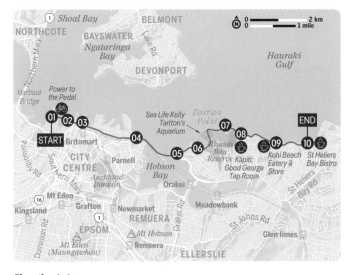

Elevation (m)

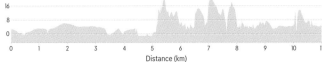

Sea Life Kelly Tarlton's Aquarium

New Zealanders are an innovative bunch, and concealed beneath Tāmaki Drive is a very surprising aquarium. Repurposing parts of Auckland's stormwater drainage system, Kelly Tarlton's – named after the late Kiwi entrepreneur whose vision it was to reuse the subterranean network – is best explored while travelling on a moving walkway through transparent tunnels. Turtles, stingrays and schools of fish all swim over and around visitors to the aquarium, while other exciting and fascinating activities include snorkelling with sharks and checking out sub-Antarctic king and gentoo penguins. Plenty of interactive exhibits are perfect for younger travellers.

02 From the Wynyard Quarter, cross the pedestrian- and bike-friendly Te Wero Bridge. You may need to wait a few minutes if it's being raised to let boats in and out of Viaduct Harbour. Passing under the *waharoa*, a traditional Māori carved entranceway, look for the bold ocean-themed murals on the exterior walls of the New Zealand Maritime Museum. Boat trips exploring the harbour leave from the museum.

03 Outside the museum is the leviathan *KZ1*, an America's Cup yacht raced by New Zealand in the 1988 regatta. On the right, Viaduct Harbour is another area with good bars and restaurants. Continue on a dedicated bike path to Auckland's historic Ferry Building. Passenger ferries depart from here to Devonport and to Waiheke and other islands in the Hauraki Gulf. Maybe grab an ice cream at Island Gelato.

04 On the left, you'll often see visiting cruise ships during summer, and Spark Arena on the right hosts big concerts from international performers. Views north across the harbour include the extinct volcanic ones of Maungauika/North Head and Takarunga/Mt Victoria, while the Parnell Baths sit inland on the edge of Judge's Bay. A pedestrian overbridge crosses the road and railway line to the popular summer destination.

05 Carry on along the bike path to the Ngapipi Estuary Bridge. Just past the bridge is a good place to stop for photos of Rangitoto, the 700-year-old volcanic island rising from Auckland's Hauraki Gulf. A railway causeway crosses Hobson Bay and the Ōrākei Basin, while historic boat sheds line the edge of the bay. During summer, pōhutukawa trees are enlivened with crimson blooms.

06 Just before Okahu Bay, Ferg's Kayaks offer kayak rental, and on summer weekends you might see paddleboarders negotiating the compact cove. Note the bike path becomes a shared space around Okahu Bay – watch out for pedestrians – and weekends are busier along this stretch of Tāmaki Drive. Okahu Bay is a good swimming beach and there are barbecues for public use.

07 After Okahu Bay, the shared pathway widens considerably and continues around Bastion Point to Mission Bay. At the northern end of Okahu Bay, Sea Life Kelly Tarlton's is a unique underground aquarium built in former stormwater drains. Look for WWII-era defensive fortifications in the cliffs just after the inland road uphill to Bastion Point. Right before Mission Bay, the historic Tamaki Yacht Club is a popular events venue.

08 Featuring a waterfront esplanade, grassy lawns and an art-deco fountain, Mission Bay is Tāmaki Drive's most popular beach. A dedicated bike path is reintroduced at Mission Bay, but you'll probably be sharing it with rollerbladers and e-scooters. Built in 1859, the historic Melanesian Mission now houses Azabu, an excellent Japanese-Peruvian restaurant, and Mission Bay Watersports offer kayak and paddleboard rental and lessons throughout summer.

09 After Mission Bay comes the shallow arc of Kohimarama, offering more shade than other Tāmaki Drive beaches, and another good spot for a swim. A wooden waterfront boardwalk reduces pedestrian numbers on the shared bike path, and island profiles on the near horizon include Rangitoto, Motukorea (Browns Island) and Motuihe. There are a few eating options near the intersection of Tāmaki Drive and Averill Ave.

10 Lined with towering palms, St Heliers is Tāmaki Drive's second-most-popular beach after Mission Bay. There's a good range of cafes and restaurants, and also an excellent kid's playground at the eastern end of the beach. From St Heliers, the TāmakiLink bus runs frequently back to downtown's Britomart Transport Centre. To explore further, Cliff Rd continues for 800m uphill for excellent harbour views from Achilles Point.

☕ Take a Break

From Mexican, Thai or Japanese cuisine through to fish and chips, Mission Bay has a wide range of cafes and restaurants. Refuel with an ice cream from Kāpiti or kick back with a craft beer or cider on the deck at the Good George Tap Room. There's also a smaller dining enclave around Kohimarama. The Kohi Beach Eatery & Store is recommended for brunch and coffee. Celebrate completing the ride with lunch or an early dinner at the St Heliers Bay Bistro.

STEVE TODD/SHUTTERSTOCK ©

Auckland skyline, Bastion Point

Bastion Point

Between Kelly Tarlton's and the Tamaki Yacht Club, detour 500m uphill for elevated views of Rangitoto Island and the Waitematā Harbour. Amid manicured lawns, Bastion Point's clifftop mausoleum honours Michael Joseph Savage (1872–1940), New Zealand's first Labour prime minister, and the architect of popular left-wing social-welfare reforms following the Great Depression. More recently, Bastion Point was the location of an extended land occupation by Ngāti Whātua Ōrākei, the local Māori hapū. Ending after 506 days in May 1978, it's regarded as a seminal moment in the discussion and subsequent recognition of land injustices in New Zealand.

02

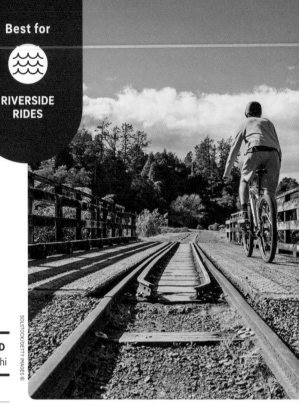

SOLSTOCK/GETTY IMAGES ©

Hauraki Rail Trail

DURATION	DIFFICULTY	DISTANCE	START/END
2-3hr	Easy	24km	Paeroa/Waihi
TERRAIN		Gravel pathway	

Hauraki Rail Trail, near Karangahake

Very popular with riders heading south from the Big Smoke of Auckland, the Hauraki Rail Trail is one of New Zealand's most accessible bike rides. A total of five sections make up the full trail, but the most scenic and most popular route is the spur heading east from Paeroa through the Karangahake Gorge to Waihi. Sublime river scenery, a historic tunnel, and attractions en route including canyon walking trails and an optional railway journey make it a firm favourite of Kiwi families. Visit outside the school holidays for the best experience on this fun and very achievable trail.

Bike Hire

Based in Paeroa, Hauraki Bike Hire can arrange mountain bikes, e-bikes and shuttle transfers. Similar services are offered by Waihi Bicycle Hire in Waihi and Thames-based JollyBikes.

Starting Point

Begin this section at Hauraki Bike Hire's Wharf Rd location in Paeroa. It's a short ride to join the trail as it travels south through town from Thames.

01 From Wharf Rd in Paeroa, make the short ride uphill to join the trail as it begins its initial shadowing of the meandering Ohinemuri River. This part of the trail is elevated and you'll have excellent views of the shaded banks of the river on your right, and vistas of Paeroa's heritage shopfronts on your left. If you're keen to explore Paeroa's reputation for good vintage and retro clothes shopping before setting off, check out Second Thoughts and Upstairs Treasure in the Theatre.

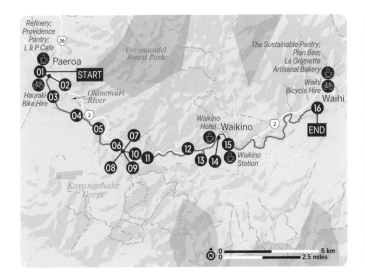

TOP TIP:

Close to Auckland, Hamilton and Tauranga, this section of the Hauraki Rail Trail gets busy during summer, and on holiday weekends including Easter and Auckland's Anniversary weekend in late January. Try and visit on a weekday.

Elevation (m)

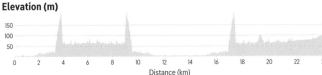

Hauraki Rail Trail

Paeroa to Waikino and Waihi through the Karangahake Gorge is the most popular section of the Hauraki Rail Trail, but four other routes also make up the trail's total length of 160km. Popular sections include Thames to Paeroa (34km), starting amid Thames' heritage gold-mining-era streetscape and including a stop at the Matatoki Cheese Barn, and the 53km stretch along the southern edge of the Firth of Thames from Kaiaua to Thames. This section includes the Pūkorokoro Miranda Shorebird Centre where migratory birds – some travelling from as as far as Siberia – can be observed from special viewing hides.

02 Approaching Paeroa's McDonald's, divert left from the trail – just before the burger restaurant's lane for drive-in orders – and follow the grassy path underneath the road bridge. This leads to the back of a park framing Paeroa's Giant L & P bottle, and ensures you avoid crossing a busy road. An essential selfie before departing Paeroa is with the towering brown bottle, a classic slice of Kiwiana referencing Lemon & Paeroa, a popular New Zealand soft drink (soda) first made with mineral water from the town's natural springs in 1907. Now the (very) refreshing drink is made in Auckland by multinational Coca-Cola, but it's still an essential part of Paeroa's heritage.

03 Leaving the Giant L & P bottle, return under the bridge and cross the river on the pedestrian lane of the right-hand side of the bridge. Continue along Te Aroha Rd for 250m before turning left onto Rotokohu Rd to begin this section of the Hauraki Trail through the Karangahake Gorge to Waihi. Note: if you chose to stay on Te Aroha Rd and not divert east through the gorge to Waihi, you'd be on another of the trail's five sections, which travels south through lush farmland for 23km to Te Aroha.

04 Keep riding alongside Rotokohu Rd. Bucolic rural views include the rustic A-frame outline of St John's Tamatera Anglican church, originally consecrated in 1932,

☕ Take a Break

In Paeroa, seek out the Refinery for coffee and gourmet sandwiches. Don't forget to check out the retro 1970s furniture and play some vintage vinyl on the stereo. Paeroa's best pies are baked daily at Providence Pantry. Flavours include chicken and bacon. At the L & P Cafe there's a whole menu infused with Paeroa's fizzy famous export. Try the crunchy onion rings with L & P batter. On the ride, refuel at the Waikino Hotel or the cafe at Waikino Station.

and now only used on special occasions. After travelling for 1.7km beside Rotokohu Rd, the trail diverts left along Te Moananui Flats Rd. On this section, you'll need to negotiate a few stock gates on the dairy farm that the trail runs through. Views include a brace of dilapidated farm buildings, and forested hills hinting at the more rugged scenery that's to come.

05 From the Te Moananui Flats, the trail again starts to run near the southern banks of the Ohinemuri River. Highlights include a lovely forest glade, guaranteed to provide cooling shade, and a simple bridge for both walkers and cyclists. Completing this journey in a reverse direction – heading north from Waihi to Paeroa – is also popular, so you may see some oncoming traffic.

06 Continuing alongside the river, the trail passes the compact riverside settlement of Karangahake to the left. Look across the river to see the State Hwy 2 (SH2) meandering through the Karangahake Gorge. It's one of the most scenic drives on New Zealand's North Island.

07 Just after the houses, a combination road, bike and pedestrian bridge crosses the river. This bike and pedestrian section of the trail then leads to the entrance of an historic 1.1km-long tunnel.

08 Before entering the tunnel, consider an optional detour from the Hauraki Rail Trail. Halfway across the bridge, a sign indicates various walking trails exploring this section of the gorge. Rich in gold-mining history, the Windows Walk takes in suspension bridges, valley and canyon views, and a cliff-face railway tunnel formerly used to transport ore. A torch (flashlight) is recommended for negotiating the tunnel. Bordering the Waitawheta River, the Windows Walk is accessed by the Karangahake Gorge Historic Walkway. A second bridge on the walkway crosses to the northern side of the Ohinemuri River, and a couple of eating options are located across the road on the northern side of SH2. Take care crossing the road.

09 If you're exploring this part of the gorge as a detour from the Hauraki Rail Trail, you'll need to negotiate a few stairways with your bike. Note you're not able to take your bike on either the Windows Walk (one hour) or the equally popular 45-minute Karangahake Loop Walk. Leave your bike at the main Karangahake car park while you complete these walks.

MICHAEL YOUNG/GETTY IMAGES ©

Karangahake Gorge

10 Back on the Hauraki Rail Trail, continue at the end of the road, bike and pedestrian bridge to enter the 1.1km-long tunnel. There are a few overhead halogen lights to illuminate the way ahead, but the considerable distance to the light at the end of the tunnel is deceptive. Keep to the left of the tunnel, and if you don't have a light on your bike it's recommended you walk your bike. Expect a few drops of water to slowly drip, drip, drip from the roof as you negotiate the tunnel, first opened in 1905 and still in use up to 1978.

11 Exiting the tunnel, the dual-purpose trail – now incorporating both the Hauraki Rail Trail and the Karangahake Gorge Historic Walkway – crosses another short bridge to follow the southern side of the Ohinemuri River. Stop for a moment as you exit the tunnel for excellent views of the road traffic

Waihi's Gold-Mining Heritage

Gold was first discovered around Waihi in 1878, and until 1911 the town's Martha Mine was one of the world's most important gold mines. Ore from more than 170km of tunnels was transported by train to the Victoria Battery in Waikino. Other mining batteries were in the hills and valleys fringing the nearby Karangahake Gorge. Explore Waihi's gold-flecked history at the town's Gold Discovery Centre. Look forward to plenty of interactive wizardry – including holograms – and book ahead online (golddiscoverycentre.co.nz) for Waihi Gold Mine Tours. Fascinating tours include a peek into central Waihi's massive open-pit Martha Mine.

TOMAS PAVELKA/SHUTTERSTOCK ©

on the SH2 coursing through the Karangahake Gorge.

12 Welcome to the most scenic section of the Hauraki Rail Trail, meandering right alongside the river, and shaded by dappled sunlight. Along some parts of the trail you'll see rusted sections of the original railway line peeking through the forest litter. Provided by the Thames Valley Deerstalkers Association, wooden boxes marked 'TVDA' are traps designed to catch predators including rats, stoats and ferrets. The use of the traps has helped to increase the number of native birds along the trail.

13 Reached via a short 100m detour up Waitawheta Rd, the Owharoa Falls are one of New Zealand's most photogenic cascades. Leave your bike at the top of the 90m track down to the falls. It's an excellent spot for an on-the-trail picnic, and a good place for a swim if the weather is hot. A further 100m uphill along Waitawheta Rd, the Falls Retreat offers cottage accommodation and two- and three-course lunch menus. Check online for opening hours.

14 Continuing on the trail, it's a further 1km along the river to the Victoria Battery. Just before the historic site where gold ore from Waihi's Martha Mine was processed from 1897 to 1954, a bridge crosses the river to the Waikino Hotel. Consider a detour for a pub lunch or to try the hotel's award-winning Eliza's Claim Gold Gin. On Saturdays and Sundays, tram rides and guided tours of the Victoria Battery are on offer (see vbts.org. nz). The spookily derelict site can be visited independently daily.

15 Another optional detour from the trail is around a bend at the nearby Waikino Railway Station. Cross to the northern side of the river by bridge and underpass and consider catching the Goldfields Railway for Waihi as an alternative to the final ride to Waihi station (see waihirail.co.nz for details). There's a good cafe in the historic station building relocated from Paeroa.

16 Back on the trail on the river's southern side, it's another 9km to Waihi, continuing to follow the river closely before cutting through farmland, tracking through historic railway cuttings, and finally segueing to a sealed concrete trail that heads uphill and along quiet residential streets to the Waihi railway station. With a restored station house and many other historic structures, it's actually New Zealand's most well-preserved historic railway precinct. This platform where trains from Waikino terminate is the official end of the Hauraki Rail Trail spur from Paeroa to Waihi. It's a further 1.7km from the station to central Waihi for visiting the Gold Discovery Centre and Martha Mine.

☕ Take a Break

After completing the ride in Waihi, there are some standout eating options to recharge in. The Sustainable Pantry offers excellent coffee, salads and smoothies, while a few doors down, Plan Bee's sandwiches are deservedly world famous in Waihi. Pick up European-style baked goods at La Grignette Artisanal Bakery. After completing the ride you've definitely earned one of their brioches. If you're kicking on a further 11km by road to Waihi Beach, the Surf Shack teams delicious gourmet burgers with craft beer and kombucha.

Martha Mine

03

Te Awa River Ride – Day 1

DURATION	DIFFICULTY	DISTANCE	START/END
3–4hr	Easy	23km	Ngāruawāhia/ Hamilton CBD

TERRAIN	Shared paved path and boardwalks

TRISTANBNZ/GETTY IMAGES ©

Te Awa River Ride, near Hamilton

Beginning in Ngāruawāhia, the journey south along the Waikato River to Hamilton is an opportunity to see a side of the Waikato region usually concealed when travelling in a car. A brace of bridges – one built especially for the trail – criss-cross the river. Stops on this first section of the Te Awa River Ride include a historic Māori *pā* (fortified village) site, and the final approach into central Hamilton runs along a shaded shared path located right beside the river. Note that continuing an additional 3.5km into the Hamilton Gardens is a popular variation on this section of the trail.

Bike Hire

Bike rental and shuttle transport can be arranged with Lake Karapiro–based Riverside Adventures, and River Riders operating out of Ngāruawāhia, Hamilton and Cambridge. River Riders also offer overnight e-bike recharging.

Starting Point

Te Awa begins near the Point in Ngāruawāhia where the Waipa and Waikato rivers meet. From the car park, follow the paved path under the rail bridge to the official starting place.

01 Leaving Ngāruawāhia, Te Awa passes by recent housing subdivisions and upstream along a riverbank framed by willow trees. Look forward to gently undulating terrain, an accurate indicator of the upcoming experience while riding on this trail into Hamilton. Various trail-side information panels detail the Māori and colonial history of the Waikato River.

02 After skirting the river-facing side of the Ngāruawāhia Golf Course – there's often a few locals lining up putts on the 11th and

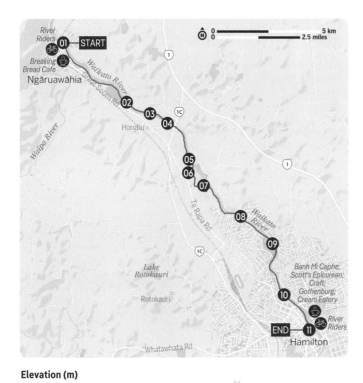

Elevation (m)

Ngāruawāhia

Ngāruawāhia is the base of New Zealand's Kīngitanga (Māori King) movement. On the Waikato River's eastern shore is the impressive Tūrangawaewae Marae, the location for *waka taua* (war canoe) races during mid-March's Regatta Day. Near the Point, check out the 1919-era exterior architecture of Tūrangawaewae House. Nearby, the Durham Precinct offers food trucks – try the burgers at Phat Pattie – and there's bike rental from River Riders. To explore Ngāruawāhia's creative side, visit the adjacent Hākarimata Boutique for clothing, homeware and jewellery inspired by Māori culture. The town's Te Whare Toi o Ngaaruawaahia art centre has occasional exhibitions from local artists.

12th greens – the trail crosses to the other side of the river on the spectacular Perry Cycle Bridge. Opened in 2017, the bridge spans 130m and is an integral part of Te Awa. Highlighting the spiritual connection of Māori to the river, colourful mosaics at both ends of the bridge were created by local schoolchildren. The bridge's spearmint-green hue contrasts against the olive-green colour of the river.

03 Bordering prime Waikato dairy-farming country, Te Awa continues on a paved path alongside the river's northern bank. Occasionally flightless pūkeko, New Zealand's indigo-coloured swamp hens, can be seen patrolling pastures enlivened with sword-like stands of harakeke (flax). During spring and summer, towering harakeke blooms are frequented by other birds including tui and korimako (bellbirds).

04 Cross back to the southern side of the river on the Horotiu Bridge, a more prosaic concrete structure. You'll need to dismount to negotiate the narrow pedestrian lane on the left-hand side of the bridge.

05 Descending back down to the river, continue along Te Awa on a combination of paving and wooden boardwalks. After a riverside section framed by pine trees, stop at the entrance to the Mangaharakeke Pā. Secure your bike at the bottom of the hill and make the short walk to the *pā* site. In earlier centuries, it was one of the most important *pā* along the Waikato River, and is now marked by carved *pou whenua* (land posts). Just after the *pā* is a shaded picnic table.

06 After Mangaharakeke Pā, Te Awa diverts away from the river, continuing on rural roads past the back of Fonterra's Te Rapa dairy factory, a sprawling reminder of the Waikato region's most important industry.

07 From Meadow View Ln, turn left onto Pukete Rd, and then make another left downhill past the Waikato Equestrian Centre and rejoin the riverside shared path just after the Pukete boat ramp. You'll often have a few curious equine observers on this part of the journey. After rejoining the trail, a pleasantly weathered Te Awa River Ride sign – looking like a rusted circular sawmill blade – is a great spot for a photo.

08 Continue along the riverside shared path, and then after a brief elevated section through a residential area on Pukete Rd, take the Te Awa trail left back down to the river. Travel through leafy Braithwaite Park and under the Flagstaff footbridge, a convenient way to link walking trails on both sides of the river.

09 Travelling alongside some of Hamilton's flashiest riverside suburbs, Te Awa continues in a southerly arc past the St Andrews golf course. Look across the river to more ritzy houses lining popular River Rd. The next section of the riverside trail is very low-lying and can be flooded after heavy rain. If need be, follow any temporary signage to make a short diversion along Ann St.

10 Now firmly within Hamilton's city limits, Te Awa continues along the river and passes under the Fairfield and Whitiora road bridges. Shaded by forest, this part of the trail is also very popular with walkers, so slow down and keep an eye on the shared path.

11 From the riverside pathway, there are various options to divert from the river and complete the day's journey in Hamilton's CBD. Recommended is the pedestrian route up onto Alma St, just past the Claudelands bridge. Continue past the Novotel hotel to reach Victoria St, central Hamilton's main thoroughfare.

☕ Take a Break

There are no eating and drinking options along this section of Te Awa so grab sandwiches or wraps before you leave from Ngāruawāhia's Breaking Bread Cafe. Recommendations for a post-ride lunch in Hamilton include Vietnamese street food at Banh Mi Caphe or cafe classics at Scott's Epicurean. Toast a successful day's ride with beers at Craft bar before dining on tapas and shared plates at Gothenburg's riverside location. Breakfast at Hamilton's Cream Eatery is recommended before continuing Te Awa on to Cambridge and Lake Karapiro.

Waikato Museum

Waikato Museum

With a central Hamilton location overlooking the river, the Waikato Museum is one of regional New Zealand's best cultural institutions. Highlights include galleries showcasing Māori *taonga* (treasures) from the Tainui *iwi* (tribes) who call the region home. Housed in a spectacular atrium with river views, Te Winika is a magnificent *waka taua*. In front of the museum is a statue of Riff Raff from *The Rocky Horror Show*. Creator Richard O'Brien grew up in a city also known as Kirikiriroa in the 1950s and 1960s. Check the museum's website for regular special exhibitions, including international collections visiting from overseas.

04

EMAGNETIC/SHUTTERSTOCK ©

Hamilton Gardens

Te Awa River Ride – Day 2

DURATION	DIFFICULTY	DISTANCE	START/END
4–6hr	Easy	42km	Hamilton CBD/Lake Karapiro

TERRAIN	Shared paved path and boardwalks

Beginning in central Hamilton or a few kilometres further in the Hamilton Gardens, day two of the Te Awa River Ride incorporates some of New Zealand's finest cycleway engineering. Wooden bridges and boardwalks both border the river and rise high above it, while smooth pathways rise and fall like a gently undulating roller coaster. Stops include the cafes of Tamahere and Cambridge and New Zealand's Velodrome, before the trail bisects a flat, rural landscape to wind downhill past the Karapiro Dam and on to the expanse of Lake Karapiro.

Bike Hire

Hamilton CBD-based River Riders also have a convenient Hamilton Gardens location. Both River Riders and River Adventures can also arrange experiences further south on the Waikato River Trails.

Starting Point

From Victoria St in Hamilton's CBD, follow the zigzag downhill shared path leaving from the Victoria on the River Precinct down to the riverbank. Te Awa continues upstream to the right.

01 Leaving Hamilton's CBD, the Te Awa River Ride continues alongside the Waikato River. Located below the Waikato Museum, five of the city's Māori hapū are represented by a colourful sculpture on Hamilton's floating central jetty, and just before the steel arch of the Victoria Bridge, the Hamilton Rowing Club and *waka ama* (outrigger canoes) are more indicators of the city's ongoing links to the river.

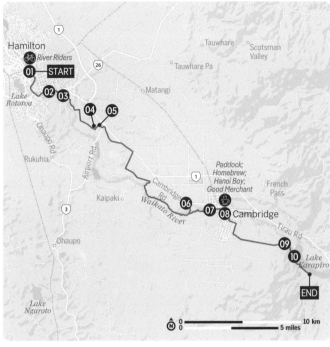

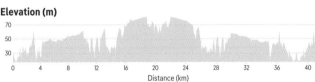

Elevation (m)

Distance (km)

Hamilton Gardens

Arrayed over 50 hectares southeast of the city centre, it's worth exploring the world-class Hamilton Gardens while undertaking the Te Awa River Ride. You'll spend most of your time in the fascinating and diverse Enclosed Gardens. Spectacular themed displays re-create Italian Renaissance, Japanese and Chinese gardens, and the intriguing Modernist and Surrealist gardens are both arty and a little confounding – in a good way. The Te Papapara garden showcases traditional foods and rongoā (natural remedies) harnessed by Māori. Book ahead online for excellent 75-minute guided tours of the gardens' highlights, and fuel up at the cafe before rejoining Te Awa.

02 Continue on the paved pathway alongside Hillsborough Tce and Cobham Dr before crossing to the river's northern bank on the Cobham traffic bridge. There's a shared path for bikes and pedestrians. Turn right to follow the Te Awa trail along the northern edge of the Hamilton Gardens – definitely worth a stop. From the gardens use the brick-red pedestrian and cycle bridge to cross Wairere Dr, and follow the Te Awa signs on the shared path to Hammond Park.

03 High above the river, Hammond Park features one of Hamilton's last remaining stands of native forest. Walk your bike for 500m on the shared boardwalk through this precious natural reserve – including many native birds and a long-tailed bat colony – before negotiating a paved path framed by wooden banking and then traversing a wooden bridge over forested gullies. Continue on another spectacular elevated boardwalk before linking to Riverglade Dr.

04 Continuing on a paved path past rural lifestyle properties, turn right down Newell Rd and stop at the Punnet Eatery. There's plenty of secure cycle parking at this bike-friendly cafe, and it's ideal for coffee and cake, or for a more leisurely brunch. A children's playground and an on-site provedore and gift shop are other distractions before rejoining the trail.

05 From Punnet, continue beside Newell Rd before turning left along Devine

Rd to the Tamahere shopping centre. Good cafes include Poppy Peach and Forever Bound. Turn right at the shops and follow Wiremu Tamihana Dr to use the underpass under Airport Rd to link to Tamahere Dr.

06 Rural lifestyle properties give way to emerald-green farming country on an extended flat ride of around 7km via Tamahere Dr, Pencarrow Rd and Hooker Rd. Te Awa then continues through private property – thank local farming families for the access – with elevated views of the river segueing to more wooden boardwalks descending through forested glades. Following a few uphill zig-zags is a recommended 1km detour to the Velodrome. Stop for a coffee and check out the progress of New Zealand's highly ranked national track-cycling team.

07 Returning 1km to the main Te Awa trail, it's another 3km into Cambridge, following a paved shared pathway near the river. Just before turning inland to the historic Gaslight Theatre, the grey arches and massive pipes of a water bridge loom like a giant insect.

08 Riding through Cambridge is the only section of the trail to use public roads. From the Gaslight Theatre, continue uphill on Alpha St and then turn right at the town's Edwardian-era Clock Tower to follow Cambridge's main drag of Victoria St. Stop for lunch and then continue via the steel arches of 1907's Victoria Bridge across the Waikato River.

09 Follow the Te Awa River Ride signs via Shakespeare, Wordsworth and Carlyle Sts to the Leamington Rugby Sports Club on the rural outskirts of Cambridge. Back in farming country, it's another flat ride for 5km for ice cream made with seasonal strawberries and blueberries at the Karapiro Berry Box. It's probably the trail's most uninspiring section, and can sometimes be windy, but it's definitely worth it for the Berry Box's refreshing treats.

10 The river is soon back in view, and downhill past the Karapiro Dam and hydroelectric station is Mighty River Domain, the Lake Karapiro training centre of New Zealand's very successful national rowing crews. Podium Cafe has river views, and it's then a final ride along another raised boardwalk, this one right above the water, followed by a 500m paved roller-coaster to reach the end of the trail on Maungatautari Rd.

☕ Take a Break

Leafy Cambridge is an ideal lunch stop on day two of the Te Awa River Ride. Recommended cafes include Paddock for gourmet bagels and virtuous superfood smoothies, while the town's best coffee is at Homebrew. Head to Hanoi Boy for Vietnamese street food, or refuel with craft beer at Good Merchant's location in a former church. On Saturday morning, Cambridge's weekly farmers market enlivens Victoria Sq. Around 800m past the popular Punnet Eatery, the Tamahere shopping centre also features good cafes and bakeries.

NATMINT/GETTY IMAGES ©

Karapiro Dam

Waikato's Town of Cycling

More than anywhere in the Waikato region, cycling is hugely popular in leafy Cambridge, and it's the one part of the Te Awa River Ride where you're guaranteed two-wheeled company most days of the week. They're justly proud of the Olympic, Commonwealth Games and world cycling champions nurtured at the nearby Velodrome, and you'll see probably a few 'Wāipa – Home of Champions' billboards around the region. On certain days, it's possible to join a 'Have-a-Go' session riding on the Velodrome's banked track, and guided tours of the cycling facility are also offered. See velodrome.nz for more information and bookings.

05

Twin Coast Cycle Trail – Day 1

STEVE TODD/SHUTTERSTOCK ©

Pou Herenga Tai Twin Coast Cycle Trail

DURATION	DIFFICULTY	DISTANCE	START/END
4–6hr	Easy	45km	Ōpua/Kaikohe

TERRAIN		Gravel cycleway

Beginning in the historic and scenic Bay of Islands, the first half of the Pou Herenga Tai Twin Coast Cycle Trail incorporates tunnels, a train ride and spectacular wooden bridges to end at the inland town of Kaikohe. Terrain varies from gentle hills to a rolling forest trail, and along the way there's the opportunity to learn about a world-renowned artist who called this region home and endowed the area with a quirky and idiosyncratic architectural legacy. Before heading off west, learn about Aotearoa's history at Waitangi, and spend a few hours experiencing one of the country's best mountain-bike parks.

Bike Hire

See twincoastcycletrail.kiwi.nz for details of operators offering bike hire and shuttle transport to and from trailheads. E-bikes are an increasingly popular option for travellers undertaking the full 87km of the trail.

Starting Point

Bike-hire companies provide shuttle transport to the Ōpua Marina. Also popular, and with a gentle downhill gradient, is to complete this route starting from Kaikohe east to Ōpua.

 01 Begin the trail's journey west at the southern end of Ōpua Marina, around 6km south of Paihia. Following a railway line that once linked Ōpua to Kaikohe and on to Ōkaihau – look down to still see rusted steel tracks – the elevated trail runs through mangroves and after 1.4km crosses a wooden bridge.

 02 The old railway line continues through the Te Ake Ake tunnel. At the time of writing, the tunnel was closed for safety issues, so the cycle

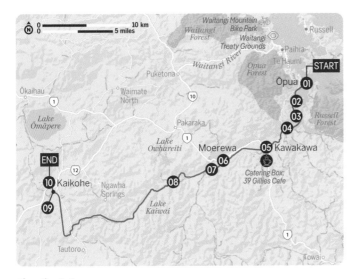

Elevation (m)

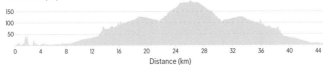

Distance (km)

trail follows a short, but steep, up and down diversion to the left of the tunnel. Dismounting on the way down is recommended. After the diversion, the trail continues past the Kawakawa River to the Te Ake Ake railway stop.

03 Departures from Te Ake Ake on the Bay of Islands Vintage Railway run from Friday to Sunday year-round, and daily across summer. Check the Twin Coast Cycle Trail website for the latest schedule. The first train of the day usually leaves Te Ake Ake at 10.50am. Drop a $1 or $2 coin in the donation bucket, load your bike on the special bike carriage, and continue by train across the long wooden bridge to the Taumarere train station. Future plans include developing the cycle trail to run alongside this

railway stretch from Te Ake Ake to Taumarere. Currently, when the train's not running, an 18km on-road diversion – only recommended for more experienced riders – links Ōpua to Kawakawa.

04 After checking out the heritage photographs in the Taumarere railway station, you have two options. Stay on the train for the 3.2km run into Kawakawa – an additional fare applies – or rejoin the cycle trail. Get away before the train departs Tamahere – it's a thrill to ride alongside the train as it courses through the rural countryside.

05 The train continues right down Kawakawa's main street, and the town's other claim to fame – public

Waitangi Mountain Bike Park

With 50km of well-planned trails, Waitangi Mountain Bike Park's forested coastal location is one of New Zealand's best destinations for bumping around the berms on two knobbly wheels. Trails range from undulating tracks for beginners right up to challenging options for MTB experts. If you've grown to love the ease of e-bikes while exploring the Pou Herenga Tai Twin Coast Cycle Trail, Paihia Mountain Bikes rent our electric-powered two-wheeled options that make it a cinch to climb the trails to the park's scenic lookouts. Convenient shuttle services make it even easier to just focus on the park's thrilling downhill sections.

toilets designed by the Austrian artist and architect, Friedensreich Hundertwasser, a local resident for two decades until 2000. Kawakawa's Te Hononga Hundertwasser Memorial Park features an interactive museum showcasing the eco-visionary's life and work.

06 From Kawakawa, the cycle trail exits the town west through farmland across the Moerewa Flats. Look out for egrets before passing by the malodorous Moerewa abattoir. Along this stretch you'll need to dismount regularly to negotiate gates designed to prevent motorcycle access to the trail. A sign indicates a 300m detour into Moerewa village. The burgers at Moerewa's Hati's Cafe are a perennial favourite of Twin Coast cyclists.

07 After passing the Otiria *marae* (Māori meeting house), the trail follows Otiria Rd before diverting through the Ngapipito valley, a rugged area combining forests and backblocks pasture.

08 Continue across the tannin-stained tea-brown waters of the Orauta stream on the historic 74m-long Kawiti Truss rail bridge – on your right are a few gentle cascades – and after a second shorter bridge,

the trail loops back to follow Ngapipito Rd. Just after the junction, a hill is crowned with the Maungarangi *urupa* (Māori cemetery). Forestry plantations provide a backdrop to the ongoing journey following a gradual incline towards Kaikohe.

09 Approaching Kaikohe, the trail again diverts from following the road and makes a southern loop around the grassy expanse of the Kaikohe aerodrome. Originally established by the US Marines as a WWII bomber base in 1942, it's the southern hemisphere's largest grass airstrip. At its southern end, the trail runs north through farmland to reach the now-abandoned concrete pad that was once Kaikohe's railway station, an important stop on the route linking Ōpua to Ōkaihau.

10 Continuing north alongside Station Rd, it's a further 600m into central Kaikohe, passing the town's Pioneer Village en route. The entrance to the interesting historical precinct is on Recreation Rd. To ease your leg muscles, consider a 6km detour east of central Kaikohe to the soothing geothermal pools at Ngawha Hot Springs (p47). Book online for session times from Thursday to Sunday.

☕ Take a Break

Leaving from Ōpua and catching the day's first train at Te Ake Ake, riders usually arrive in Kawakawa at around 11.30am. After checking out the town's Hundertwasser-related attractions, it's a fine place for a lunch stop. Popular cafes include the Catering Box – try one of the burgers made with Māori-style 'fry bread' – and 39 Gillies Cafe. Menu highlights include plenty of trail-friendly counter food. There's also a convenient water fountain out the front if you need to fill your water bottle.

CHAMELEONSEYE/SHUTTERSTOCK ©

Haka, **Waitangi Treaty Grounds**

Waitangi Treaty Grounds

Before departing Ōpua, make the journey 3km north of nearby Paihia to the Waitangi Treaty Grounds. In 1840, New Zealand's founding document, the Treaty of Waitangi, was signed between the British Crown and *rangatira* (chiefs) representing the country's Māori *iwi* (tribes). The leafy grounds offer superb coastal views of the Bay of Islands, and excellent museums chart the proud role of Māori in New Zealand's armed forces, and the treaty's ongoing importance at the heart of New Zealand government legislation. Definitely book a guided tour including a Māori cultural performance held at Waitangi's exquisitely carved Te Whare Runanga (meeting house).

06

Best for

OFF THE BEATEN TRACK

Twin Coast Cycle Trail – Day 2

DURATION	DIFFICULTY	DISTANCE	START/END
4–6hr	Easy	42km	Kaikohe/ Horeke

TERRAIN	Gravel cycleway

Hokianga Harbour

DAVID STEELE/SHUTTERSTOCK ©

Slightly shorter, and also more downhill than the Ōpua to Kaikohe section of the Pou Herenga Tai Twin Coast Cycle Trail, the trail's continuation from Kaikohe to Horeke is arguably more scenic and also more popular. Sleepy Ōkaihau is an essential stop for world-famous-in-Northland pies, and from there it's just a short ride before negotiating steep switchbacks to join a shaded trail running alongside a lovely river. The riverside glade of Snow's Farm is a perfect picnic stop before the trail continues past traditional Māori *marae*, and along a mangrove boardwalk to Horeke and the historic Mangungu Mission House.

Bike Hire

Operators offering bike hire, accommodation bookings and shuttle services include Ōpua-based Mullarkey Bike & Hire, and Top Trail & Tours and Twin Coast Adventures, both based in Kaikohe.

Starting Point

From Kaikohe to Horeke, the Twin Coast Cycle Way begins at the northern end of Station Rd. Cross Takehe Rd (SH1) and then continue west on the dedicated gravel trail.

01 Leaving Kaikohe, the Twin Coast Cycle Trail is marked by the town's famous 'bike fence', a rustic collection of two-wheeled transport arrayed along a rickety fence line. It's a good photo opportunity with your own bike, hopefully more trustworthy than the slowly rusting assemblage of abandoned bikes. The grassy peak to the right is Monument Hill, crowned with a memorial to Hōne Heke, a 19th-century *rangatira* (chief) of Northland's Ngāpuhi *iwi* (Māori tribe). The hill is accessed along

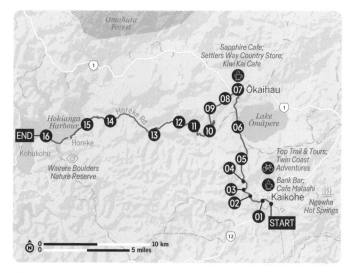

TOP TIP:

If you're overnighting in Horeke, the *Ranui*, a motorboat first launched in 1945, offers occasional history cruises on the Hokianga harbour. The vessel can also be hired by cyclists for transport across the harbour to tiny Kohukohu. From Kohukohu, a vehicular ferry continues to equally historic Rawene.

Elevation (m)

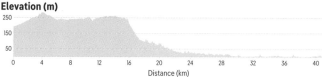

Monument Rd, west of the town centre.

02 Travelling along a red gravel pathway, the trail zips through farmland past another Twin Coast photo op. Showcasing views of a verdant valley is a giant picture frame celebrating the region's diversity of trees and plants. Along the next few kilometres framed by forest, look out for trailside information panels – in both English and te reo Māori, New Zealand's indigenous language – highlighting native trees and shrubs.

03 Exiting from the forest, a narrow and undulating single-track mountain-bike trail hugs the left-hand side of the main trail for a stretch. It's a good

opportunity for some exciting alternative two-wheeled action.

04 Climbing gradually to the highest point of the trail at 280m, enter the curved 80m-long Tahuna Tunnel. It's worth spending a few minutes in the tunnel's entrance for your eyes to adjust, and a flashlight is also a good idea. The tunnel was constructed in 1915 and was originally designed to link the railway all the way north to Kaitaia. In fact, the line only ever made it as far as the nearby village of Ōkaihau. Inside, the tunnel can be wet and muddy, especially after rain, and dismounting and walking through is recommended. Exiting the tunnel, the train continues through another magical glade of shaded native forest.

Ngawha Hot Springs

A popular end-of-day option for cyclists overnighting in Kaikohe is a visit to the nearby Ngawha Hot Springs. Sixteen different geothermal hot pools feature different medicinal and healing properties. Locals' use of the springs dates back several centuries, and warriors from Northland's Ngā Puhi *iwi* (tribe) are said to have bathed here after battles. The springs are open from Thursday to Sunday, and booking ahead online is essential to secure one of the five two-hour bathing sessions spread throughout the day from 7am to 9pm.

☕ Take a Break

Recommended overnight accommodation in Kaikohe is at the Left Bank, a heritage bank building with spacious double rooms and good-value shared accommodation for groups. There's also secure bike storage and overnight charging for e-bikes. Evening dining opportunities in Kaikohe are limited to the Bank Bar – the town's local pub – and a Thai restaurant. The New World supermarket has a good deli section with takeaway salads. Before hitting the trail, gas up at Cafe Malaahi with excellent coffee, eggs Benedict and regular breakfast specials.

05 From 1935 to 1945, the next part of the trail was the location of the number 3 Roswell & Roswell sawmill, one of four sawmills set up from the 1880s to fell the region's giant kauri, kahikatea and totara trees. Centuries-old kauri gum was also dug up from the ancient fallen forests framing the shores of nearby Lake Ōmāpere. In past decades, the area was enlivened by bullock trains and steam-powered saws, but now local bird life is a more subdued soundtrack. Look out for energetic tauhou (wax eyes), a compact and curious bird with an olive-green head. Just past an information sign for the sawmill, the Waihōanga sign indicates another optional detour to a mountain-bike pump track running parallel to the main trail.

06 The trail now runs alongside Lake Rd north to Ōkaihau, travelling through a dairy farm where you'll need to dismount to traverse a few shared gates and fences. Good luck also steering around the occasional fresh cowpat on the trail. To the right is the silvery expanse of Lake Ōmāpere, Northland's largest lake, and an important breeding area for squat pūkeko (indigo-coloured swamphens). In earlier centuries, the lake was also an important food source, with local Māori harvesting eels from its shallow depth of 2m to 3m.

07 Just before Ōkaihau, the trail diverts from following Lake Rd, and instead traces a downhill line through a shaded glade. It's soon decision time – cross a wooden pedestrian bridge or surge through the shallow waters of a river ford – before emerging at a creek-side picnic area just downhill from the village. Stop to read the information panel about Ōkaihau's history – the name translates to 'Feast of Winds' from te reo Māori – before continuing uphill on a short on-road section to Ōkaihau's sleepy main drag. There's good eating at a concise array of cafes, and a scattering of accommodation options.

08 Leaving Ōkaihau, follow Settler's Way, the village's main street southwest for around 3km, riding on a dedicated gravel bike path on the left-hand side of the road. Along this largely straight stretch, there's plenty to see, including historic Anglican (St Catherine's) and Catholic (St Patrick's) churches on the right-hand side of the road, and a giant puriri tree beside the trail on the left of the road.

JT888/SHUTTERSTOCK ©

Wairere Boulders

Wairere Boulders

Around 1km before the end of the trail at Mangungu Mission House, an unsealed road travels for 3.2km up the Wairere River to the Wairere Boulders Nature Reserve. The most popular option to explore the reserve's idiosyncratic basalt formations shaped by river erosion is the one-hour Boulder Loop trail. From the trail, there's a short forested walk to a bush swimming hole. Don't dive in as there are submerged rocks. Also popular is the longer Magic Rock trail for elevated views of the volcanic lava flow that originally formed the basalt. Overnight camping is available and kayaks can be rented.

09 Just before the road curves to the right, the trail diverts left to enter a macadamia-nut orchard framed by towering stands of bamboo used as windbreaks for the precious trees. Meander through the macadamias with views down across rural valleys before entering the most spectacular section of the trail.

10 For around 1.6km, a series of downhill switchbacks travel down the hillside to finally emerge beside a gently rushing brook. The first part of the switchback is steep so consider dismounting and walking down this section if you're not confident negotiating steeper inclines. Past the brook, there's

another bridge vs ford decision to make, this time crossing the Utakura River, which is on the right of the trail for the next few kilometres.

11 Look forward to dappled light along this section, traversing a few gentle ups and downs, and combining

VERONIKA HANZLIKOVA/SHUTTERSTOCK ©

glimpses of the river with a few more technical mountain-bike-style sections through shaded forest. It's definitely worth getting off your bike for a few minutes and quietly submerging yourself in the sylvan tranquility. Look out for the handwritten sign to the 'Lily Pond', reached by a short walking track to the right off the main trail. The lilies overlap each other to completely cover the pond and it's a good chance to stretch your legs. Near an uphill section, there's another smaller 'bike fence' to seek out.

12 Continuing to follow the Utakura River, the next recommended stop on the trail is at Snow's Farm, a shaded picnic stop with a few riverside tables. It's a good spot for snacking, so hopefully you've packed lunch or picked up some counter food from the cafes in Ōkaihau. Before hitting the trail again, it's worth visiting Snow's Farm's rustic museum, framed by forest and farmland, and on the banks of one of Northland's prettiest rivers.

13 From Snow's Farm, the Utakura River continues to be a constant presence before the trail begins to run alongside the unsealed route of Mangataraire Rd. A few undulating sections combine with occasional road crossings.

14 Linking to run alongside Horeke Rd, the trail continues through a backblocks landscape of farms and *marae* representing several of the hapū of this remote region of Northland. Some of the *marae* fly Te Kara, a distinctive white, red and blue ensign also known as the flag of the United Tribes of New Zealand, and originally adopted by northern Māori chiefs in 1834.

15 Following Horeke Rd west towards the Hokianga Harbour, a few kilometres before Horeke, the trail diverts to another memorable section by continuing across a spectacular raised boardwalk through the mangrove forests of the Wairau River estuary. At 1.1km, it's the longest boardwalk on New Zealand's Ngā Herenga network of 22 Great Rides. There's a photo-worthy Twin Coast Cycle Trail gateway to ride through, but it's still actually few kilometres more to the end of the trail.

16 Exiting the boardwalk, the trail continues on an on-road section through the sleepy hamlet of Horeke, established around 1826 as New Zealand's second European settlement. There's accommodation at the Riverhead Villa Bed & Breakfast and the Horeke Hotel, and around a final headland the trail ends at the historic Māngungu Mission House, established in 1839. On the grounds of the historic building, more than 70 northern Māori chiefs signed New Zealand's Treaty of Waitangi in 1840 – actually the biggest single signing of the country's founding document.

☕ Take a Break

Tiny Ōkaihau – population just 350 – packs in plenty of opportunities for great eating. Delicious slabs of pie are served with good coffee at the Sapphire Cafe – flavours could include pecan or strawberry and rhubarb – while at the Settlers Way Country Store, ice cream with seasonal blueberries are perennial favourites. The burgers at Ōkaihau's Kiwi Kai cafe are legendary, and 2km northeast of town there's comfortable overnight accommodation in renovated railway carriages at the Ōkaihau Rail Stay. Trailhead shuttles can also be arranged.

Wairau River estuary boardwalk

Also Try...

Waiheke Island

Waiheke Island

DURATION	DIFFICULTY	DISTANCE
2–3hr	Easy	24km

Catch the ferry from downtown Auckland to Waiheke Island and embark on a two-wheeled journey taking in five different bays and several vineyards. The first part of the ride from Matiatia Wharf uphill to the shops and cafes of Oneroa village is steep, so renting an e-bike from Eride Waiheke is recommended. Book ahead and pick up a bike at the Matiatia ferry terminal. Highlights of their 24km loop ride around the western part of the island include the broad arc of Onetangi Beach – ideal for bodysurfing – island-brewed craft beer at Alibi Brewing's Tantalus Estate location, or archery, *pétanque* and claybird shooting a short ride away at Wild on Waiheke. For island-distilled whisky, check out the Heke.

Lake Karapiro to Arapuni

DURATION	DIFFICULTY	DISTANCE
1hr	Easy	11.5km

Starting at the Pokaihwhenua Bridge, around 10km upstream from the southern end of the Te Awa River Ride on Maungatautari Rd, the 11.5km ride from Lake Karapiro is the first of five sections making up the total 104km length of the Waikato River Trails. Sections two and three of this track are more challenging, but this initial stretch is achievable by most cyclists. Highlights include riding alongside Lake Karapiro before crossing 500m of boardwalk through the Huihuitaha Wetlands and negotiating the 152m-long Arapuni Suspension Bridge for coffee at Arapuni's Rhubarb cafe. Plans are underway to link the southern trailhead of Te Awa with the northern starting point of the Waikato River Trails, creating a single river trail of almost 200km.

JORDAN TAN/SHUTTERSTOCK ©

Waikato River, Whakamaru

Mangakino to Ātiamuri

DURATION	DIFFICULTY	DISTANCE
4–5hr	Easy	38km

Following the more technical second and third sections of the Waikato River Trails (from Arapuni to Waipapa Dam and then from Waipapa Dam to Mangakino), the final two sections continuing from Mangakino to the Whakamaru Dam, and then on to Ātiamuri, are easier riding. There are a few steeper sections and an overall gradual uphill gradient, but riders are rewarded with crossing a suspension bridge over the Mangakino Stream, passing through the protected area of the Lake Whakamaru Reserve, and exploring millennia-old volcanic landscapes around Ātiamuri. Mentioned in the oral histories of the Arawa and Ngati Raukawa *iwi*, Pohaturoa Rock is a culturally significant volcanic outcrop near Ātiamuri. See waikatorivertrails.co.nz for planning details, accommodation, bike hire and transport operators.

Twin Coast Trail Combo

DURATION	DIFFICULTY	DISTANCE
8–12hr	Easy	87km

Not often do you get the chance to ride right across a country, but the 87km journey from Ōpua in the Bay of Islands to the remote Hokianga Harbour presents that exact opportunity. Timings with train departures from Te Ake Ake to Kawakawa mean it's difficult to complete the ride in a single day – even with the convenience of an e-bike – so plan it as a two-day ride. The classic cross-country route is from Ōpua to Horeke, overnighting in Kaikohe and finishing in Horeke, but some riders prefer to use Kaikohe as a starting point for rides to both the east and the west, taking advantage of the better downhill gradient of the section linking Kaikohe with Ōpua.

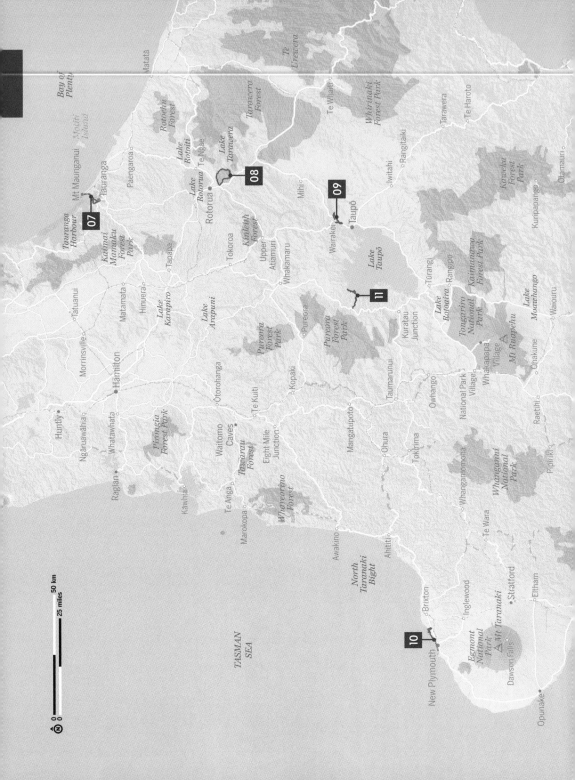

TASMAN SEA

Bay of Plenty

Te Urewera

Matata

Rotoehu Forest

Mt Maunganui
Motiti Island

Tauranga
Tauranga Harbour

07

Kaimai Mamaku Forest Park

Paengaroa

Lake Rotoiti
Lake Rotoma
Te Ngae

Tarawera Forest

Lake Rotorua

Lake Tarawera

08

Rotorua

Te Whaiti

Whirinaki Forest Park

Tarawera

Te Haroto

Iwitahi

Rangitaiki

Mihi

Otamauri

Kaweka Forest Park

Kuripapango

Tatuanui

Hinuera

Matamata

Tapapa

Tokoroa

Kinleith Forest

09

Wairakei

Taupō

Turangi

Morrinsville

Hamilton

Lake Karapiro

Lake Arapuni

Upper Atiamuri

Whakamaru

Pureora

Lake Taupō

Lake Rotoaira

Tongariro National Park

Lake Moawhango

Waiouru

Te Kuiti

Otorohanga

Pureora Forest Park

Pureora Forest Park

Kuratau Junction

Kaimanawa Forest Park

Rangipo

Raglan

Whatawhata

Ngaruawahia

Huntly

Pirongia Forest Park

Waitomo Caves

Taeraroa Forest

Eight Mile Junction

Kopaki

Mangatupoto

Taumarunui

Owhango

Raetihi

Mt Ruapehu

Whakapapa Village

National Park Village

Ohakune

Kawhia

Te Anga

Te Wara

Ohura

Toktma

Whangamomona

Whanganui National Park

Pipiriki

Marokopa

Whareorino Forest

Awakino

Ahititi

North Taranaki Bight

10

Brixton

New Plymouth

Inglewood

Egmont National Park

Mt Taranaki

Dawson Falls

Stratford

Eltham

Opunake

11

50 km

25 miles

N

ANDREW PEACOCK/GETTY IMAGES ©

Lake Taupō, Great Lake Trail (p74)

Central North Island

Explore

Central North Island

The Central North... Land of provision and productivity. Of mysterious forms and ancient norms. Here, verdant and sprawling farmlands transition into ancient sleeping giants that rise up from the earth below, spilling out into the broad waterways and piping geothermal vapours, making this region one of the most renewable and resourceful patches of Aotearoa. The diverse variations in the terrain ensure that riders of all ages and stages are spoilt for choice, with trails tracking volcanic ridges, navigating sacred lake vistas and sheltering under native canopies of prehistoric proportions.

Taupō

Taupō is ground zero of the Central North region, if we're talking geography. With a population of around 37,203, the lakeside district is a great hub for tourists wanting to base themselves in town before branching off on day trips and wild explorations. There's a handful of large supermarkets, rental-car companies, ample cafes and restaurants, and an airport here. Rotorua is a 40- to 50-minute drive (or bus ride) away, where visitors can get up close and personal with geothermal geysers, soak in natural hot springs and try some adrenaline pumping adventure activities. Just over an hour south of Taupō is the spectacular Tongariro National Park – one of New Zealand's most dramatic dual World Heritage areas and oldest national parks.

Mt Maunganui

Just over 2½ hours from New Zealand's capital city Auckland is the beachside utopia of Mt Maunganui. Situated on a long and sprawling coastal spit with its prominent namesake (Mauao) keeping watch over holiday makers, surfers, cruise ships and active outdoor locals, Mt Maunganui is a favourite summer destination for Kiwis and visitors from faraway lands. Downtown you'll find surfboard-hire stores, fashion boutiques, beachfront accommodation and a generous selection of healthy eateries, seafood restaurants and ice-cream shops. This is the perfect place to find your groove and take a deep breath before venturing deeper into the more remote beauty of the Central North Island.

WHEN TO GO

December through to April is when this region really takes off. With ample sun and surf shifting the atmosphere, lakeside days and bush walks become the hobbies of choice for many. This time of year is also peak season, with tourism overriding the sometimes sleepy local feel of the towns. Bear this in mind when booking accommodation and activities.

New Plymouth

Less of a place you'll simply 'happen upon' as you travel this region, New Plymouth is a destination in its own right. Tucked away and hugging the wild west coast, this region of 80,679 is a short flight from Auckland, or a four-hour drive from Taupō. Once you arrive, you'll be greeted with the inimitable melange of coast, culture, traditional values and retro-Kiwi architecture. Much of New Plymouth's urban charm comes from the dedication to preserving a laid-back local feel, despite geographical size and the diversity of its denizens. Awarded 'most liveable city' in the International Awards for Liveable Communities (2021), New Plymouth has mastered the balance we all seek to find. There are ample supermarkets, supply stores, parks and gardens, cafes, friendly beaches and shuttle services (taranakidriven.nz/mountain-shuttle) to and from more remote regional gems on offer here.

TRANSPORT

The Central North is easiest to trip around by car, but also has air-travel access points by way of small regional airports. Connecting flights from Auckland head to Tauranga, Rotorua, Taupō and New Plymouth within 45 minutes of the capital. InterCity buses also connect these main regional hubs, but limited service times require pre-booking your best route in advance.

 WHERE TO STAY

Canopycamping.co.nz features a selection of thoughtful cabins, yurts and unique tiny homes dotted around Rotorua and Taupō. One serious off-the-beaten-path standout is **Kanuka** on Lake Tarawera in the Rotorua region – a glamping site set on Māori land that is only accessible by water taxi or foot. Closer to civilisation there's **Totara Perch**, a four-bedroom cabin just 10 to 20 minutes from Kinloch and Taupō, or **Treetops** tiny home in Acacia Bay – complete with outdoor shower and east-facing views out to the Kaimanawa Ranges. Alternatively, there are hotels and backpackers in the main towns if you're not after anything too fancy.

 WHAT'S ON

Festival of Lights

(festivaloflights.nz) Twice yearly New Plymouth is bathed in lights, with luminous installations transforming Pukekura Park and the CBD.

Le Currents

(lecurrents.co.nz) Every December in Taupō a festival of art, music and culture ushers in a full expression of classic summer vibes.

Flavours of Plenty

(flavoursofplentyfestival. com) A festival of culinary and environmental delights each March/April. Events range from micro-green-growing workshops to honey spinning, plus lots of regional *kai* (food).

Resources

Visit Rotorua (*rotoruanz. com/visit*) Rotorua official tourism website and guide.

Love Taupō (*lovetaupo.com/ en*) Official Taupō tourism website and guide.

NZ Pocket Guide (*nzpocket-guide.com/10-new-plymouth-must-dos*) A list of things to do in New Plymouth.

Never Ending Voyage (*never-endingvoyage.com/things-to-do-in-new-plymouth-tarana-ki*) Blog feature on New Plymouth.

07

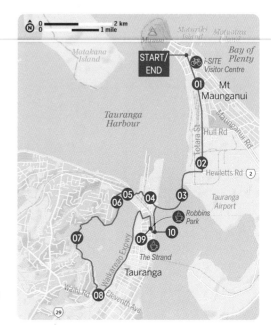

Daisy Hardwick Loop

DURATION	DIFFICULTY	DISTANCE	START/END
2–3hr	Easy	25km	Maunganui Rd, Mt Maunganui Town Centre

TERRAIN		Urban footpaths, boardwalk

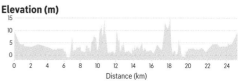

New Zealand beachside summers typically recall the famous Tip Top Ice Cream commercial: 'undies, undies, togs'. But in Mt Maunganui, all rules fly out the window. Biking here is tropical, leisurely and can quite comfortably be done in board shorts or bikini, surfboard at your side à la 1960s Venice Beach. Slap on sunscreen and bike around town, working up a sweat. If you're after something more urban, head over the bridge to learn about Tauranga's history and see restorative eco efforts in action on the Waikareao Estuary (aka the Daisy Hardwick Loop). It's a nice alternative to beachy days.

Bike Hire

The i-SITE Visitor Centre in Mt Maunganui rents e-bikes for one- to eight-hour sessions ($30 to $90). Book ahead in peak season, as there are only a few bikes on-site.

Starting Point

Downtown Mt Maunganui is the most accessible base point. You'll complete the mission right next to the beach admiring mighty Mauao, with plenty of cafes to replenish your energy.

01 Begin your ride heading southeast, away from the Mount, on the downtown streets among cafes and shops. Passing two roundabouts, you'll meet a third linking Rata St to the right. Take this turn and continue down until you meet Totara St.

02 As you cruise down Totara St, you'll be afforded a slightly faster pace as you cycle alongside traffic instead of downtown pedestrians. This first area is predominantly indus-

Pitau Road
Pōhutakawa

Take a detour via Pitau Rd
before you return your bike just
around the corner. Here you can
marvel at one big little-known
gem that has been humbly
standing guard for an estimated
500 years. The rākau (tree) you
will see before you is thought
to be one of the oldest in the
country, and the only remaining
pōhutukawa tree in the Maunganui area that pre-dates early
settlement. To stand inside
the arms of such a mighty
and enchanting form that has
weathered many storms, trans-
muted through environmental
changes and stood protective
over neighbouring houses is
quite an experience.

trial, so look out for trucks as you pass entranceways. You'll see green-and-white cycleway markings on the footpath from here, indicating you are on track to the Tauranga bridge. Cross the few necessary roads using the traffic-light system and keep to the left of the footpath. This is a high traffic zone with lots of cars, so be careful.

03 Passing a couple of shipping yards you'll come to Tauranga Bridge Marina. There are picnic tables and some pop-up food and coffee stores here if you fancy a break already; otherwise continue towards the bridge. The footpath splits to lead either downhill or up over the bridge. Take the latter, and enjoy a scenic pedal or push over the water with views of both Tauranga city to your left and the back side of Mt Maunganui to your right.

04 Descending the bridge section, you'll come to a busy intersection. Take extreme care crossing as there are no traffic lights for walkers or cyclists. Once you're on the other side of the road you'll veer right on Mirrielees Rd until you reach a road sign with options for Port, Marina, Matakana Ferry or Otūmoetai. Follow the cycle symbol towards Otūmoetai, which will immediately take you left on Cross Rd.

05 Once you hit Marine Park, continue left towards the water until you reach a small marine hub. There are a couple of restaurants set up here. You'll need to walk your bike over the puzzle-like bridge, coming out the other side and continuing to Chapel St bridge over the Otūmoetai Channel.

06 Carry on left once you reach Maxwells Rd, which will take you to the best starting point for the Waikareao Estuary trail. The 8.7km loop itself is fairly self-explanatory. During this section of your larger journey, you'll enjoy riding under and through an abundance of native foliage, listening to the quintessential summer soundtrack of cicadas clicking, and smell the heady salted scent of the inlet you are skirting. There are a couple of grassy areas with picnic tables for a rest along the way, or to dismount and take in the sights.

07 You'll shortly transition onto the boardwalk section of the track. Riding over the top of the Category 1 ecological area is a unique experience – it's a narrow bridge-like structure with no railing, so adopt a gentle pace. There are information boards along this route explaining how the ecosystem works in more detail, should you want to indulge in a bit of eco-science.

08 You'll come to a residential area. Cross left over Kopurererua Stream to continue on a footpath parallel to the motorway on your right. The estuary is now on your left. Once you get to the Takitimu Dr intersection, you'll see a Mobil petrol station – turn right up Chapel St. Take a left on Mission St to stop by the Elms Mission House – one

PHOTOS BRIANSCANTLEBURY/SHUTTERSTOCK ©

Waikareao Estuary

☕ Take a Break

A great option if you've pre-packed a picnic is to perch at one of the tables or on the lush grass under the memorial trees next to Robbins Park. Admire the 28-bed rose garden in full bloom in spring and summer, or find refuge in the tropical display house with its begonias, orchids, bromeliads and palms. Another option is a quick detour down to the Strand to grab takeaway, or enjoy full service at one of the many stellar cafes and restaurants along the waterfront.

of New Zealand's oldest heritage sites.

09 Keep going down Cliff Rd where you will take a right towards the Strand in Tauranga's downtown. You'll soon pass Robbins Park Rose Gardens and Monmouth Redoubt where you can read up on the early history of the area.

Waikareao Estuary

The Waikareao Estuary is regarded by New Zealand's *Resource Management Act* to be a 'Special Ecological Area'. This means it has high biodiversity value and requires the protective care of passers-by in order to continue thriving against invasive species and weeds. It is home to two species of native birds classified as threatened, and also four regionally uncommon native plant species. Beyond that, the estuary is where the river and sea meet and form a specialised environment influenced by tide and saltwater. There's a lot more going on than you might think when viewing from afar!

10 Descending down a short-cut, you'll come to a Wake Shelter immediately before a railway crossing, facing the water with the Strand and CBD to your right. Stop and explore the waterfront of Tauranga, or take a left and head down Dive Cres to the bridge where your ride back to Mt Maunganui will become the reverse of where you started.

08

Whaka-rewarewa Forest (Redwoods)

DURATION	DIFFICULTY	DISTANCE	START/END
3–5hr	Easy	35km	Waipa Whaka-rewarewa Forest car park

TERRAIN	Mountain-bike dirt trail

FRANKIEFINDS/SHUTTERSTOCK ©

Mountain-biking, Whakarewarewa Forest

Rotorua is best known for its strong connection to Māori culture, geothermal activity (along with the accompanying sulphuric aroma!), adventure tourism and impressive Jurassic Park–esque ponga trees. Ensconced in a jungle of native flora, curling around corners on the Whakarewarewa Forest Loop – also known as the Redwoods – is a perfect way to get in touch with it all. Your enthusiasm may undulate as much as the trail, but just remember: what goes up must come down.

Bike Hire

Mountain Bike Rotorua have a variety of kids and adults bikes available for hire in two-hour, half-day, full-day, or multi-day time blocks. Prices start from $40.

Starting Point

Start the loop from the Rotorua Mountain Bike car park at Waipa. Here you'll find toilets, water taps and friendly staff to set you off on your way.

01 Begin at the main Waipa entrance, which takes you deep into the forest. Ensconced inside the canopy of unfurled native ferns, fanning ponga and prominent Californian redwoods, you'll make your way through a series of gentle inclines, winding corners and flowy downhill segments for the first 3km. There are lots of intersections where other trails meet, so slow down as you approach and listen for mountain bikers crossing.

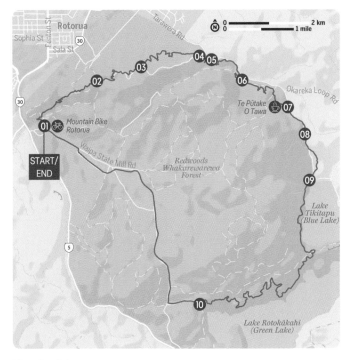

Post-Ride Pampering

A great place to debrief your ride Rotorua-style is at Secret Spot Hot Tubs, which are located directly across from the entrance to the trail. Order a drink and some food, whip off your shoes, and let your hard work soak in...literally. Owned and operated by local brothers Keith and Eric, the hot tubs have been set up to cater to those who like to gather together and tell tales of adventure while also connecting with nature. You'll soak in your own cedar tub overlooking the Whakarewarewa Forest and the Puarenga Stream.

Elevation (m)

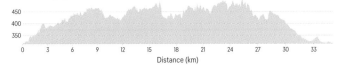

Distance (km)

02 Continue for another 5km. Things start to open up as you climb out of Waipa to a long traverse of the Tokorangi Pa ridge. You'll come across a gravel logging area at the top of Radio Hut Rd, which makes things a little confusing. Keep following the trail icon (orange arrow signage with accompanying 'Loop' text). You'll soon return onto the curl of the bike trail, edged with towering ponga and an easy surface to navigate.

03 A couple of minutes in, there's a rest-stop seat made of a long horizontal log – a good place for a quick drink in the shade. Be careful stopping in spontaneous places on this trail. Practise good trail etiquette – it's a popular trail with lots of traffic, so if you need a breather, make sure you're well tucked into the side, preferably not on a corner. Other riders appear out of nowhere very fast.

04 Pedalling onwards you'll make a gentle climb towards Chubbo's Pass, a nice spot to stop for a snack should you need one. Look out for an old wooden bridge. You'll soon see signage indicating a viewpoint up ahead. In 50m you'll have expansive views of Lake Rotorua and the city below.

05 Around 100m from this point is a sign with the option to head left onto the 'Tank to Town Trail' or continue right on the Whakarewarewa Loop. Go right and enjoy picking up speed as a fun downhill segment takes you through the bush once again.

06 Coming out of the bush you'll see a large fenced water cylinder and a Linkmore Link sign. There's a bench seat if you need a break, otherwise head in the direction of the orange arrow with the main road to your left. You'll duck in and out of forest for a while on a segment called Kurawai ki Tarawera, tracking towards the 12km mark at Te Pūtake O Tawa Forest Hub. There's a large information board around 10km in, offering a choice of trails to reach it. The most consistent choice is to stay on the single-track trail or the orange line, called Te Koropu Trail.

07 At the 12km mark you'll reach Te Pūtake O Tawa Forest Hub and car park – a good spot to dismount and starfish out on the grassy field for a quick power charge. Be sure to check out the powerful artworks created by local Tūhourangi people, including Katore by Tāwhanga Rika and Umukaria by Tukiri Tini.

08 Follow the signs through the car park and you'll soon be led back into the forest for a section of the trail called the Feeder. This part of the ride is free-flowing with ample moments of downhill reward. It gets pretty dark and jungle-like in the dense bush, so take extra care and look out for oncoming riders and walkers. After your fun run on the Feeder, you'll come out at stunning Lake Tikitapu, also known as the Blue Lake.

09 You can organise a pickup from here if you've had enough, or continue to the next segment around the lake called Tangaroamihi trail. A few kilometres in, there's a signpost to the right leading you onto a one-way section of the track. Soon you'll hit Tikitapu Rd and begin the signposted route to Te Kōtukutuku trail above Lake Rotokākahi, also known as the Green Lake, 22.5km in.

10 Passing by a redwood grove and a picnic area, this loop leads you into the Baja Trail section and ushers you out onto Te Ara Ahi – a concrete cycle path that will guide you (mostly downhill) back home alongside the road to Waipa.

☕ Take a Break

Looking at a map of the trails on offer within this Forest Loop is like looking at the neuro-circuitry of a busy brain. With so many options and side tracks to zip in and out of, it's smart to pace yourself and return to a home base. Midway in, Te Pūtake O Tawa is a large reserve area with toilets, showers, bike-rental information, artworks and a cafe. There's the option to end or start your ride here, depending on shuttle service timetables.

Lake Tikitapu

≈ Sacred Waters

Lake Tikitapu is one of Rotorua's most popular recreational lakes, catering to all manner of local water activities including boating, fishing and jet skiing. The lake is a collapsed volcanic crater with a pumice and rhyolite underlayer, resulting in a shallow depth of 27m, and causing the brilliant aqua-blue hue that inspired its common name the 'Blue Lake'. Lake Rotokākahi, or the 'Green Lake', sits adjacent and is considered *tapu* (sacred) by Tūhourangi descendants – a sub-tribe of the wider Te Arawa tribe. No access or water activity is permitted in or on this lake, to respect the *tikanga* of the local people.

09

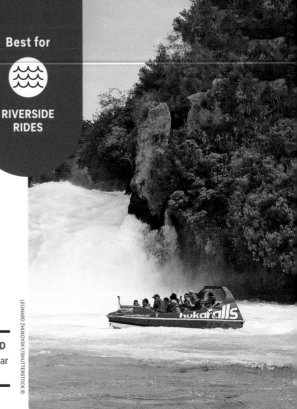

Best for

RIVERSIDE RIDES

Aratiatia Dam Loop

DURATION	DIFFICULTY	DISTANCE	START/END
1–3hr	Easy	14km return or 7km one way	Huka Falls car park

TERRAIN	Mountain-bike dirt trail

LEONARD ZHUKOVSKY/SHUTTERSTOCK ©

Huka Falls

Taupō is known for being the biggest riding hub of the North Island, and mountain-bike racks on the backs of cars are a ubiquitous sighting around these parts. Naturally, hopping on two wheels in such a place may seem intimidating, but once you hit the Aratiatia trail, you'll be ushered through the looping scene with one very wise and powerful local at your side – the Waikato River. With a handful of small climbs uphill, many humbling vantage points, and a generous dose of scientific observation thrown in, this track's sure to keep you honest without breaking you in pieces.

Bike Hire

FourB Bike Hire, just up the road from Huka Falls, offers bike tours and hire and shuttle services to and from most of the rides around the Taupō area. Prices start from $35.

Starting Point

The Aratiatia Loop begins just beyond the thunderous Huka Falls, 200m or so down the road from FourB and the Hub. Cross the bridge over the deluge and follow the first trail arrow.

01 Enter the bush, follow the blue Huka Trails bike symbol and veer right towards the Aratiatia Dam Loop. There are plenty of signs guiding your way during this first section of the ride. After a short climb you'll come to an elevated vantage point of Huka Falls that is worth stopping to take in as you ride through a clearing a couple of minutes in.

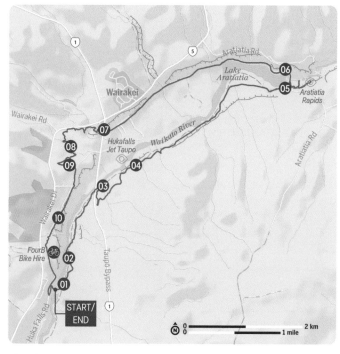

Additional Adrenaline

If riding beside the river doesn't feel quite enough, how about a high-speed cruise on top of it? Hukafalls Jet Taupo runs 30-minute jetboat rides on the Waikato river. Your expert driver will jumpstart the adrenaline rush with 80km/h speeds and 360-degree spins as you travel past Huka Prawn Park, the Wairakei Geo-Thermal Power Station and Aratiatia Dam, tracking the river to get close and personal with the power of nature under the gushing tail of the renowned Huka Falls. It's an excellent way to break up the pedalling and rest your legs as you consider the trail from a more novel vantage point.

Elevation (m)

02 After this, you'll jump back on the narrow dirt trail surrounded by plush native bush including rata, manuka and tī kōuka, complemented by the deafening thrum of cicadas. You may come across people making their way in the other direction here, so be on the lookout, ready to navigate oncoming foot traffic or fellow cyclists.

03 Coming out of the bush section you'll end up at the Red Bridge and the busy road above. Continue to the left, following the signage that indicates Aratiatia once again. After you cross under the bridge you'll find yourself among a series of ponga trees that lead into the first big hill climb moment.

04 There is a bench seat overlooking the river about 4km in, where you can stop for a drink or a snack. From here, a flowing descent down the hill leads into an open meadow that soon returns you to a familiar bush scene for the next few kilometres.

05 Around 7km in you'll come to a steel bike barrier – you'll need to dismount here and pass through. The path then widens into a gravel road, with options for either continuing straight or taking a left. Carry on straight ahead for about 200m and pop out at the Aratiatia car park and bridge.

06 Once you've taken in the sights and stretched your legs with a bit of walking, head over the bridge, which will take you to the opposite side of the river you've been tracking so far. You'll follow a side road with a small power plant to your left and then come to a gate with a bike barrier to pass through. This will get you back on track for the next section, which skirts some paddocks and the river to your left, with some large pine trees to your right. There is also one more bike-barrier gate at the end of this section, taking you up on a tar-sealed main road to pass under a large bridge. Just keep looking out for the blue bike icon to guide you back onto the bush trail about 200m from here.

07 You'll come off the trail again shortly and be led onto a busy main road that crosses over Wairakei bridge. Take extra caution here as there is only a narrow cyclist lane and car traffic passes by at high speed.

08 You'll now be riding through a short and sinuous forest section with a hidden geothermal stream that trickles alongside you to your left. It's worth stopping on the short

upcoming bridge to observe the colours of this natural phenomenon and watch the hot steam rising.

09 The next section is jungle-like, winding through a family of elegant native ponga trees, which then transform into a series of eucalyptus trees standing tall like apparitions. You'll come to a sign with multiple directions on offer. If you're feeling like extending the ride you can head right towards Crater's MTB Park, otherwise carry on left following the arrow towards Hub Cafe.

10 Returning to the main highway, you'll pass a honey shop called the Honey Hive on the right-hand side before crossing over in about 150m when you see the Hub with its big Sikorsky helicopter. Stop off for lunch or a coffee here and then pedal forth for about one minute down the road so you can return your bike to the shop.

☕ Take a Break

Once you reach the Aratiatia car park, hop off your bike and cross the road to the Aratiatia Rapids Walk, which takes about 10 to 15 minutes to complete. Definitely don't attempt this one on your bike as there are some rocky patches, and a fair bit of foot traffic on a busy day. With lower and upper viewing platforms, you'll experience the full splendour and terror of the thunderous rapids from the clifftop. Seats are also set up here should you fancy a snack as you marvel.

PHOTOS BRIANSCANTLEBURY/SHUTTERSTOCK ©

Waikato River, Aratiatia

River People

Before the dam action of today, Aratiatia was – and still is – a location of great significance to the people of Ngāti Tahu – Ngāti Whaoa. This river *iwi* (tribe) once used the river as an access point to reach the region's *wāhi tapu* (sacred) sites containing natural resources. The most established settlement that lay just beyond the rapids was called 'Atahaka' and was home to numerous cultivations, cherry trees, burial places and a river crossing. Tourism around the rapids started as early as 1877, when local people belonging to Opunga, one of the other settlements, began offering visitors canoe rides across the river.

10

New Plymouth Coastal Trail

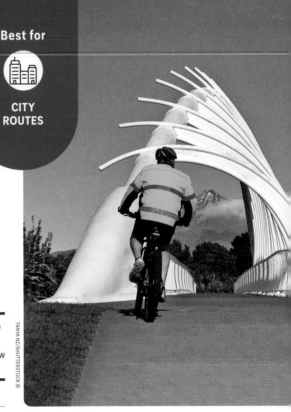

CITY ROUTES

DURATION	DIFFICULTY	DISTANCE	START/END
2–3hr return	Easy	13.2km one way, 26km return	Bottom of Liardet St, New Plymouth

TERRAIN		Paved walkway

TANYA NZ/SHUTTERSTOCK ©

Te Rewa Rewa Bridge

Making your way from Pioneer Park at Port Taranaki all the way to the eastern side of Bell Block Beach is one heck of a way to become au fait with the inimitable and diverse spirit of New Plymouth. Cruising the pavement in seaside promenade fashion among the walkers and talkers and Sunday-stroll-takers of the 'Naki', you'll be convinced you're a local in no time. Stopping for a swim at one of the surf clubs, or rolling out the picnic rug for a spot of *kai*, this ride is an open book for all brands of bike-led leisure.

Bike Hire

Cycle Inn on Devon St East rents city bikes, e-bikes and kids' bikes for either two hours or a full day. It's $10 for a child, and $15 to $55 for adults.

Starting Point

Right around the corner from Cycle Inn is Liardet St. Access to the Coastal Walkway is right down the end of the street – just follow your nose to the ocean!

01 Head right on the promenade, keeping the ocean to your left. The path's design makes the ride fairly intuitive. Straight away you'll be bobbing around other friendly path users – the route is New Plymouth's hot spot for scenic dog walking, running, cycling, skateboarding, skating and scooting. Pack your swimwear. East End and Fitzroy beaches are both lovely for a dip – be it a preventative cooling down at the beginning of your ride, or a rewarding float on your return. Along this first stretch you'll see people fishing off the bordering rocks.

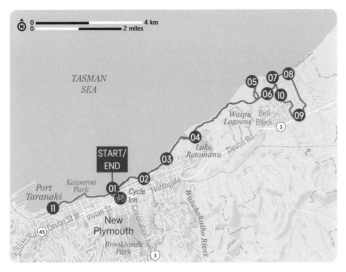

Elevation (m)

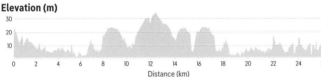

Around 2km in you'll cross a short bridge over Te Henui Stream to reach the 'official' entrance, with toilets, a playground and skate park. Learn a little about the Te Henui Stream, which runs 15km inland and once served as a food-source location for upper and lower river settlements, ideal for catching piharau or inanga (whitebait). Near here you'll begin to notice plaques cemented into the path letting you know how far into the ride you are.

03 Catch your first sight of decent waves as you pass East End beach, and transition onto the wooden boardwalk that takes you through to neighbouring Fitzroy beach dotted with beach towels and the bustle of beachgoers

in summer. Plenty of Kiwi-style pop-up coffee-shed opportunities are here.

04 Continue on the path to a gentle sinuous section with a golf course to your right, beach to your left. The soundtrack of cicadas and strategic placement of harakeke (flax bush) will guide you to the famous Te Rewa Rewa Bridge. You can't miss the bridge – 83m long, the bold white structure, which opened for public use in 2010, was designed to resemble a wave breaking, or a whale skeleton. On the return journey it also perfectly frames Mt Taranaki as you venture towards it. In New Plymouth, everyday life is a work of art, and every corner extends a chance for artistic expression.

Nature's Prompts

More than just a mere walk or cycle path, careful design and consideration is behind the Coastal Walkway. Owing to the often harsh reality of coastal living and the character of the surrounding landscape, robust materials, textures and simple forms were required to bring the design vision of Richard Bain Landscape Architects and the Isthmus Group to life, on a planning journey that began back in 1997. The edgeless promenade section aims to punctuate the feeling of being 'on the edge of the ocean', with its seawall strategically in place to preserve the path and its people from the break of often harsh west-coast waves.

05 Things now start to feel more rural, as you head away from the shore and meet your first little sloping effort through the verdant green farmlands of Hickford Park. You'll then reach the 8km mark, and be reacquainted with residential life as you pass Taranaki Cycle Park and the BMX Club track. An open-air velodrome and 1.7km cycle road circuit is here, plus a pump track for the kids. It's a nice stop for a play, or to clock up some extra kilometres.

06 Continuing past the action, you'll be riding through wetlands. Some great bird-watching is likely here, and a different scene to all you've been taking in so far.

07 Follow the signs and turn left, heading back towards the ocean through a section of big trees. You'll shortly come out at Bell Block Beach car park, with toilets, and a slightly more private spot for a picnic or swim.

08 Continue up Tiromoana Rd for 500m. You're now more elevated on the coastal cliff, with phenomenal views at the 10km official finishing point. There are plenty of grassy patches and tables to perch at while rewarding your efforts with a picnic.

09 Either return the way you came, or for a little extra, at the end of the road take a right and head down Wills Rd for 1km, and then turn right on Penrod Dr. This will take you through residential streets.

10 Turn right onto Sunnyvale St, which soon links onto Mangati Rd. Follow this road in the direction of the ocean and go through the gate to your left. You'll once again return to the wetlands intersection from earlier. From here, the path will be familiar as you head back the way you came.

11 Back at the start, if you continue to the port end of the walkway there's a classic boatie scene. Tucked among the marine shops are some hidden gems if you'd like a classic Kiwi favourite – 'fush and chups'. Catch & Co on Ocean View Pde cooks the freshest *kaimoana* (seafood) in town. For a sit-down alternative, Bach on Breakwater Cafe & Restaurant is a couple of pedals away.

☕ Take a break

If you fancy mixing in a little artistic contemplation, be sure to carry on towards the port once you return to the starting point after your main ride. You'll soon pass Len Lye's iconic *Wind Wand* sculpture – a 48m kinetic form made of red fibreglass, towering above the coast like a wavering antenna. And if you want more, you can also take a detour to the Govett-Brewster Art Gallery (Len Lye Centre), situated downtown on Queen St, to see the full contemporary collection.

JAM TRAVELS/SHUTTERSTOCK ©

Coastal Walkway, New Plymouth

An Enlightened History

The Coastal Walkway has been enhanced by a project named Te Ara Puāwai – which translates from Māori to mean 'the pathway to enlightenment'. A series of panels identifying sites that are of deep significance to the pre-colonised region have been set up to shine light on forgotten Māori landmarks, and provide insight into keeping the world of their ancestors alive. Ngati Te Whiti, the local *hapū* (sub-tribe), developed Te Ara Puāwai to remind the public how vital it is to restore the *mouri* (life essence) and history of the walkways in and around the city.

11

Best for

OFF THE BEATEN TRACK

Great Lake Trail

DURATION	DIFFICULTY	DISTANCE	START/END
7–9hr	Difficult	39.2km	Kinloch

TERRAIN	Purpose-built mountain-bike trail

Great Lake Trail

It's been said that if you want to go fast, go alone, but if you want to go far, go together. The Great Lake Trails may just be the poster trail for such a slogan. On this hearty ride best done in a group, you'll traverse the ridgeline of volcanic escarpments fringing Lake Taupō's Western Bays, journey through sections of dense virgin bush, and cap the day off with some waterfall ogling and a well-earned water-taxi cruise across the water.

Bike Hire

FourB Bike Hire outside Taupō has bikes, including e-mountain bikes, from $35. You can book a shuttle package there to the start of the trail in Waihaha, with a taxi-cat ride across the lake for the K2K.

Starting Point

Starting at FourB Bike Hire or meeting one of their shuttle drivers in Kinloch, you'll be transported by van to the more remote starting point of the trail in Waihaha on SH35.

01 The Waihaha to Waihora or 'Waihaha Link' section of the Great Lake Trail starts with an immediate crossing of a scenic bridge over the Waihaha River to bless the journey ahead. You will be greeted with dramatic views down into the canyon as you make your way around the ridgeline, becoming acquainted with the plant life that will become your constant companion. From this early stage you can start listening out for the call of native birds, including tui, ruru (morepork), tauhou (silvereye), pīwakawaka (fantail), toutouwai (North Island robin) and kereru (native pigeon).

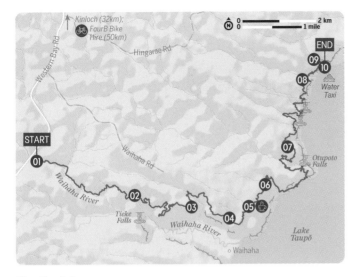

Elevation (m)

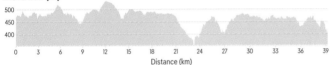

Distance (km)

02 Impressive formations fill this early section, leading you to the first bench seat and viewing spot 7km in, with a gushing waterfall and lagoon nestled deep in the valley below.

03 Continuing on, you'll soon come to your first view of impressive Lake Taupō, and begin to contemplate the ancient activity that's gone on around here. The escarpment edges you're standing in front of are actually a hidden volcano, with the caldera incognito within the lake waters, formed after the last eruption 1800 years ago – what's known to be the largest eruption on the planet in 5000 years. A brief stop is worthwhile to read all about the soil beneath you – actually pumice from the volcano, and how the lack of

mud on the trail is thanks to its free-draining essence.

04 Meandering on through lush forest from here you'll come to a steel bike barrier, which you'll need to dismount and pass through. This marks the official end of 'the first section', after approximately 13km. There is an artful toilet made of red corrugated iron, with a bike chain for a handle – some excellent Kiwi artisanship, and a tip of the hat to the hobby you're partaking in! This is the only toilet stop on the Waihora part of the trail, so be sure to take advantage.

05 A small wooden sign pitched in the centre of what appears to be a dirt crossroads and an information

K2K – The Final Push

Kawakawa Bay is a secluded curved beach that marks the start of the K2K (Kawakawa to Kinloch) stretch of the ride. This shoreline spot has toilets and a shelter for campers to prepare food and gather under a make-shift roof. Continuing on your route, you'll climb up the undulating pathway through native bush before being rewarded with sweeping panoramic views of Lake Taupō from Codgers Rock lookout. The return to Kinloch from here is snug inside the canopy, tracking a fun and flowy ride downhill.

board identify the direction – the Waihora Link to Waihora Bay boat landing. This 17km section has plenty of rest stops, and an unforgettable lunch location in 2km. Here things get more technical, too. So take your time on the trickier corners.

06 It's now a challenging little climb, levelling up your vantage point of the region out beyond the lake. The gradient of the trail also begins to vary from this point, with a few more tight switchbacks and avoidable obstacles thrown in.

07 The track plateaus after you pass the next bench seat, and leads into a more exposed and expansive segment known as Darwin's Corner. Here you'll feel like you're back to Gondwanaland, or your own hidden world. The descent from here has a series of very sharp corners. If you aren't a confident rider, it's best to get off and walk your bike.

08 Around 12km from Waihora Bay is the Echo Rock landmark, a sonic mystery, reverberating the trickling sounds of the stream below. The climb after Echo Rock begs the use of the battery if you're on an e-mountain bike, or a bit of extra juice in the tank, to make it to the next stop.

09 You're now nearing the latter part of the journey, and the most unforgiving. As you make your descent alongside Kotukutuku Stream, the nature of the terrain means concentration is key as the surfaces change. If it has recently rained, take extra care on the sharp downhills, and watch for mossy slips, erosion, and often two-tiered sections of pumice rock splitting the path into uneven gradients.

10 Around 29.5km in, you'll come to a wooden platform overlooking the beautiful Kotukutuku Waterfall flowing down to Kotukutuku Landing in Waihora Bay. This tranquil piece of paradise is only accessible by boat, so if you're ahead of schedule and your taxi hasn't yet arrived, it's well worth a refreshing celebratory soak in the water to revive those limbs.

☕ Take a break

Green and blue become the thematic backdrop on the Waihora Link. Around 2km in, the trail will take you up and over outcrops elevated along the edge of the lake, through to a lunch spot complemented by rocky ravines and clifftop lookouts facing south towards Tongariro, Ngāuruhoe and Ruapehu (the volcanoes of Tongariro National Park). Make sure you fuel up well here, and rest and digest for a quick minute as there's a hilly moment ahead once you're back on the bike.

Mine Bay, Lake Taupō

From Bike to Boat

Travelling between the trails, you'll have time to recharge in a leisurely fashion as you board the taxi-cat water-taxi service from Waihora and boat across the lake. You'll typically be greeted by a cheery and knowledgeable driver armed with locally roasted coffee, tea and Tim Tams – what service! This is a great chance to take in the waterfalls in full glory as they cascade from the cliffs. You'll cruise around the Western Bays, renowned for being the most beautiful part of Lake Taupō, and only accessible by boat. You'll also hear historical anecdotes about the geography and Māori mythology integral to the area.

Also Try...

Tongariro River

Timber Trail

DURATION	DIFFICULTY	DISTANCE
2 days, 5–7hr per day	Intermediate	85km

You're in for real adventure on the Timber Trail. Best completed over two days and most popularly tracked from Pureora to Ongarue, you'll set off on a historical reconnaissance and stop for a night's rest either camping or in one of the on-track lodge accommodation options among the secluded flats of Piropiro. Highlights include the trail itself, which has been set up to follow old logging roads and tramlines, crossing a handful of suspension bridges, through virgin rainforest, and even spotting a historic Crawler Tractor from the 1940s. This trail is remote, so riders are expected to be self-sufficient – come stocked with provisions, toilet paper and ample water. Your best option for a pre-departure stocktake is in Te Kūiti or Taumarunui.

Tongariro River Trail

DURATION	DIFFICULTY	DISTANCE
2–3hr	Easy	15km

The Tongariro National Park is a World Heritage area with mind-blowing scenery. Bike-wise, tracking through lush native forest and over a couple of swing bridges, this straightforward and comfortable loop is a great choice for families or those looking for a more leisurely exploration. Starting in Turangi, at the southern end of Lake Taupō, this rustic ride follows the riverbank, winding up back where you began. A nice way to take in more of the history, culture and proportions of the river is to tack on a white-water rafting expedition, allowing you to experience the Tongariro River from two angles. Rafting adventures can be booked at Tongariro Mountain Biking base in Turangi, who also offer shuttle services and bike hire.

W2K – Great Lake Trail

W2K – Great Lake Trail

DURATION	DIFFICULTY	DISTANCE
2½–3½hr	Intermediate	21km

Part of Ngā Haerenga – the New Zealand Cycle
Trails network, the W2K, or Whakaipo to Kinloch
section of the Great Lake Trail – is a fantastic 'next
day' journey once you've tackled the aforemen-
tioned Waihaha to Waihora segment. It can be cy-
cled either way, but it's best to start at Kinloch and
ride to Whakaipo Bay and catch either a returning
water taxi or shuttle back to base, or, if you're not
defeated, you can spin around and follow the trail
in reverse. We recommend to also do the Headland
Loop detour, adding 9.5km to your journey as you
circuit the headland and relish panoramic views
over the lake to the distant Tongariro National Park
and Kaimanawa Ranges.

Whakamaru Trail

DURATION	DIFFICULTY	DISTANCE
6hr	Intermediate	26km

Whakamaru Trail is a 30-minute drive north of
Taupō and is one of five rides making up the Waikato River Trails. Beginning at Lake Ātiamuri boat
ramp and concluding just past Lake Whakamaru
Reserve, this undulating and at times windy track
passes native bush, pine forest, clifftop ridges and
open country as it traces the banks of the Waikato
River. Replete with native bird life and diverse
natural phenomena, there's much to marvel at as
you journey towards the historic Whakamaru Dam,
which concludes this section of the ride. There are
toilets and a couple of secluded campsites dotted
along the way if a night off-grid is appealing; the
most idyllic is Dunham's Point Reserve.

YIUCHEUNG/SHUTTERSTOCK ©

Pencarrow Coast Road

Southern North Island

12 **Pencarrow Coast Road**
Return trip along a ruggedly beautiful stretch of rocky coastline to a lighthouse and sights beyond, with city and ocean views. **p84**

13 **Hutt River Trail (Remutaka Cycle Trail)**
A relaxed and accessible ramble the length of the Hutt Valley between rural Upper Hutt and urban Petone. **p88**

14 **Water Ride (Hawke's Bay Trails)**
Meander along this Hawke's Bay favourite, exploring water features and great bird

life near Napier traversing coast, river, and wetlands. **p94**

15 **Remutaka Rail Trail (Remutaka Cycle Trail)**
Explore the old railway and settlement history along this gentle climb with forest and river views, rail tunnels and great picnic spots. **p98**

16 **Havelock North to Clifton (Hawke's Bay Trails)**
A Hawke's Bay sampler with rural and coastal landscapes, and an abundance of mouthwatering local winery and food options. **p104**

Southern North Island

Both the Wellington/Te Whanganui a Tara and Hawke's Bay/Te Matau-a-Māui regions are some of the best bases in the country for lovers of outdoor adventures, fueled by excellent food and drinks. The regions are, however, poles apart when it comes to the population, politics, landscapes and, famously, the weather. Hawke's Bay is known as one of the sunshine hubs of the country while Wellington wears its title of world's windiest capital with something between pride and resignation. This makes the Hawke's Bay trails a reliable bet, with Wellington's rides needing a little more luck on your side.

Wellington

New Zealand's vibrant capital is a compact city, constrained by steep hills, green spaces and the harbour. They say you can't beat Wellington on a good day, and it really does sparkle when the sun shines. Cycling is experiencing a surge in popularity with e-bikes, but the centre is very walkable too. There's a thriving arts, culture and culinary scene, so knock back some coffee perfection, then explore the museums, galleries, food and some waterfront or hilltop vistas. The national museum, Te Papa Tongarewa, Wellington Museum and City Gallery have excellent exhibitions, and there's likely a gig or a show on somewhere. Cafes, bars and restaurants are loosely centred around quirky Cuba St and Courtenay Pl.

Brunch is a favourite meal of Wellingtonians – try Floriditas, Fidel's or Egmont Street Eatery. The brewery scene is impressive, and craft-beer darlings Garage Project are based in charming Aro Valley. For more everyday supplies, two centrally located New World supermarkets are most convenient.

While Wellington has more to entertain travellers, the notable rides are situated north of the city, so Petone can also make a logical base and can be linked by train or bus.

Napier

Napier has fully embraced an identity around its unique art-deco architecture, the result of the devastating 1931 earthquake and the flurry of rebuild-

WHEN TO GO

December to April are great months to visit. Hawke's Bay typically has warmer, calmer and more forgiving weather, making it possible to ride year-round. In Wellington, the ideal season is shorter, as winter (June to August) is colder, and the city's famous wind can be especially volatile in spring (September to November).

ing that followed. The elegant streets are a rare gem, and with its coastal location, weather and wineries, it has a year-round seaside holiday-resort feel. The flat landscape and investment in fantastic cycling infrastructure make it a very accessible and welcoming destination for exploring on two wheels, for adults only or families. Napier's centre and art-deco precinct encompass about 10 city blocks, centred on Tennyson and Emerson streets, where you'll find great wandering, shops and food, with favourites like Vinci's Pizza, Hapi Organic Cafe, and Mister D. The long beachfront is backed by parks, and cycle and walking paths along Marine Pde. North of Bluff Hill, Ahuriri is another hub with waterfront nightlife, shops and a beach.

Hastings & Havelock North

Around 12km from more glamorous and coastal Napier, Hastings is its humble, inland twin city,

and Havelock North is a ritzier satellite village. While most choose to base themselves in Napier, Hastings and Havelock North are surrounded by the majority of the region's wineries, and have a top-notch selection of cafes and restaurants.

TRANSPORT

Wellington is a major transport hub, serviced by train, bus, ferry (to the South Island) and international and domestic flights. Hawke's Bay is off the main trunk (railway) line, but big enough to have intercity buses and domestic flights. Buses link Wellington and Napier daily. Your own wheels are helpful but not essential.

 WHAT'S ON

Napier Art Deco Festival February

Harvest Hawkes Bay Food & Wine Festival April

Napier Night Fiesta Friday nights in summer

Wellington Pasifika Festival February

New Zealand Fringe Festival February–March; Wellington

Aotearoa New Zealand Festival of the Arts February–March in even-numbered years; Wellington

Cuba Dupa street festival March; Wellington

Wellington on a Plate May

Matariki ki Pōneke June or July; Wellington

Resources

Wellington Regional Trails (*wellingtonregionaltrails. com*) Showcases walking and cycling trails.

Wellington NZ (*wellingtonnz. com*) What to see and do in the region.

Hawke's Bay Trails (*hbtrails. nz*) Handy info on the cycle trail network.

Hawke's Bay New Zealand (*hawkesbaynz.com*) General information and advice.

 WHERE TO STAY

Hawke's Bay has no shortage of luxury digs, from B&Bs in immaculately restored villas like Hawthorne House, art-deco delights like the Art Deco Masonic Hotel or the Dome Boutique Hotel, fancy vineyard stays and scenic rural glamping like Clifton Glamping. For more budget-friendly options, there are hostels, motels and a holiday park.

Wellington's accommodation is less diverse, with downtown hostels, hotels and B&Bs. The Marion, Dwellington and YHA are quality, budget-friendly hostels, while the QT Wellington and Ohtel are more upmarket spots that are well-located near Oriental Bay and the waterfront.

12

Pencarrow Coast Road

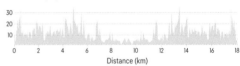

DURATION	DIFFICULTY	DISTANCE	START/END
1½hr	Easy	18km return	Start and end at Burdan's Gate, just south of Eastbourne
TERRAIN		Flat, wide, gravel trail	

Elevation (m)

It's common to see people happily cruising south towards the Pencarrow lighthouse on this traffic-free stretch of coastal gravel road, breathing in the salty seabreeze, enjoying the views across the sparkling blue Wellington Harbour mouth to Miramar Peninsula and the Cook Strait, blissfully unaware that they are being propelled along, not by their powerful thighs, but by a ripping tailwind. It's worth remembering that this is a return trip, though, so take heed of what the wind is up to if you fancy a jaunt along this otherwise ruggedly beautiful stretch of coastline.

Bike Hire

At the start of the trail, hire bikes are available from Wildfinder, ranging from $30 for an hour to $60 for the day. You can book at wildfinder.co.nz.

Starting Point

Burdan's Gate is the end of the drivable road. From Wellington, take central bus 81. If you're coming on the ferry, try organising a lift with Wildfinder from the Days Bay wharf.

01 The end of the road and start of the ride is marked by a car park, Wildfinder bike hire and Burdan's Gate. A toilet is about 150m up the road, and drinks and snacks are available at Wildfinder if you need any more supplies before heading off. Duck through the pedestrian and bike gate, and start heading along the gravel road past the first bay, Camp Bay. There's no navigation required, so just enjoy following the coast to Pencarrow head, 6.5km away.

Pencarrow Lighthouse

At the exposed, wild entrance to Wellington Harbour, Pencarrow was New Zealand's first permanent lighthouse. It's a historically significant landmark with a rich story of early settlement, shipwreck and hardy souls. The lighthouse you see today was opened in 1859, but the first lighthouse, built about 1852, was actually just the lighthouse keeper's house with a lamp in the window. George and Mary Bennett lived here with their five children in harsh, isolated conditions. When George died in 1855, Mary (pregnant with her sixth child) took over for about a decade, becoming New Zealand's first and only female lighthouse keeper.

02 After 2km you'll reach the Pipes picnic area just above the trail on the left. On the surrounding hillsides, keep an eye out for goats along the sheer slopes. Unfortunately, these characters are a pest, hindering efforts to regenerate the native plant life on the hillsides.

03 Keep winding around the coast, and as you near Pencarrow Head, the lower lighthouse will come into view. The historic lighthouse is on the hill above here. Just under 6km from Burdan's Gate, a shortcut to the Lighthouse Track will start on the left. This is the shortest route to visit the lighthouse and is best done on foot, but going via the lakes further on is the main, more scenic track.

04 Another 700m on stands the lower lighthouse. It was commissioned in 1906, as the hilltop lighthouse was frequently obscured by fog and clouds. This automated light stands 17m tall and is still in use today. You'll see rocks offshore, visible above the water – this is why this coastline was so treacherous. Many people ride here and then return, making a 13km round trip.

05 Turning the corner after the lighthouse, the track continues along the bay and the foot of the sheer hills, past Bluff Point. The trail from here on can be a little variable with areas of soft sand that are tricky to ride through, so you may need to push through some short sections.

06 Signs mark the turn-off to Lake Kohangapiripiri; 1.5km later, the track passes Gollans Stream and the turn-off to Lake Kohangatera.

07 Carry on for another 500m to see the rusted shipwreck of the *SS Paiaka* right next to the trail. The *Paiaka* was a steamboat wrecked here in Fitzroy Bay in a severe storm in 1906, in full view of the lighthouse keepers. Fortunately there was no loss of life, but this is only one of many ships that are buried along this coastline.

08 From here, you can retrace your route and head back to Burdan's Gate the same way, or explore a few short detours to the lakes and historic lighthouse.

09 You can take an detour to Lake Kohangatera. Just before crossing back over Gollans Stream, turn right onto the Kohangatera track. Although this trail continues for over 3km (and returns the same way), you only need to go a short way to get views over the lake and wetland that are largely hidden from the coast. The track can get boggy and flooded in areas after rain.

10 Another detour is to the historic Pencarrow lighthouse via Lake Kohangapiripiri. Backtrack further on the main coastal trail until you reach some signs and a sharp turn to the right onto the Kohangapiripiri trail along the lake edge. It's 1.5km to

STEVE TODD/SHUTTERSTOCK ©

Lake Kohangapiripiri

☕ Take a Break

On a nice day, there are plenty of great spots for a picnic on the rocky beaches. There is no shortage of views, but the challenge may be finding some shelter from the sun or wind. The lower lighthouse next to the trail at Pencarrow Head makes a good destination for a break, and you should find a wind break on one side at least! Remember to bring everything you need with you, including water, food, sun protection and warm clothing, so you can take your time.

lighthouse with some climbing on a grassy farm track. Again, just a few hundred metres along, views of the lake open up. Start climbing and continue straight onto the Lighthouse Track where the trails fork, and follow this up the grassy trail, hooking around to the left for the last stretch. You can continue on foot if you prefer – the views

are worth it! The old cast-iron lighthouse last shone in 1935, after 76 years of service, when it was replaced by an automated light further east. It's a picturesque sight, occupying an exposed spot with sweeping harbour, ocean and hill views.

The Lakes & Early Māori Occupation

Despite their proximity to Wellington, the two lakes here are considered some of New Zealand's most unspoiled freshwater wetlands, with both lakes dammed by gravel and sandbanks as a result of historic earthquakes. The area has rare native plants, fish and wetland birds, and also has evidence of early Māori occupation dating back hundreds of years. Terraces, hut sites, oven deposits and tools have all been discovered around the lakes. Kohangapiripiri means 'a nest clinging very strongly' and Kohangatera means 'a nest basking in the sun', suggesting that Kohangatera was the more sheltered and hospitable spot.

13

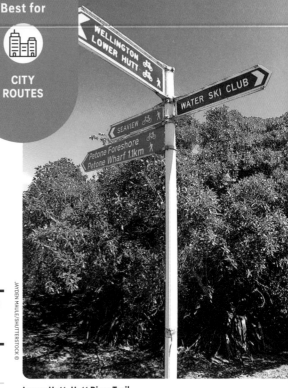

JAYDEN MAULE/SHUTTERSTOCK ©

Hutt River Trail

DURATION	DIFFICULTY	DISTANCE	START/END
3hr	Easy	33km one way	Te Marua/ Petone

TERRAIN	Flat, wide, paved and gravel cycle trails, with a few narrower sections

Lower Hutt, Hutt River Trail

Roll along the riverside and watch the scenes transform from the leafy, rural upper valley to beachfront Petone, with its views over Wellington Harbour. The easygoing, family-friendly Hutt River Trail can be sliced and diced to suit you – make a shorter loop somewhere along the valley using the eastern and western river trails, take on the whole trail and more with the full Remutaka Cycle Trail adventure or, as suggested here, make a relaxed day of riding its full length, taking in the sights along the way, including riverside parks, swimming holes, a nearby art gallery and cafes.

Bike Hire

Wildfinder can meet you at Petone wharf if you book ahead. If you're coming from Wellington, Switched On Bikes at Queens Wharf is a good option. Both offer full-day hire from $60.

Starting Point

Te Marua is at the northern end of the trail. You can catch the Wairarapa Line train to the nearby Maymorn Station. Riding south, it's ever-so-slightly downhill, often with a tailwind, but either direction works.

01 If you're coming by train to Maymorn Station, you may feel like you've arrived in the middle of nowhere. Leaving the station, take a left onto Maymorn Rd for the 10-minute ride to reach the start at Te Marua. This section is on the road but sees very little traffic.

02 Te Marua is marked by a small convenience store on the corner, where you can top up on snacks or drinks for your ride – there are surprisingly few trailside options further south,

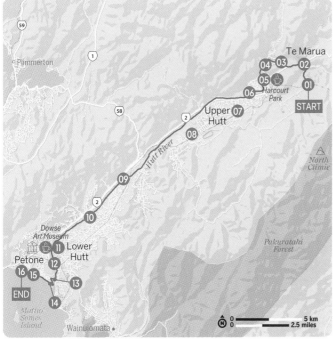

Sample a Shorter Ride

Over 70km of trails follow the Hutt River if you're after shorter trip options. The Upper Hutt–Birchville loop (12km) heads over the bridge to Totara Park. Follow the trail north, staying on the western side to Bridge Rd, cross the Akatarawa bridge, then follow the leafy trail back to Upper Hutt. The Melling–Waione loop (8km) is an accessible and easy Lower Hutt loop around the river between Melling and Waione bridges. For the Petone–Seaview return route (10km), start at Petone Wharf, follow the water's edge to Hikoikoi Reserve, over Waione Bridge, and right to Seaview Marina and Compass Cafe.

Elevation (m)

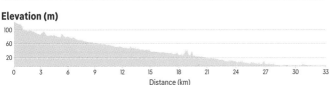

though there are cafes a little off route. Briefly follow the wide shoulder along the highway until the trail veers left on Beechwood Lane and over a footbridge. Take a right onto Beechwood Way, then the short, sharp track that takes you safely under the highway and onto the trail.

03 Wedged between the river and the highway at first, the trail soon leaves the road and ducks through the trees, where it travels between backyard farms and the river. As the trail takes a sweeping left turn, keep

an eye out for a path across the grass and through the trees to the stony riverside, where there's a peaceful spot to take a break or a dip.

04 Approaching the Akatarawa Bridge and where the Akatarawa River flows into the Hutt River/Te Awa Kairangi, the trail again drops down and loops under the road, and heading back up you'll find a sheltered picnic area and toilets. The river confluence is a good swimming spot, and a few hundred metres further along

near the car park, Big Rock is also popular with a deep pool. Take care in the currents, which can be strong.

05 A peaceful section through the trees follows, with glimpses to the lovely section of narrow river below, along with more backyard glimpses over fences. The trail gets narrow in places, so look out for oncoming walkers and cyclists. It widens again when you get to Harcourt Park, a pretty spot with lots of trees. As you reach the road just south of the park, take a

☕ Take a Break

Harcourt Park is one of the nicest along the length of the trail, with rolling grounds and mature trees creating lovely nooks and private, shady spots. It's popular with families for its great facilities, including a splash pool, adventure playground, kids' bike park, Frisbee golf, barbecues and picnic tables. *Lord of the Rings* film fans might recognise the park as the Gardens of Isengard from the trilogy's first film. The films also transformed the Hutt River into the Great River Anduin.

right over the pedestrian and cycle bridge to the suburb of Totara Park on the western side of the river. There are trail options on both sides for this next section, but crossing over keeps you a little further from the motorway.

06 Ride through the grassy parkland, behind the suburbs, for 2km until you reach the next bridge at Totara Park Rd. For a challenging but rewarding detour, you can ride or walk up to check out the view from the Cannon Point trig (345m). The trail starts from Tulsa Park, at the end of Totara Park Rd (take a right instead of left at the bridge), along lush, ponga-fern-clad hillsides.

07 From Totara Park, cross back over to the east bank. If you want to head into Upper Hutt, make sure to cross the motorway straight after coming over the bridge, as there are few places to cross. The main street has several cafes; let Dough Bakery and Cake & Kitchen tempt you with some treats. On the far side of the train tracks is Brewtown, a craft-beer lover's paradise that's home to several excellent breweries, food options, go karting, ice skating, bowling and even axe throwing. It also hosts a Sunday farmers market.

08 Back by the riverside, continue heading south. The trail travels along close to the main road for about 2km, then passes through the grassy Poet's Park and Moonshine Park, where there are toilets. Another 1km further is a fork in the trail. The main route goes straight, staying next to river, and the left turn leads through the park and out to the suburb of Heretaunga if you're looking for a rest stop. Follow Barton Rd to the busy Fergusson Dr, briefly take a right, and you'll find the Fig Tree Cafe occupying an old chapel across the road. Retrace your route back to the park and the riverside.

09 For the next 7km the trail cruises along the riverside, behind golf courses and suburbs, on a mix of paved and gravel trail. Occasionally the trail diverges, with one path closer to the river and one nearer the road, but they come back together so you can choose. There are few places to detour to until Taita Rock, though the Silver Stream Railway Museum might lure train enthusiasts over the road (check the infrequent hours). Taita Rock is another popular swimming spot and is named after the rock outcrop on the far side of the river.

Hutt River

Colonial Settlement

New Zealand Company surveyors arrived in Petone in 1840, and were met by local Māori. Sent ahead to establish Wellington as the new colony's capital, they found the proposal of a Thorndon township and a rural area around the Hutt Valley problematic – Thorndon was too hilly, and travel between them was difficult. The Hutt Valley was chosen as the main site and immigrant boats started arriving soon after. The new settlement was called Britannia, but it was short-lived – within months it was flooded by the Hutt River and the settlement moved across the harbour, with only a few remaining at Petone.

10 Another 4km on, approaching the underpass, there's a crossing to get to Avalon Park. A great stop for kids, this multi-million-dollar destination playground has an impressive variety of experiences including water-play features, large climbing structures, Colin the giant 12m-long Tyrannosaurus Rex, flying foxes, a cheap and cheerful mini golf and a miniature train on the weekends, and even an app-based augmented-reality game called *Magical Park*.

11 Winding trails through wide-open green spaces take you further to Lower Hutt. Just beyond Melling Bridge, the Saturday Riverside Market (until 2pm) has fresh produce, baked goods, coffee and street food. Behind the car park and market is central Lower Hutt, the main shopping hub of the Hutt Valley and home to the Dowse Art Museum. Food options a short distance from the trail include tasty Korean at Han River and Fix Federation bakery.

NEW ZEALAND TRANSITION/GETTY IMAGES ©

12 The trail splits into multiple paths again, so take your pick of gravel or pavement, but make sure to head under the next two bridges, rather than up to cross them. It's a relaxed and pleasant spin overlooking the river where it widens and nears the harbour, as you approach Waione Bridge.

Petone Wharf

13 Loop under the bridge and up to cross it on the separated path on the south side. Pass the turn to the Estuary Boadwalk, continue briefly on the footpath, then take a left onto the Hikoikoi Walkway trail, which roughly follows the water's edge. This area feels quite industrial – from the late 19th century Petone was a thriving, working-class town and there were large industrial sites located here, including car assembly plants, meat, wool and tobacco processing plants, and soap and toothbrush factories.

14 Pass behind a row of boat sheds and keep following the trail as it loops around near the headland, going from the river-mouth to the foreshore through Hikoikoi Reserve. As you start following the beach, there are some lovely spots to pop down to the sand and pebble beach, which is more peaceful here than further along next to the esplanade and road. At the end of the reserve are sports fields, a miniature railway, playground, toilets and Mariana's Kitchen kiosk (coffee, drinks and Argentine food).

15 The Esplanade continues along the bay, with just a few buildings dotting the shore. The first of these is the striking Wellington Provincial Centennial Memorial

TOP TIP:

A visit to Seashore Cabaret makes a great start or end to the ride. This vibrant, lively institution of a cafe is based upstairs in the Petone Rowing Club with epic harbour views. Feast your eyes on its eclectic decor and treat your taste buds.

building, which commemorates the arrival of British immigrants in 1840 and was also designed as a bathing pavilion. It houses the Petone Settlers Museum Te Whare Whakaaro o Pito-one (free entry), featuring displays about the history of Māori and British settlement in the surrounding area and the history of Petone.

16 Continue past some nice rest areas and the Seashore Cabaret cafe on the way to Petone Wharf. Although the route ends here, it's worth also visiting Jackson St. Running parallel to the esplanade one (long) block back, this is Petone's heart, with boutiques, cafes, bars and restaurants.

☕ Take a Break

The Dowse Art Museum is a free public gallery, well worth a visit for art lovers. Its collection focuses on studio craft, including ceramics, textiles and weaving, with exhibitions showcasing contemporary local artists. The experience is a complete package with its modern architecture, thought-provoking exhibitions, on-site Bellbird cafe and outdoor spaces. *Fallen Robot*, a giant robot sculpture by artist Ronnie van Hout, lies partly submerged in a pool outside, both a nod to Hutt Valley's industrial history and a playful space for all ages to enjoy.

14

Water Ride

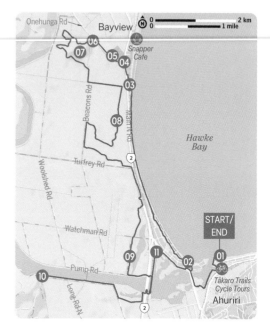

DURATION	DIFFICULTY	DISTANCE	START/END
2½hr	Easy	32km	Start and finish in Ahuriri

TERRAIN	Paved and gravel cycle trails

Elevation (m)

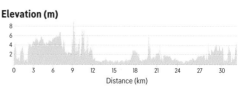

Ahuriri's urban, harbourside bar and restaurant buzz gives way to suburban beachfront cruising towards Bayview, with views of the Pacific Ocean. Peaceful trails through the backblocks follow, with rare migrating birds, historic maritime beacons, Māori history and the lasting effects of 1931's brutal earthquake all on display. The Water Ride is a flat and accessible section of the Hawke's Bay Trails, making it popular with families and all abilities. This route describes a shortened take on the usual route which is made up of two loops, but there are options for making it shorter or longer to suit.

Bike Hire

Tākaro Trails Cycle Tours are conveniently based in Ahuriri. Fishbike are closer to Napier's centre, adding a few extra kilometers along the cycleway. Prices from $30 for a half day.

Starting Point

Perfume Point in Ahuriri is a nice spot to get your bearings. It juts into the water between ocean and estuary, with views up Westshore beach towards Bayview.

01 From the lighthouse at Perfume Point in Ahuriri, follow the cycle path that winds around the harbour. A cluster of bars and restaurants lines the waterfront, which makes for a lively spot to watch the world go by and grab a bite before or after your ride.

02 Keep an eye on the signs and follow directions to Bayview (via the coast). You'll cross the bridge by the sailing club, turn right back towards the ocean and join the cycle path at the coast.

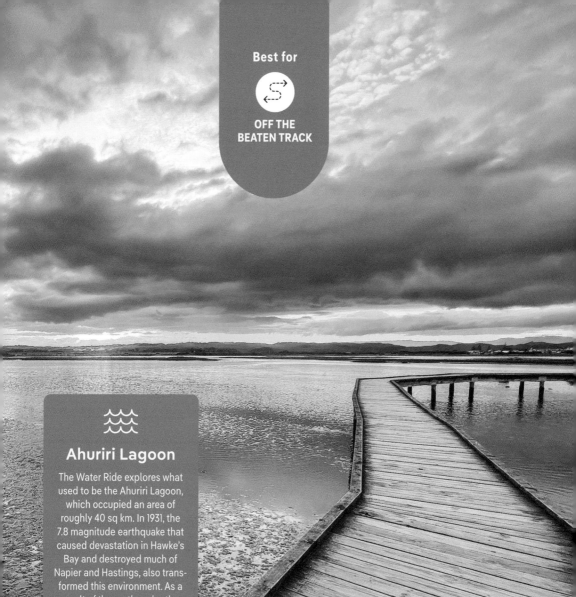

Ahuriri Lagoon

The Water Ride explores what used to be the Ahuriri Lagoon, which occupied an area of roughly 40 sq km. In 1931, the 7.8 magnitude earthquake that caused devastation in Hawke's Bay and destroyed much of Napier and Hastings, also transformed this environment. As a result of the earthquake, the land rose by about 1.5m, mostly draining the water, and left a much smaller estuary. With additional land reclamation and drainage work, the estuary is about a quarter of the size of the original lagoon. Most of the area is now home to the airport, suburbs and agriculture.

From there it's plain sailing all the way towards Bayview, cruising along the paved cycle and pedestrian path. You'll pass some toilets, a water fountain, picnic tables and shady trees.

03 The trail is sandwiched between Esplanade Rd and the coast for the most part, but then runs adjacent to the highway for a short section before it reaches the southern fringes of Bayview. Join Ferguson Rd at the end of the cycle trail, then veer left, approaching the highway crossing.

04 From here you can take a detour to Snapper Cafe, 1.2km off route on quiet roads, before returning the same way. To continue, cross the highway at the marked crossing, following signs to Taradale. At the intersection with Onehunga Rd the trail turns left. Another detour option is Crab Farm Winery, a charming, rustic restaurant (open Thursday to Sunday for lunch). Instead of turning onto Onehunga Rd, continue straight for half a kilometre until you reach the winery on the left, the return to the trail the same way.

05 Heading down Onehunga Rd, the inland section of the trail begins and the trail changes from paved to smooth, limestone gravel. Pass Petane War Memorial domain, a sports field with toilets and a playground.

06 After 1km on Onehunga Rd, turn left at the signs for the Whakamaharatanga Walkway and Westshore (via wetlands). You'll also start seeing signs for the Water Ride. There are several gates throughout this next section. It crosses a working farm and animals may be roaming, so be sure to leave the gates as instructed.

07 Go through the gate and turn right. Roro o Kuri is the hill in front of you, but prior to the 1931 earthquake, which raised a huge area of land in the area, it was actually an island. You can leave your bike and walk up to the summit in about 15 minutes to get a view of the surrounding area. It's a culturally and archaelogically significant place, with multiple *pā* (fortified village) sites, so keep to the marked trails.

08 The trail traces the edge of Roro o Kuri through farmland, then picks its way through wetlands and water channels. The two unusual towers that punctuate the flat landscape are known as the Beacons. They predate the earthquake, and served as leading lights to guide ships into the Port of Napier.

09 Pass by the airport car park and after 1km cross the road. Continue through the Westshore Wildlife Reserve, following signs to Taradale via Water Ride until you pass under the expressway. From here the route explores the estuary, then comes back the same way, so for a shorter option, you can take the left here to return straight to Ahuriri.

DONA SHIELL/GETTY IMAGES ©

Ahuriri estuary

☕ Take a Break

The Snapper Cafe at the Napier Beach Top 10 Holiday Park in Bayview is one of the only places to get food and drinks once you leave the bustle of the Ahuriri waterfront behind. It's just over a kilometre off the route, but well-signposted from the trail, and it makes a reliably friendly break. Find a shady spot in the pleasant garden and grab a drink and a treat from the counter selection, or order lunch off the menu. Open 8.30am to 3pm.

10 To continue along the estuary for some more bird-watching opportunities, take the old bridge and wind back under the expressway. After a few hundred metres there's a basic bird hide – a wall with some cutouts to observe the birds. Take the right turn that follows and continue along between the estuary and wetlands for a few more

Bird-Watching

The Ahuriri estuary has a wide array of habitats and supports diverse birds, fish, invertebrates and plant life. Over 70 bird species can be found here. Many birds arrive each year from their arctic breeding grounds, before returning for the next round of nesting and chick-raising. Others gather here over winter for the abundant food supplies. Sightings might include the pied stilt, black-billed gull, white-faced heron, paradise shelduck, royal spoonbill and bar-tailed godwit. The bar-tailed godwit travels around 11,500km from its breeding grounds in the Alaskan tundra to this estuary – a nonstop flight of about nine to 12 days!

kilometres until you reach another, more impressive bird hide.

11 Head back towards Ahuriri by retracing your steps, crossing the bridge again, and continuing straight. After half a kilometre turn right at the cycleway junction, and you'll soon rejoin the early part of the route at the first bridge and sailing club.

15

Remutaka Rail Trail

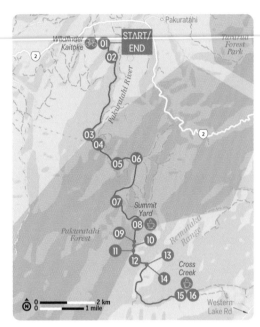

DURATION	DIFFICULTY	DISTANCE	START/END
3hr	Intermediate	30km return	Kaitoke trailhead

TERRAIN	Gravel trails with some climbing

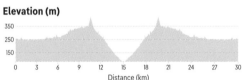

Elevation (m)

The Remutaka Rail Trail is a highlight section of the full Remutaka Cycle Trail adventure that makes a great day trip for nature lovers. Far away from any roads, this popular trail takes a beautiful, meandering journey through the Pakuratahi Forest and Rimutaka Forest Park, exploring the old railway line and its history, several tunnels, a swing bridge, plus swimming and picnic spots. This describes a there-and-back trip along the most scenic part from Kaitoke to Cross Creek, but there are many options to suit families, different levels, ages and budgets.

Bike Hire

Wildfinder Kaitoke at the trailhead and car park has regular or e-mountain bikes ($50/$70 for three hours). See wildfinder.co.nz for bike hire and transport options.

Starting Point

The Kaitoke trailhead and car park is on Kaitoke Summit Rd and requires a car or shuttle. The full trail starts at Maymorn (7km away, train station nearby) but has no bike hire.

01 Skirt around the barrier just beyond the car park and join the gravel road shaded by pine forest. There are occasionally service vehicles on the trail, but it's usually traffic-free from here on, though you'll likely encounter many cyclists and walkers on weekends. There's some trail information and toilets available here. Navigation for the most part is very straightforward with just a few tracks branching off the main route, but they are well signposted.

Best for

MOUNTAIN SCENERY

BLONDIE/SHUTTERSTOCK ©

Siberia swing bridge (p102)

02 Shortly after the start, pass the rifle range to the right of the trail. Don't be alarmed if you hear shots fired – they're all pointed away from the trail. Just beyond this, you catch the first views of the Pakuratahi River below the trail. The trail will trace the river's path, crossing it a few times, almost all the way to the top. The forest changes from pine to include more native bush. Pakuratahi is part of the forested corridor connecting the Akatarawa, Tararua, Remutaka and Orongorongo ranges. In this area you'll mostly find regenerating native forest, with some signs of exotic forestry.

03 The first 4km of the route is flat and easygoing, with a wide trail and just the odd pothole to dodge. Pass the turn-off to Goat Rock Rd, which bends sharply to the right – this links up with the rail-trail section before Kaitoke, via a hefty climb. The sweeping left turn with a ford across the road and a pedestrian and bike bridge is Munitions Bend. There's a picnic table here, and a glimpse of the tunnel ahead.

04 The trail begins to climb very gently as you head into the cool, dark Pakuratahi tunnel, the first of four historic tunnels on route. It's

73m long and was built in 1876 – the first concrete block structure in New Zealand. On the far side of the tunnel is the Remutaka Rail Tunnel ventilation shaft. Far underground, 116m to be exact, the 8.93km-long tunnel ploughs through the Remutaka Range connecting Upper Hutt and Maymorn Station to Featherston. The tunnel was built as part of the new route that replaced the Rimutaka Incline, which was slow and costly to run. Detailed surveys were completed in 1938–39, but the project was postponed due to WWII. Construction eventually began in 1948 and it opened in 1955.

☕ Take a Break

Take a load off, you've made it to the top! Summit yard (348m) is the ideal spot for a break. Bask in the sun (hopefully), spread out limbs and a picnic on the surprisingly manicured grass, scope out the old locomotive remnants, read the history and imagine what it was like here when it bustled with railway activity. A small shelter, picnic table and toilets are available. This is also a great spot to camp if you want to tackle an overnight or multiday getaway.

05 River views and lush, steep hillsides make for a lovely section of riding, made more atmospheric by the characterful Howe Truss Bridge, which passes over the river. Originally built in 1876, it was rebuilt in 1910 after a fire, and further restored in 2001. Look out for a short, steep access way down to the river just before the bridge.

06 Crossing a side stream, the curved, 70m-long Ladle Bend Creek Bridge is another historic landmark where the view up the valley is revealed. A trail veers left at the far end of the bridge, which leads steeply up to connect to the Remutaka Hill Rd highway, or reaches the summit via a back way. Stay on the main Rail Trail for the more scenic and gentle climb. Around 500m beyond the bridge, you can reach the river by heading right down a rougher track to the grassy picnic area and basic campsite.

07 The trail continues climbing gently on a shaded trail with some interesting sections cut deeply into the land, and mosses and ferns clinging to the steep walls. It rises higher above the river for a few kilometes, until it veers left up a neighbouring valley with just 1km to go until the top.

08 Summit yards open up to a flat, grassy expanse. The orange, rusted remains of boilers, steam pipes and train cabs sitting on display, and a cute weatherboard shelter, are the only nods to the area's bustling past life. This was once the site of five cottages, a signal box, water tank, ashpit and turntable for the train carriages. Landscaping and planting has transformed it into a pleasant park-like space, where cyclists and walkers enjoy a well-earned break. There are some fascinating historic photos displayed in the shelter, and toilets are available.

09 Just beyond the yard area, the impressive 584m Summit Tunnel travels through the hill. Many people ride to the Summit and return the same way, making a family-friendly, 20km return trip. If you're planning this, be sure to go just a little further to check out the tunnel. You'll definitely want a light for this one – the darkness is complete and disorientating.

10 Popping out on the Wairarapa side, take in the wild framing of the tunnel emerging from the hillside, covered in moss and ferns, with water trickling down the steep sides. It's the Remutaka Cycle Trail's most iconic image.

PX239/SHUTTERSTOCK ©

Remutaka Ranges

The Full Remutaka Cycle Trail

One of New Zealand's 23 'Great Rides', this 115km trail has a rich diversity of scenery and is rideable by most people over two to three days. The trail can be accessed in many places, but is commonly ridden from Petone or Days Bay, up the Hutt River Trail, over the Rail Trail, down to the coast on quiet sealed roads, then around the stunning wild coast on a 4WD track. Accommodation is available in the Hutt Valley, Featherston and the road to the coast, or there is basic camping in some fantastic locations. Find out more at nzcycletrail.com.

11 The trail begins to descend more steeply on this side; in fact, it's twice as steep as the other side with a 1:15 gradient, compared to 1:30. While this was exceptionally steep for a rail line, its consistent gradient is reasonably bike-friendly. The trail is less groomed on this side and its surface can be more variable, so keep an eye out for looser areas of gravel.

12 Take a moment to walk to the lookout point, just to left of the trail as you descend, which has a panoramic view of the old route from Cross Creek to the Summit. The Wairarapa side of the trail feels a little wilder, with views across the hills which, once stripped by logging, are again covered in regenerating forest.

13 After the lookout is the Siberia tunnel, then the modern Siberia swing bridge. The hostile weather is

BLONDIE/SHUTTERSTOCK ©

Rail Trail History

When the government set out to build links between major ports and the agricultural countryside, the rail link from Wellington to Wairarapa via the rugged Remutaka Ranges posed a challenge. A tunnel was preferred but too costly, so a steep railway was built instead, opening in 1878. From Cross Creek to Summit is the steepest section of the main railway line ever built in New Zealand, and the innovative Fell mountain railway system ran here for 77 years. Eventually high costs and the need to replace trains led to building an almost-9km tunnel, sealing the fate of the historic route.

responsible for the name, as this part of the historic track was the scene of one of New Zealand's worst early rail crashes in 1880. Howling down the gully, the wind blew three train carriages off the track and killed four children.

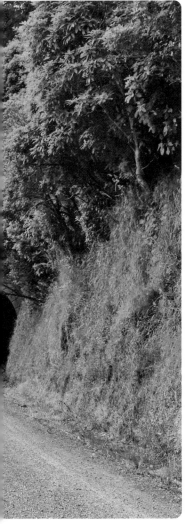

Pakuratahi rail tunnel (p99)

14 Looking into the gully from the swing bridge, you'll see a narrow track leading down and back out, which used to be a section of walking and pushing. Despite there being eight pairs of cables anchored in the gully beneath that are securing the bridge, on exceptionally windy days it's recommended to take the original low route.

15 After one final, short tunnel, it's a long, fun roll down, roughly following Cross Creek in the valley below. Be sure to keep left where you can, as you might encounter people heading uphill. A flat, grassy clearing and the bottom of the hill marks Cross Creek Station. There's a pit toilet and small shelter available.

16 Heading back over the hill will require a moderate level of fitness, or an e-bike might be a good option! The return trip is logistically simpler, but if you don't fancy riding the trail both ways, you have a couple of choices. You can organise a shuttle from the Cross Creek car park, which

TOP TIP:

Besides toilets, you won't find facilities along the route, so come prepared with everything you need, including food, water and extra layers. Hire bikes will come with lights, but if you're bringing your own wheels, remember to take a light to guide you through the pitch-black tunnels.

will need to be booked ahead through Wildfinder. To get there, veer right at Cross Creek, cross the bridge, and follow the single-track trail that winds its way through forest for another 2km. This section is a little more technical as it's quite narrow in places. From the car park, it's also possible to carry on to Featherston, 10km further on a roadside trail, to catch a train back to the Hutt Valley.

☕ Take a Break

At the bottom of the long, grin-inducing descent lies Cross Creek. This historic site was once occupied by cottages, a hall, school, library, locomotive depot and a turntable but, similar to Summit, little evidence remains of its heyday on first glance. Some remnants can still be found, like the concrete foundations of the locomotive shed and the turntable pit. It's a peaceful spot for a break, with a little shelter from the elements and a few plaques highlighting various features of the yard.

16

Havelock North to Clifton

DURATION	DIFFICULTY	DISTANCE	START/END
2hr	Easy	22km	Havelock North/Clifton

TERRAIN	Flat, smooth, gravel cycle trails, with a few sections on quiet roads

Te Mata Estate Winery

Exploring part of what's known as the Landscape Ride section of the Hawke's Bay Trail network, this route is a perfect taster of local flavours and scenery in a relaxed, fun little package. Sample wineries, cafes and trails through vibrant orchards and vineyards along the Tukituki River, then meander down the coast to Clifton through laid-back settlements with views to the cliffs around Cape Kidnappers. Bring a hearty appetite to make the most of the stops along the the way.

Bike Hire

Tākaro Trails in Ahuriri has a day trip with drop-off and pickup for $95. Hire bikes, e-bikes and shuttles from Good Fun Bike Rides in Havelock North from $40 a day.

Starting Point

Havelock North's centre fans out from a roundabout and makes an ideal starting point, with bike hire, information centre and plenty of cafes and supply options available in close proximity.

01 From the centre of Havelock North, head out of town along Te Mata Rd. Pass the Village Green park and swimming pool, then turn right to keep following Te Mata Rd, where there is a marked cycle lane on the road. There's 3km of riding along this to head out of town, but if you'd prefer to skip it, bike-hire operators can also drop you on the edge of town, such as at Black Barn Vineyard.

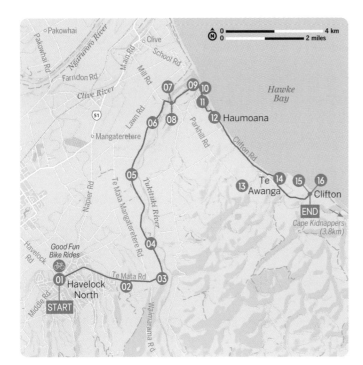

Cape Kidnappers

Down the coast from Clifton is the distinctive, crumbling coastline of Cape Kidnappers. Its English name came after Captain Cook's voyage in 1769, when Māori traders are said to have taken Cook's cabin boy, who they thought was being held against his will. The Cape is the site of a significant mainland Gannet colony, home to an estimated 20,000 birds. You can walk the beach from Clifton to the Plateau colony (19km return), though the risk of landslides and rockfall along the coast is real. It's easier to take a Gannet Safaris Overland tour ($92 for a three-hour tour from Te Awanga).

Elevation (m)

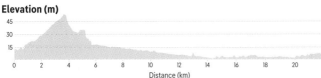

Distance (km)

02 After a few kilometres and a gentle climb, you'll reach the outskirts of town. Before you've broken a sweat, there are already vineyards and more to explore – Brother cafe (great food and coffee) and Village Vineyards are on the left, and Black Barn Vineyard is on the right. The Black Barn growers market on Saturday mornings (9am to midday) in summer makes a nice stop with freshly baked goods, coffee, produce and other local products. The separated cycle trail starts around here, too. Start descending and soon after you'll also find Te Mata Estate Winery on the left, followed by Origin Earth, a local cheesemaker.

03 Reaching the four-way intersection at Waimarama Rd, head straight on River Rd, staying on the cycle path, and follow the signs to Black Bridge (9km). As you approach the Tukituki River, this curves around to the left and leaves the road, winding through a short section of lovely shaded forest.

04 Head through the gate onto the raised stopbank, which protects the surrounding areas from flooding. The trail runs along here for 8km with slightly elevated views over abundant apple orchards and vineyards. You'll see how the region earned its title as the Fruit Bowl of New Zealand – it's the largest growing region for apples, peaches and squash. Vines were first planted in Hawke's Bay in 1851 by French Missionaries who established Mission Estate, and now with over 200 vineyards, it's the country's second-largest growing area for wine, some way behind Marlborough.

☕ Take a Break

With almost 40 wineries with cellar doors in Hawke's Bay, wine-focused visits are hugely popular in this area, best known for red blends, syrah and chardonnay. Most cellar doors charge $10 to $20 for tastings (but some can be more). This allows you to taste a range of different wines, and usually purchasing a bottle or two will waive the charge. For a tasting it's generally fine to drop in, but it pays to call ahead if there's a bigger group.

05 From the path, you'll have some occasional views of the river. Although the views are sparse, the river is an important piece of the landscape and has played vital roles in local industries. These days it's valuable for the water it provides for farms and orchards. Back in the 1880s, barges used to travel down the river carrying wool from farms to deliver to freighters off the coast of Haumoana.

06 This river section has a few more gates along the way, which help manage stock and block access to motorbikes. On the positive side, it'll give you a chance to look back and check out the views of the craggy Te Mata Peak, southeast of Havelock North, which is one of the area's most significant landmarks. It's the highest hill around at 399m and is worth a visit for fantastic views over the region in all directions.

07 As you approach Mill Rd and Black Bridge, follow the sign heading straight to Haumoana and go right over the bridge. Going under the bridge leads to Clive, 6km away, via the coast and wetlands, which is another option for a slightly shorter route or an extra detour. You may notice that Black Bridge has a curious absence of blackness – the name hails from the original 1888 bridge, brushed in tar, which was replaced by its current steel and concrete incarnation in 1956.

08 Crossing the bridge you'll get a view along the Tukituki River. The river flows from the rugged Ruahine Ranges southeast of Hawke's Bay to the Pacific Ocean for 117km. The story of the river's existence in Māori mythology describes a large lake located at the headwaters. It's said that two *taniwha* (supernatural, dragon-like creatures in Māori tradition) lived in this lake, and when a boy fell into the lake, the two *taniwha* fought over their prey. The resulting destruction on the landscape created breaks in the hills through which the lake drained away – one of the channels was the Tukituki River.

09 After the bridge, loop back underneath it or cross over the road, then continue along the riverside trail. About 1km on you'll get great views over the scenic Tukituki River mouth and out to the coast. The river-mouth is considered an important conservation area and wildlife habitat due to its high diversity of bird life, notably the large number of black-billed gulls, terns and little black shags.

10 Crossing a small bridge, you'll reach another junction. Heading left you can take a small detour to check out the stony beach, then rejoin the main route. Toilets are also available down near the beach at the Domain.

11 Keep following the signs through the settlement of Haumoana, which is spread out along this section of coast. This stretch navigates paved roads and a few turns for a short stint, so keep an eye out for the cycling signs. It follows Grange Rd N, right onto

Te Mata Peak

Haumoana Rd, then left onto Beach Rd. There's no separated cycle trail or lane, but the streets are wide and traffic sparse and slow. As you trace the coast, the views stretch out along the bay towards Te Kauwae-a-Māui/Cape Kidnappers, about 10km away with its distinctive white cliffs of crumbling sandstone.

12 Haumoana's cluster of services has a Four Square convenience store, takeaway food, a pub and coffee caravan, and can furnish you with food, drinks, ice cream and more. Kids might enjoy a visit to the Hawke's Bay Farmyard Zoo just off-route on East Rd.

13 Continue along the cycle path next to the road, following signs to Te Awanga and Clifton. Three vineyards are dotted along this next stretch to the right of the main road – Elephant Hill, Clearview Estate and Te Awanga Estate. It's recommended to book if you plan on stopping in for lunch at any of them. Keep your eyes open for the turn-offs across the main road, especially to Te Awanga Estate, 2km after the Haumoana shops. Don't be put off by the long gravel driveway – it's worth seeking out the detour. Offering a relaxed atmosphere where you can make yourself comfortable on the deck or on the shady grass slope, enjoy great pizzas, platters and wine, and just enough elevation to glimpse the sea over the rows of vines, it's a favourite place to take a break.

14 Past the vineyards, the route jumps between trail and small side roads but is reasonably well-marked. Heading into the settlement of Te

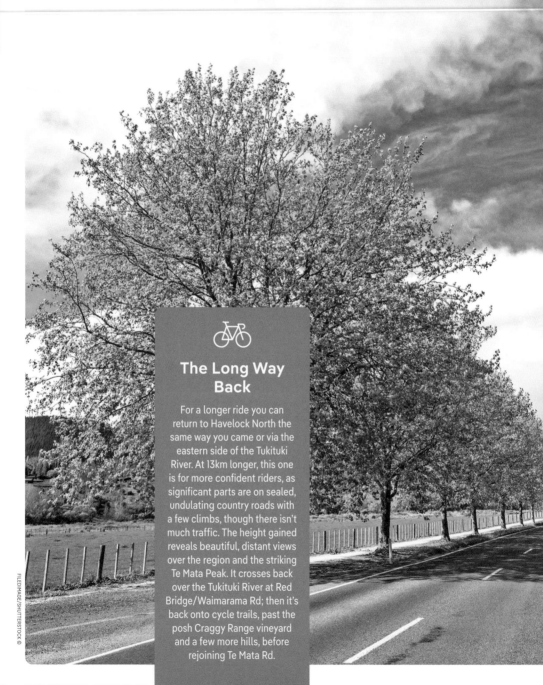

🚲

The Long Way Back

For a longer ride you can return to Havelock North the same way you came or via the eastern side of the Tukituki River. At 13km longer, this one is for more confident riders, as significant parts are on sealed, undulating country roads with a few climbs, though there isn't much traffic. The height gained reveals beautiful, distant views over the region and the striking Te Mata Peak. It crosses back over the Tukituki River at Red Bridge/Waimarama Rd; then it's back onto cycle trails, past the posh Craggy Range vineyard and a few more hills, before rejoining Te Mata Rd.

Te Mata Peak

Awanga, the trail hugs the coast and then passes the Te Awanga Holiday Park, a nice, laid-back, waterfront spot nestled between the coast and the Maraetotara River mouth. The on-site Vanilla Bean cafe provides yet another refreshment option.

15 Rejoining the main road, cross over the Maraetotara River and continue for just over 1km to Clifton. Clifton Station is a sixth-generation family operation, running glamping accommodation and a cafe here, among other things. At the end of the route you'll find some information and history panels and toilets.

16 You can continue on for a short stretch and take a peek at the grand old Clifton Homestead building opposite the beach. Otherwise, pop into Hygge at Clifton Bay, a delightful, sprawling but homely cafe where you can park up in

TOP TIP:

Don't let the tasty food and drinks end with your ride. If you have time in Havelock North, indulge in some more delights. Maina Cafe has excellent brunch, Hawthorne Coffee Roastery extracts the perfect drop and Giant Brewing will refresh you after a hot day.

the large garden or in the rustic indoor nooks, fill your belly and rest your legs. There's often live music on Sundays, too. If you've arranged to be collected by your bike-hire company, this is a great spot to wait, or recharge for the trip back.

 Take a Break

One of the trail's most scenic spots is the Tukituki river-mouth and estuary, with its plant and bird life and big coastal views. Take some time to spot birds like oyster catchers, dotterels, white heron, royal spoonbill, godwits, terns, shags and ducks. Make your way down to the stony beach at the river-mouth to take a break, dip your feet (or more) in the water, and watch the locals fishing and surfing. Keep to marked tracks within the estuary and be careful of nesting birds.

Also Try...

Mākara Peak

Puketapu Loop

DURATION	DIFFICULTY	DISTANCE
1½hr	Easy	18km

This thoroughly pleasant riverside ramble, part of the Hawke's Bay Trails, follows raised stopbanks up one side of the Tutaekuri River and down the other, with some lovely shaded sections through mature trees. A local favourite, the friendly Puketapu Pub is ideally situated at the halfway mark and offers a wide-ranging menu of tasty food catering to dietary needs and children. The Ōtātara Pā site along the route is well worth a visit. Wander up the hill and explore the significance of this historic Māori defensive settlement, and check out the expansive views. Begin in Taradale at the Pettigrew Green Arena to access the trail, and ride the loop in either direction.

Mākara Peak Mountain Bike Park

DURATION	DIFFICULTY	DISTANCE
1½hr	Medium	10km

For those keen to try mountain biking, Wellington's most-loved bike park maintains beautiful trails through native forest for all abilities from beginners to experts, from 3km upwards. The Kids and Beginners Loop and the Fern Loop are great options if you're starting out. The first is the flattest and easiest with mostly wide trails. It starts at the entrance on Allington Rd, and takes in Rimu, Miro, Big Tom's Wheelie and Magic Carpet. To add the Fern Loop, head down Lazy Fern to the main entrance, and back up Koru. From there you can roll down Lazy Fern again, or back towards Allington Rd via Miro and Rimu. Mud Cycles has bike hire nearby.

STEVE TODD/SHUTTERSTOCK ©

Te Ara o Whareroa, Queen Elizabeth Park

Queen Elizabeth Park Trails

DURATION	DIFFICULTY	DISTANCE
1hr	Medium	12km

Wind through the sand dunes and regenerating native plants of the Queen Elizabeth Park on a network of great trails, well away from the traffic on the Kāpiti Coast. Stretching between Paekākāriki and Raumati South, the Te Ara o Whareroa trail is a family-friendly, paved, 5.5km route. Return the same way, or at the southern end you can opt to loop back on the stunning Coastal Track, which is a more undulating dirt trail. The views are fantastic, encompassing coastline, hills, Kāpiti Island and even the Marlborough Sounds and Mt Taranaki on clear days. Bookend the ride at either end with cafe stops by going a bit beyond the park – Raumati Social Club and Beach Road Deli are favourites.

Martinborough Wine Touring

DURATION	DIFFICULTY	DISTANCE
1hr	Easy	5-10km

A popular weekend getaway for locals, Martinborough in the Wairarapa region has a charming square with boutiques, pubs, cafes and restaurants, and is surrounded by vineyards. It also has more reliable weather than Wellington. Bike hire is available (try Green Jersey), cycling is flat and easy along wide, quiet roads, and there are plenty of vineyards close to town for tastings and food. There's no set loop to follow – grab a map from the information centre and follow your nose. A 10km outing will take you past more places than you can visit in a day. Vineyards are all around, with many clustered near Huangarua Rd, Puruatanga Rd and Kitchener Rd, including Poppies, Moy Hall and Nga Waka.

50 km

25 miles

0

0

TASMAN SEA

Cape Farewell

Farewell Spit

Puponga

Pakawau

Golden Bay

Collingwood

Onekaka

Pōhara

Tōtaranui

Bainham

Upper Takaka

Takaka

Abel Tasman National Park

Mārahau

Kaiteriteri

Riwaka

Motueka

Kahurangi National Park

Kōhaihai

Karamea

Little Wanganui

Tapawera

Woodstock

Māpua

Wakefield

17

Nelson

Richmond

Brightwater

18

Tasman Bay

Mt Richmond Forest Park

French Pass

D'Urville Island

Marlborough Sounds

Havelock

Anakiwa

19

Waikawa

Picton

Cloudy Bay

Blenheim

Renwick

20

Wairau River

Seddon

Grassmere

Ward

Cape Campbell

St Arnaud

Kawatiri

Nelson Lakes National Park

Murchison

Lyell

Victoria Forest Park

MILOSZ MASLANKA/SHUTTERSTOCK ©

Queen Charlotte Track (p124)

Top of the South

Top of the South

Consisting of the fertile Tasman and Marlborough districts, for international visitors, the Top of the South is often the first introduction to what South Islanders refer to as 'the mainland'. If the ferry sailing across the Cook Strait from Wellington was calm, there's a sense of peace and serenity on arrival in Picton, but if it was a white-knuckle crossing, then there's more of a sigh of relief. Picton is the gateway to the gorgeous Marlborough Sounds, while chilled-out Nelson is known as Aotearoa's sunniest city. The world-renowned Marlborough wine district is based around the city of Blenheim.

Nelson

Dishing up a winning combination of beautiful surroundings, sophisticated art and culinary scenes and lashings of sunshine, Nelson (population 53,000) is hailed as one of Aotearoa's most liveable cities. In summer, it fills with local and international visitors, there to take advantage of its proximity to holiday and activity hot spots in the Marlborough Sounds, Golden Bay, three nearby national parks, well known multiday hikes, a myriad of bike trails and the diverse natural attractions of the Tasman District. It has everything you'd expect of a city this size, including a good selection of breweries, bakeries and supermarkets, and a good range of biking, outdoors and camping stores. The best restaurants congregate at the

cathedral end of Trafalgar St, while other good options spread along Hardy St.

Takaka

Boasting Aotearoa's highest concentration of yoga pants, dreadlocks and bare feet in the main street, tiny Takaka (population 1330) is a lovable little town, over the hill west of Nelson, and is the 'big smoke' for Golden Bay, the last 'big' centre before the road west ends at Farewell Spit. You'll find most things you need here, and quite a few things you don't.

Picton

Half asleep in winter, but hyperactive in summer, with Cook Strait ferries coming and going, boaty Picton (population 4300) clusters around a deep and beautiful gulch at the head of Queen

WHEN TO GO

The Top of the South soaks up some of Aotearoa's sunniest weather, with January and February being the warmest months. The region teems with Kiwi holidaymakers during the summer school holidays, so book well ahead. June and July are the coldest months, though there's often wonderful winter weather, with frosty mornings giving way to clear skies and T-shirt temperatures.

Charlotte Sound. It's the main traveller port for the South Island and the best base for exploring the Marlborough Sounds and tackling the Queen Charlotte Track. As such, there's plenty to entice visitors to linger before hitting the road and heading south. There are plenty of accommodation options, good eating spots, a supermarket plus a somewhat legendary Dutch-style bakery.

Blenheim

Blenheim (population 28,200), only 29km south of the South Island gateway town of Picton, is an agricultural town. Its name has become associated with its surrounding Marlborough wine region, producing some of the most recognised sauvignon blanc on the planet. On the pretty Wairau Plains between the Wither Hills and the Richmond Ranges, Blenheim has benefitted from the maturation of the country's wine industry, town beautification projects and an exceptional museum for aviation buffs, the

Omaka Aviation Heritage Museum, housing Peter Jackson's amazing collection of original and replica Great War aircraft. Throw in some good bike rides, and Blenheim is a great place to park up for a few days.

TRANSPORT

Picton is the South Island's main Interislander ferry port, with multiple daily sailings to and from Wellington. Nelson has the busiest domestic airport, followed by Blenheim and Picton. Buses link the region to Canterbury and the West Coast. Kiwi Rail's Coastal Pacific scenic train links Picton and Christchurch, stopping in Blenheim and Kaikōura along the way.

 WHAT'S ON

Marlborough Wine & Food Festival

Fabulous wine, cuisine and music in Blenheim in early February.

Nelson A&P Show

Going for over 125 years, the Agricultural & Pastoral Show is a late-November highlight.

Taste Tasman Beer, Cider & Food Festival

Mid-January summer fun in Nelson.

Nelson Arts Festival

11 days of exciting arts experiences in October.

Classic Fighters Omaka Air Show

Aviation buffs go gaga near Blenheim biennially over Easter.

 WHERE TO STAY

As the gateway to the 'mainland' and a ferry port town, Picton has plenty of places to stay. Some intriguing options beckon from out in the Marlborough Sounds, such as Furneaux Lodge, Punga Cove Resort and Lochmara Lodge, accessed by water taxi from Picton. Around 29km south of Picton ferry terminal, Blenheim is more of a working town, but is also the centre for the Marlborough wine industry, so it has decent accommodation options. Appealing Nelson, as the region's biggest city, has plenty in terms of accommodation to suit all budgets, with beachside holiday parks through to backpackers and hotels.

Resources

Picton i-SITE Visitor Information Centre (*marlborough-nz.com*) On the foreshore.

Blenheim i-SITE Visitor Information Centre (*marlboroughnz.com*) Beside the railway station.

DOC Whakatū/Nelson Visitor Centre (*doc.govt.nz*)

Marlborough Online (*marlboroughonline.co.nz*) On the foreshore.

Nelson Tasman Online (*nelsontasman.nz*)

17

SEASIDE RIDES

Nelson to Māpua

DURATION	DIFFICULTY	DISTANCE	START/END
2–3hr	Easy	26km	Nelson/Māpua

TERRAIN	Flat, off-road, unsealed bike trail

GUAIXINM/SHUTTERSTOCK ©

Great Taste Trail, Nelson

This easy ride from Nelson city to Māpua, on the western side of the Waimea Estuary, takes in a wide variety of coastal scenery, giving riders the chance to spot seabirds, visit an enthralling glass gallery, swim on the Tasman Bay coast of Moturoa/Rabbit Island, then hop on a small cycle-ferry to the end of the ride. Bustling little Māpua, benefitting from being on the Great Taste Trail, boasts galleries, cafes and Golden Bear Brewing to complement the fun of the ride. You can ride the trail both ways, or get transport back to Nelson afterwards.

Bike Hire

Get a package including bike rental and return transport ($110) from Nelson Cycle Hire & Tours, based at Nelson Airport. If biking back, get bike hire only.

Starting Point

Start from the Nelson Cycle Hire & Tours office at Nelson Airport (free parking), or from the centre of Nelson city if hiring a bike elsewhere.

01 Either from central Nelson or the airport, depending on where you've rented your bike, get onto the Coastal Route bike trail and head southeast. You'll soon be sandwiched between the Waimea Estuary and State Hwy 6. The estuary is quite picturesque when the tide is in, but is mostly exposed mudflats when the tide is out.

02 Just past the end of the estuary, don't miss the sign pointing right to Moturoa/Rabbit Island. This is your turn-off point and near the start of the trail there's a large sign confirming

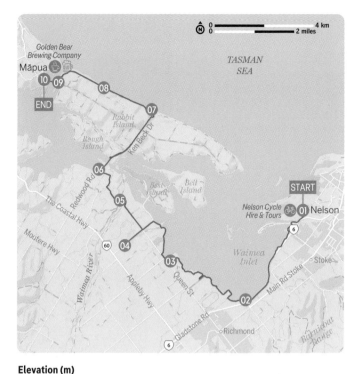

Höglund Art Glass Studio & Gallery

This art studio, only an 800m side trip off the bike trail, is an absolute stunner and well worth the extra pedalling. Swedish couple Ola and Marie Höglund have been creating glass artwork together for over 50 years, earning international recognition, and the gallery highlights their amazing skills. Son Ossian and his wife Annabel are also involved as artists. If you're lucky, you'll be able to observe glassblowing in the workshop. The gallery features vases, goblets, paperweights, platters and bowls in amazing shapes, plus handmade fused-glass jewellery. The colourful glass jellyfish are totally captivating.

Elevation (m)

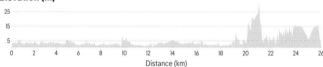

that the Māpua Ferry is operating. It's a 20km ride from here to the ferry landing.

03 The bike trail winds around the head of the Waimea Inlet, with water (or mudflats) on your right, Nelson light industry on your left, sometimes right beside the water, sometimes off-road alongside busy Lower Queen St. Keep your eyes seaward at the largest enclosed estuary in the South Island, home to seabirds such as the white heron, bar-tailed godwit, little egret, royal spoonbill,

Australasian bittern and banded rail. The bar-tailed godwits migrate from here to Alaska in late summer, the world's longest migratory flight. You'll also spot long-legged pūkeko wandering around in the wetlands and plenty of paradise ducks, the female with the distinctive white head.

04 After crossing some over-water boardwalks that create wetlands to your left, the trail will head inland to 'Speedway Corner' with Nelson's petrol-head heaven on the corner of Landsdowne Rd and Lower

Queen St. Take a short side trip 800m down Landsdowne Rd to visit the absolutely stunning Höglund Art Glass Studio & Gallery.

05 Back at 'Speedway Corner', carry on northwest along the unsealed road, along the top of the stopbank, then across the Waimea River on the impressive built-for-bikers swing bridge. This is the main river feeding the Waimea Estuary and is known for its 'white gold' or whitebait – translucent fish fry that are considered a delicacy in Aotearoa.

06 The spooky, circular, metal edifice in the middle of the trail, on top of the stopbank, has some thinking 'crashed spacecraft'. But it's actually an aeronautical radio-beacon building that helped direct aircraft to land at Nelson Airport, until it was out-of-date technologically and decommissioned in the early 1990s. Carry on along the stopbank and the trail will eventually bring you out to sealed Redwood Rd.

07 Turn right to cross a causeway over the Waimea Estuary, firstly to Rough Island, then across to Moturoa/Rabbit Island. Much of the island is pine-plantation forest, first planted in 1921, and signage will warn bikers about heading off the cycle trail. Fortunately, large swathes of land on the northern, sea-facing coast of the island were established as Rabbit Island Recreation Reserve in 1908. It's a popular play area with locals, boasting picnic spots, large grassy domains and the long sandy beach, which faces north out on Tasman Bay and the open sea. This is a great spot for a swim.

08 When you're ready, follow the flat bike trail west along the island to the ferry landing. It's a pleasant ride along the northern coast with pine plantation to your left and the sea to your right. The key here is not to have to rush to catch the ferry.

09 Keep timing in mind. On its summer schedule (daily October to April), ferry departures from Moturoa/Rabbit Island to Māpua are hourly; in winter (May to September) they're only on weekends and public holidays. It's only 200m across the mouth of the inlet to Māpua (one-way/return $12/15). There's a surprisingly strong flow of water if the tide is heading in or out of the estuary.

10 Māpua is a bustling little community, especially at the ferry landing, thanks in part to Aotearoa's biking boom. What was once a quiet little coastal community is now on a high, with an amazing terminal development housing art galleries, cafes, restaurants and a craft brewery, thanks in part to being on the Great Taste Trail. In particular, the large, former New Zealand Apple & Pear Marketing Board cool-store warehouse has been totally transformed with remarkable art on display in Coolchange Gallery, Forest Fusion and Coolstore Gallery. Munch out on fish and chips at the Smokehouse, have a sit-down meal at Jellyfish Restaurant, or enjoy a pick-me-up at the Rabbit Island Coffee Co.

☕ Take a Break

While there's nowhere to get refreshments along the trail, there are plenty of options once you get to Māpua. Best in our books is Golden Bear Brewing Company, virtually right on the waterfront. Here you'll find enticing outdoor seating overlooking the ferry landing, plus indoor seating within view of the brewing operations. Enjoy tasty Mexican food, including tacos, quesadillas and burritos, and chill out with some top Golden Bear brews. The Bear Menu includes Smokin' Otter IPA, American Wheat Ale and the Industrial Haze Hazy IPA.

ROBERT CHG/SHUTTERSTOCK ©

Moturoa/Rabbit Island

Great Taste Trail

One of Aotearoa's 23 Great Rides, the Great Taste Trail is a 200km loop trail starting and finishing in Nelson. The Nelson to Māpua ride we describe here is the first section of the trail, while the Spooners Tunnel to Nelson ride on the following pages is the last stage of the Great Taste Trail. Besides the mix of rural, urban, coastal and riverside scenery, there are plenty of tasty attractions along the way, including fruit stalls, cafes, craft-beer pubs and winery restaurants. Two-thirds of the full trail is rated easy and many riders take four days to complete it.

18

Spooners Tunnel to Nelson

DURATION	DIFFICULTY	DISTANCE	START/END
4–5hr	Easy	40km	Spooners Tunnel/Nelson

TERRAIN	Unpaved and paved cycle trail

PETER UNGER/GETTY IMAGES ©

Spooners Tunnel

Enjoy a cruise through the 1.35km Spooners Tunnel, the longest unused rail tunnel in the country, then ride back to Nelson following the route of the former Nelson Railways tracks. Enjoy all sorts of interesting things along the way, including rural scenery and animals, historic buildings and excellent pies in Wakefield, the Ernest Rutherford birthplace and memorial near Brightwater (check out the $100 note!), apples and fruit galore near Richmond, plus Aotearoa's historic first craft-beer brewery in Stoke. An extremely satisfying day with highlights to remember.

Bike Hire

You can get a one-way bike and transport package from Nelson Cycle Hire & Tours ($125), conveniently based at Nelson Airport, 7km southwest of the city centre.

Starting Point

The ride starts at the western end of Spooners Tunnel, about 40km by road from Nelson. You'll need transport there. It's easiest to get a bike-and-transport package in Nelson.

01 You'll be dropped off near the western portal of the 1.35km-long Spooners Tunnel, a highlight for any bike ride. Aotearoa's longest unused rail tunnel was in active service from 1893 until the rail line was closed in 1955. It sat unused for 60 years before becoming a part of the Great Taste Trail in 2016. To build the tunnel, a team of men worked three shifts with picks and shovels to dig the tunnel while a separate team made concrete blocks for its walls and roof. Many workers were Chinese, Japanese and Italian immigrants. It's an amazing piece of workmanship. While the present

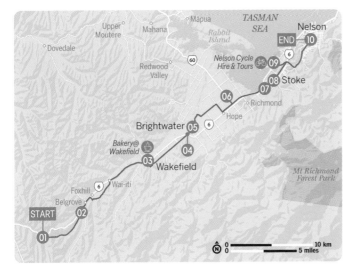

Elevation (m)

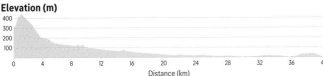

Distance (km)

riding surface is smooth, it's dark and you'll need a light (provided by the bike-hire company). Also, keep away from the walls, which are still sooty and dirty.

02 Once you're out of the tunnel, it's a 5km downhill cruise through pine forest and past farmland until the trail joins up with the SH6 just short of Belgrove. The next 10km to Wakefield is a fascinating rural ramble, often crossing the main road and river bridges, travelling past pigs, sheep, cattle, horses, free-range egg farms and the Wai-iti Estate Apiary, with honey for sale.

03 Wakefield, considered one of the oldest inland settlements in the country, is a top place to stop, especially if you're getting peckish. Bakery@

Wakefield's meat pies are the stuff of local legend. Make sure to explore the small township before heading out. The school, established in 1843, is the oldest continuously running school in the country. Other notable buildings include St John's Church (1846), the second oldest church in the country, the Wakefield Hotel of 1865 and the post office (1910).

04 Follow the trail beside rural roads, continuing north for 7km towards Brightwater. Before the township, just before your first underpass for the day, look left to see the impressive Lord Rutherford Memorial. Be sure to drop in here. The famous physicist, considered the first to 'split the atom', was born here in 1871, and went on to win the Nobel Prize in Chemistry in 1908. As the

McCashin's Brewery

Aotearoa's first craft-beer brewery was set up by ex–All Black Terry McCashin in the old Rochdale Cider factory in 1981. It's in a perfect spot for some thirst-quenching, right next to the Old Railway Route near the end of the ride in Stoke. McCashin dared to take on the duopoly of NZ's two big beer companies, and became so successful that one of them bought his brand 18 years later. Happily, his son relaunched under the name Stoke Beer in 2010. Drop in for some refreshing tap beer or cider and enjoy the convivial atmosphere in the historic old brewery.

country's most famous scientist, his face features on the $100 note. The memorial features a statue of Rutherford as a young boy and has fascinating information panels.

05 The trail winds its way through the small township of Brightwater. Headquarters Cafe & Bar is a popular local coffee spot here, so drop in for a boost. Through town, the trail continues north past vineyards and farm country to Richmond.

06 The Appleton Hwy Over-bridge is a good spot to make a side trip by turning left (northwest) and cycling 800m to 'Old Factory Corner' at the McShane's Crossroad intersection. You're in apple country. Here you'll find a cluster of interesting shops and outlets. Nelsonians love shopping at Connings Food Market, while outside you'll find Berrylands for ice cream, yoghurt and sorbets, the Junction for artisan cheese, jams and preserves, and the Grape Escape Cafe, should you be in need of a coffee and cake break.

07 Head back down the Appleton Hwy to the bike trail, turn left and continue on the cycle path towards Nelson. Shortly after an intersection with the bike trail heading west to Māpua, the Waimea Estuary appears on your left, and you'll get the opportunity to ride through an underpass inland below SH6 at Orphanage Stream.

08 Follow signage for the Old Railway Route. Should your thirst get the better of you, don't miss the chance to turn right and drop off the Old Railway Route at Byron Pl to take a break at McCashin's Brewery & Tap Room. Head right at Byron Pl, then right again on Main Rd Stoke. The brewery is only 200m down the main road.

09 Back out on the Old Railway Route, continue northeast. If you're on a Nelson Cycle Hire bike, there'll be the opportunity to follow signage to head back west to the airport to return your bike.

10 If you're heading into Nelson city, follow the Old Railway Route as it curls around to the right, climbs up past the hospital and deposits you in central Nelson. Alternatively, take cycle lanes on roads to pass Tahunanui Beach and the port on your way into the city. It's all clearly signposted.

Take a Break

If you love that Kiwi champion of cheap eats, the meat pie, it will be difficult not to get excited as you park your bike at the Bakery@Wakefield. These local legends make and sell over 800 of their spectacular pies daily, ranging from butter chicken to steak and stout, to lamb's fry and bacon. They're innovative and have a sense of humour, too. In the dessert cabinet you'll find delicious dark chocolate 'Poo Emoji Mousse Cups' shaped like, you know, poo!

Railway to Nowhere, Glenhope

Railway to Nowhere

With the ambitious plan of linking Nelson to the West Coast, work started on the Nelson Railway in 1873. Starting with a hiss and a roar, the tracks stretched from Nelson across the Waimea Plains to Wai-iti by 1876, then up to Spooners Tunnel by 1897. The track eventually reached Glenhope in 1912, then just past it, but that was the end of the line, so to speak. Costs of construction outweighed the benefits, development of truck transport for freight blossomed and what was known as the 'railway to nowhere' was closed, amid much protest, in 1955.

19

SEASIDE RIDES

Mistletoe Bay to Anakiwa

DURATION	DIFFICULTY	DISTANCE	START/END
3–4hr	Intermediate	13.5km	Picton

TERRAIN	Rough mountain-bike trail

PERRETEN/GETTY IMAGES ©

Onahau Bay

This is an excellent introduction to mountain biking on a narrow, single track, the last 12.5km of the world-renowned Queen Charlotte Track in the Marlborough Sounds. While relatively easy in good weather, it can be a tad tricky in the wet, when the trail becomes muddy and slippery. Think of this day more as an adventure than just a bike ride. The ferry to the start at Mistletoe Bay and back from the end of the track at Anakiwa is part of the fun and you'll enjoy a look at the sound from out on the water.

Bike Hire

Get a full package from Marlborough Sounds Adventure Co with rental mountain bike, helmet, return ferry transfers plus a QCT Land Co-op Pass, which you'll need for the ride. Book ahead online.

Starting Point

Start on the Picton waterfront, out front of the Marlborough Sounds Adventure Co, by hopping on the small ferry for the 15-minute cruise over to Mistletoe Bay.

01 Make sure you have everything you need in terms of food, snacks and liquids before you hop on the ferry in Picton, as there's nothing available on the track. The 15-minute cruise, initially north out of busy Picton Harbour, then west across Queen Charlotte Sound, is an absolute joy. You'll likely be sharing the ferry with other bikers, walkers and supplies such as clean linen and baggage being dropped off at small resorts around the Sounds. It's said that the Marlborough Sounds make up 20% of Aotearoa's total coastline with its intricate maze of waterways.

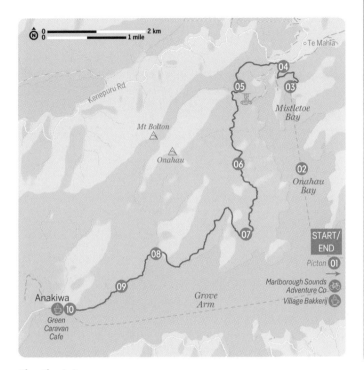

Queen Charlotte Track

This 74km, dual hiking and mountain-biking trail in the Marlborough Sounds has a big reputation. Most take two or three days to bike the whole track, two-thirds of which is considered intermediate to advanced. The ride from Mistletoe Bay to Anakiwa is the last section of the track, graded easy to intermediate. If you want a longer ride and are experienced and confident, consider the 21km Torea Saddle to Anakiwa ride – the ferry leaves Picton at 9.30am. The ferry from Picton to Mistletoe Bay leaves at 11.30am. Both return to Picton from Anakiwa on the 4pm ferry.

Elevation (m)

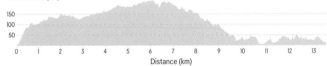

02 The small ferry turns north up into Onahau Bay. The number of houses along the coast is surprising, each with its own small jetty and most with only boat access. At the end of the inlet sits gorgeous Mistletoe Bay.

03 Hop off at the jetty, where, after pedalling along the flat waterfront trail, you'll find Mistletoe Bay Eco Village, which offers camping and cabins. Your first major mission on your bike is a 1km climb up on the road to where

it meets the Queen Charlotte Track. Think of it as a worthy warm-up!

04 Eventually, you'll reach the Queen Charlotte Track, heading into the native bush to the left. There'll also be a sign stating that you need a QCT Land Co-op Pass from here. This is because you'll be passing over private land on the ride. The operator will have presented you with one of these as part of the day package, so make sure it is displayed somewhere on your gear.

05 Head into the bush on the single, narrow track. The first 3km is the toughest bit of trail for the day. If it's a sunny, blue-sky day and there hasn't been any rain for a while, the track will be hard and fast, and a relatively easy ride. If, however, it's raining or has been raining heavily for the past few days, the clay-based, rocky trail can be very slippery, with deepish mud and puddles, and you may curse us for labelling this an 'easy' ride. If you're inexperienced and the operator has told you that they don't advise you to ride because of track conditions, accept that advice. Otherwise, this bit of track may feel a bit like 'the endless trail to hell!'

06 If it's a good-weather day, this is a great ride, which now climbs gently up to the Onahau Bay Lookout. There are no signs but you'll know when you've reached it – with glorious views down on the bay below and even across to Kenepuru Sound.

07 The next 3km of the trail then flattens and turns to face south over the Grove Arm of Queen Charlotte Sound. Views out to the far side of the sound and the small settlements in Ngākuta Bay and Momorangi Bay are impressive. There's an information panel and picnic table at Grove Arm Viewpoint, a good spot for a break.

08 The trail descends through beautiful native forest for the next 3km to Umungata/Davies Bay. This stretch is known for its proliferation of tall, thick black beech

trees and mamaku, a tree fern that can reach up to 20m in height. While the flora along the trail is lush and enthralling, bird life is equally so. You're likely to encounter vocal tui, with their distinctive white throat tuffs, twittering pīwakawaka (fantails) and kererū (wood pigeons). At Umungata/Davies Bay, you'll find a peaceful waterfront camping and picnic area.

09 The last 3km to the end of the trail at Anakiwa is an easy ride on a wide track. Keep an eye out for dog-walkers and kids, though, as dogs are allowed on this stretch of the trail, and plenty of families walk along to Umungata/Davies Bay.

10 When you arrive at Anakiwa, you'll find the friendly Green Caravan Cafe, offering refreshments, plus bike-wash facilities, picnic tables and the jetty that your ferry will leave from at 4pm. It's a 30-minute cruise back by boat to Picton.

 **Take a Break**

There's nowhere to get refreshments on the track. Stock up for a picnic before you go at Picton's excellent Village Bakkerij, a NZ Bakery of the Year winner, with everything you'd expect, plus delicious Dutch treats. The ham and cheese baguette is tasty and easy to carry. At Anakiwa, right at the end of the track, is the Green Caravan Cafe, in (surprise, surprise) a green caravan. The coffees are good, but if it's a hot day, it's hard to go past the selection of ice cream.

Ngākuta Bay, Grove Arm

Outward Bound School

The name Anakiwa resonates with generations of Kiwis who learnt their outdoor skills at the Cobham Outward Bound School, set up here in Anakiwa in 1962, right at the end of the track. Chances are you'll run into or see groups of youngsters running, sailing on the sound (rowing if there's no wind!) or simply jumping off the end of the ferry jetty. Courses involve expeditions at sea, in the mountains, and on rivers, as well as community service and solo experiences – with the goal of helping people understand their potential and making the world a better place.

20

Blenheim & Wither Hills Circuit

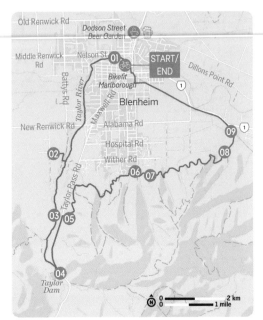

DURATION	DIFFICULTY	DISTANCE	START/END
3–4hr	Intermediate	27km	Central Blenheim

TERRAIN	Paved and unpaved bike paths

Elevation (m)

A wonderful loop ride around the Marlborough city of Blenheim and its southern hills. Ride 10km along the Taylor River trail to Taylor Dam, then traverse across the base of the Wither Hills towards the coast, before biking back into Blenheim on a paved rail trail. Visit the fascinating Omaka Aviation Heritage Museum along the way. You'll be congratulating yourself if you've splurged on an e-bike when you get to the Mapp Track in the Wither Hills. Views from its higher points extend out over vineyards to Te Koko-o-Kupe/Cloudy Bay, Cook Strait and even to Te Ika-a-Māui/North Island.

Bike Hire

Bikefit Marlborough is Blenheim's big bike shop on Market St in the middle of town; book an e-bike or mountain bike online. There are lots of options.

Starting Point

Roll out the door from Bikefit and return your bike here after cycling the loop; staff will point out the best way to get onto the Taylor River trail.

 01 The Taylor River shared-use trail runs right through the middle of Blenheim. This lovely riverside route runs west, then curls around to the south towards the Wither Hills, south of the city. You'll likely be sharing the trail with dog-walkers, joggers and mobility scooters. The ride will take you past large stones with plaques featuring local poetry and plantings of tree species from all over the world. The Trees of the World Arboretum saw 428 trees planted in memory of local horticulturist Ralph Ballinger as part of the Taylor River Enhancement Project.

Omaka Aviation Heritage Museum

Omaka Aviation Heritage Museum

You don't have to be an aviation buff to find this place totally mesmerising. Academy Award–winning film-director Peter Jackson's collection of WWI and WWII aircraft, along with lifelike displays created by special-effects film-studio Weta Workshop, may be a highlight of your visit to Aotearoa. The working Omaka airfield also hosts its Classic Fighters airshow over the Easter Weekend, biennially. This is a worthy side trip, just off the bike trail along the Taylor River. Drop in here, but be warned, you may use up a fair bit of your day. There's a cafe should you need refreshments.

02 After about 5km, Wither Rd comes down to the river from the east, offering a river crossing over to the western side of the river at Omaka Aerodrome. If you have even the vaguest interest in aircraft, head over for a visit to the mind-boggling Omaka Aviation Heritage Museum. Cross the river, turn right at the top of the small hill, then ride 200m along the fence line to the small gate with entry to the aerodrome. Ride back to the eastern side of the river after visiting the aviation museum.

03 Carry on south beside the river. You'll have left the dog-walkers behind by now. Stay right when a track heads up left to Wither Hills Mountain Bike Park. The trail enters gorgeous planted vineyards for the next stretch before a short (though sharp!) climb up to Taylor Dam.

04 There's a nice circuit around the small pond behind the dam, which is likely to be inhabited by a huge flock of seagulls, along with ducks and swans. The dam was constructed in the 1960s to control water flows and reduce flooding in Blenheim and adjacent farmland in times of high rainfall.

Head out to nearby sealed Taylor Pass Rd and cruise downhill, back north, for 2km to the Wither Hills Mountain Bike Park entrance.

05 A huge mountain-bike park has been created on what is a working farm. Bikers are asked to respect farming operations and take extra care when near stock or farm equipment. You'll be biking eastwards, initially at the foot of the hills, on the Stockyard Track. The easy-to-follow, easy-to-ride single track curls around, with housing developments down to your left on the flats and brown hills and trees rising above to your right. It's a fun trail, but be aware that other cyclists may be coming towards you from the other direction.

06 The track then becomes the Forest Hills Track and then the Lower Farm Track, before depositing you out on Redwood St in the southern suburbs of Blenheim. Turn right and ride up the street for 200m to the Redwood St park gateway.

07 If you've splurged on an e-bike for the day, it's from here that you'll be glad you did so. At the lower end of the car park, drop down, then follow signage for the Mapp Track. There's an initial steepish climb, then a drop into a gully, another climb, another gully, and so on across the face of the lower Wither Hills. It's an enjoyable ride, but you'll want to keep your speed under control on some of the downhill drops into gullies.

☕ Take a Break

The only place to stop for refreshments on the trail itself is at the small cafe at the Omaka Aviation Heritage Museum. We suggest saving your hunger and thirst for a visit post-ride to Blenheim's excellent Dodson Street Beer Garden. This German-style place is home of the Renaissance Brewing Co with brewing on site, an outside biergarten, a rustic inside restaurant and 24 brews on tap. It serves German, Italian and Kiwi cuisine all day long. The beef, vegetable and spice gulasch suppe is particularly good.

Sauvignon Blanc winery, Blenheim

08 At the end of each climb, the views are tremendous, sometimes north out over vineyards and the city of Blenheim, sometimes out east over vineyards to Te Koko-o-Kupe/Cloudy Bay and even glimpses of the North Island on the far side of Cook Strait. Eventually, there's a flattish curve in the trail before a final drop into vineyards at the eastern Cob Cottage Rd entrance to the park.

Marlborough Wineries

Many come to Marlborough to visit the wineries, world-renowned for producing excellent sauvignon blanc. It's said that Marlborough accounts for 75% of the country's wine production and 85% of its wine exports. Although cycling around the wineries is extremely popular, particularly around those on the Wairau River plains around Blenheim and Renwick, take note that most of the riding is along sealed roads shared with regular traffic and trucks. 'Biking under the influence' is not recommended for safety reasons. Pick up a map of wine-trail cycle routes from the i-SITE Visitor Centre in Blenheim.

09 The road heads north towards the SH1, but just before passing over the railway line, you'll find the sealed Riverlands Rail Trail to finish the circuit, a flat 4km ride next to the rail line into central Blenheim. In the future, this stretch will become part of the Whale Trail, an ambitiously planned, off-road bike trail that will link Picton, Blenheim and Kaikōura.

Also Try...

Picton

Coppermine Trail Experience

DURATION	DIFFICULTY	DISTANCE
3-4hr	Intermediate	23km

This ride is the first section of the Coppermine Trail, one of Aotearoa's 23 Great Rides. It involves a lengthy, though fairly friendly climb to the Third House shelter, high in Mt Richmond Forest Park, east of Nelson. This is an excellent spot for a picnic, before a thoroughly enjoyable descent back into the city on the same trail you came up on. Enjoy some stunning views, beautiful forest and bird life on the ride. Make sure to take sufficient food and water. The full Coppermine Trail experience is a 43km ride that is rated 75% intermediate, 25% advanced, so consider taking this on only if you're fit, confident and experienced.

Snout & Waikawa Bay Trails

DURATION	DIFFICULTY	DISTANCE
1-3hr	Easy	10km

These two rides are perfect for travellers with a bit of time up their sleeves while waiting for a ferry departure from Picton. Head down to Marlborough Sounds Adventure Co on the waterfront and discuss your options. With only a couple of hours, consider riding the easy bike trail out to beautiful Waikawa Bay. With a few more hours in the bank, think about riding out to the Snout, the end of the peninsula that protrudes north into the sound and separates Picton and Waikawa bays. This is a harder, longer ride, but offers gorgeous views of Queen Charlotte Sound and a couple of trail options.

STARGRASS/SHUTTERSTOCK ©

Tahunanui Beach

Nelson City Trails

DURATION	DIFFICULTY	DISTANCE
1–3hr	Easy	14km

The Tasman District's main city, Nelson boasts a set of excellent off-road bike trails based around its Old Railway Route, which extends south through the suburb of Stoke and onwards. This is one of those 'make it up as you go along' rides. We suggest making a loop using the Old Railway Route, the Coastal Route and a number of cycle lanes on roads in the city. Make sure to visit Tahunanui Beach and the fabulous Suter Art Gallery, and find a way to squeeze McCashin's Brewery into your schedule. For a longer ride, consider heading out to Old Factory Corner at the McShane's Crossroad intersection, near Richmond.

Link Pathway

DURATION	DIFFICULTY	DISTANCE
5–7hr	Intermediate	42km

This trail connects Havelock and Picton in the Marlborough Sounds, with the opportunity to also bike up to Anakiwa, at the end of the Queen Charlotte Track. European settlers and miners originally created a bridle path for horses to link the two townships in the 1860s, but much of it disappeared when Queen Charlotte Dr was built in the 1920s. The old bridle trail now forms around one-fifth of the Link Pathway. You'll bike through lush native bush and open farmland, and enjoy sea and mountain views. This is a great ride, but if you bike the whole way, you'll need to figure out transport to get back to where you started.

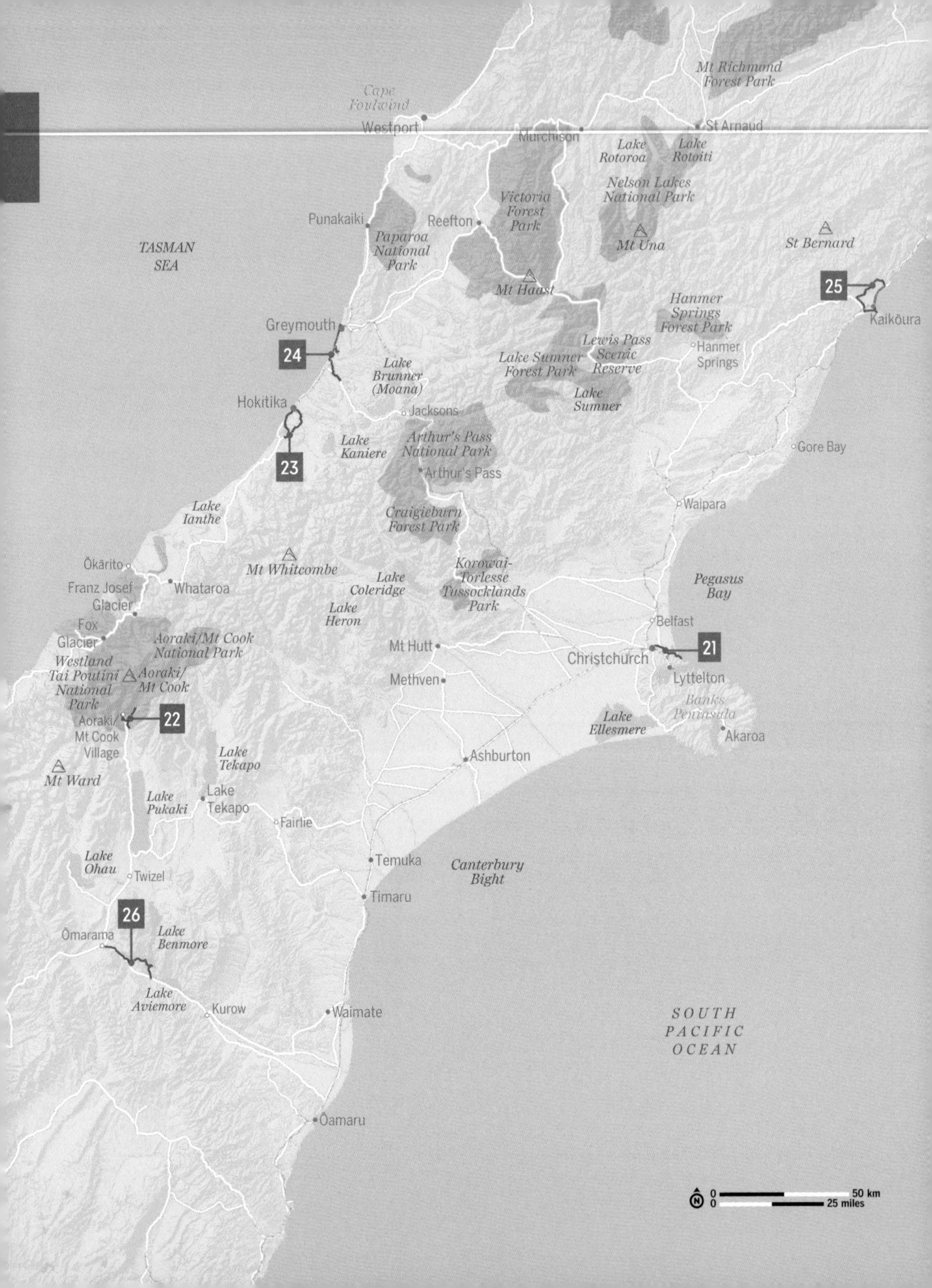

TASMAN
SEA

*Cape
Foulwind*

Westport

Murchison

St Arnaud

*Mt Richmond
Forest Park*

*Lake
Rotoroa*

*Lake
Rotoiti*

*Nelson Lakes
National Park*

Punakaiki

Reefton

*Victoria
Forest
Park*

*Paparoa
National
Park*

△ *Mt Una*

△ *St Bernard*

Greymouth

24

△ *Mt Haast*

*Hanmer
Springs
Forest Park*

25

Kaikōura

*Lake
Brunner
(Moana)*

*Lake Sumner
Forest Park*

*Lewis Pass
Scenic
Reserve*

Hanmer
Springs

Hokitika

Jacksons

Lake Sumner

23

*Lake
Kaniere*

*Arthur's Pass
National Park*

• *Arthur's Pass*

Gore Bay

Waipara

*Lake
Ianthe*

*Craigieburn
Forest Park*

Ōkārito

△ *Mt Whitcombe*

*Lake
Coleridge*

*Korowai-
Torlesse
Tussocklands
Park*

*Pegasus
Bay*

Franz Josef
Glacier

Whataroa

*Lake
Heron*

Belfast

Fox
Glacier

*Aoraki/Mt Cook
National Park*

Mt Hutt

Christchurch

21

*Westland
Tai Poutini
National
Park*

△ *Aoraki/
Mt Cook*

Methven

Lyttelton

*Banks
Peninsula*

Aoraki/
Mt Cook
Village

22

*Lake
Tekapo*

Akaroa

△ *Mt Ward*

*Lake
Pukaki*

Lake
Tekapo

*Lake
Ellesmere*

*Lake
Ohau*

Twizel

Fairlie

Ashburton

*Canterbury
Bight*

26

Omarama

*Lake
Benmore*

Temuka

Timaru

*Lake
Aviemore*

Kurow

Waimate

*SOUTH
PACIFIC
OCEAN*

Ōamaru

Ⓝ 0 _____ 50 km
    0 _____ 25 miles

JUSTIN PAGET/SHUTTERSTOCK ©

Lake Pukaki (p168)

Canterbury & the West Coast

Explore

Canterbury & the West Coast

Straddling the Southern Alps that form the backbone of the South Island, these two geographically linked regions offer contrasting climates and diverse topography. Take your pick of the temperate rainforests tucked under the mountain ranges of the West Coast or the dry eastern-side agricultural tapestry of the Canterbury Plains, stretching to the Pacific Coast. Early European settlers left a legacy of narrow tramway corridors through the dense primaeval rainforest. Crossing to the eastern side, you'll find the cultivated plains of the Canterbury region, stretching north to Kaikōura and south to the arid Mackenzie Country, where big sky vistas, ice-blue glaciers and turquoise lakes await.

Christchurch

Christchurch is the largest city in the South Island and a stop-off point for many. The post-2011 rebuild of the earthquake-damaged city centre is restoring and future-proofing much of the historical heritage. In the process it's acting as a catalyst for a renaissance of this spacious city that has somehow retained the feel of a town. This is the place to get organised for your South Island adventure. It's a major hub for domestic and international air travel, plus there are road and rail connections north to Kaikōura, and on to Picton for the Interislander ferry, or west over Arthurs Pass to the West Coast.

Lake Tekapo, Mt Cook & Mackenzie Country

There are only roads or bus transport south to Lake Tekapo, Mt Cook and Mackenzie Country,

but these iconic areas may be on your route further south to Queenstown anyway. Many of the small settlements in this sparsely populated region, such as Tekapo, Twizel and Omarama, owe their existence to the hydropower-scheme construction period in the 1950s to 1970s, but were ghost towns once the workers left. Tourism has come to their aid with constantly evolving new facilities, outdoor activities and tourist attractions to entice visitors. The old dam workers would smile seeing the canals that they built now supporting salmon farms that export to the world and cycle trails following the shores of the storage lakes. The least changed place is Mt Cook village. It was protected from development due to being within a national park that's part of a Unesco World Heritage Area. This does mean that facilities in the village are

WHEN TO GO

The West Coast is famed for rainfall punctuated by periods of fine weather, but any local will tell you that winter is the best season to enjoy 'The Coast' with mild temperatures and long settled spells. Canterbury is less dramatic in its weather patterns, with wind direction dictating conditions, with the famed nor'wester bringing sweltering hot, dry weather.

limited to the absolute minimum and it's best to come prepared.

Kaikōura

Marine life abounds at Kaikōura, but the town, recovering from a 2016 earthquake, is broadening its tourism base with biking on the agenda. With a constant stream of tourists passing through for whale-watching, swimming with dolphins, seabird-spotting or kayaking with seals, it has most of the facilities you'll need, albeit on a small-town scale. The same can also be said of the two largest towns on the West Coast, Greymouth and Hokitika. The former serves tourists thanks to its *TranzAlpine* rail link with Christchurch, while the latter is best known for its glorious sunsets and *pounamu* (greenstone/jade) carving studios. Both towns have a good range of supplies, supermarkets and accommodation, so make one of them your base while exploring the area.

TRANSPORT

The Southern Alps are crossed by two east–west passes, the Lewis Pass and the more dramatic Arthurs Pass, with scenic trains connecting Christchurch with Greymouth and Kaikōura. From Greymouth and Hokitika the remote Glacier Hwy beckons you south along the coast to the glacier towns of Fox and Franz Josef. A highway also runs through the interior between Tekapo and Queenstown.

 WHAT'S ON

The peak summer months see many regional events on the West Coast while Canterbury spreads the occasions a little more evenly.

Christchurch Cup & Show Week

Seven days of events that take over the city.

World Buskers Festival

Local and international street performers hit Christchurch.

Kaikōura Adventure Race

Test your endurance and navigational skills.

Hokitika Wildfoods Festival

Explore your dietary boundaries.

Omarama Rodeo

Join the locals for a *yeeha* fun time.

 WHERE TO STAY

Christchurch is a regional city and offers various accommodation options to suit everyone, as does Kaikōura on a town scale. Mt Cook village is a tiny settlement within the national park with various options but limited by the number of beds, so book ahead, or be prepared to use the towns of Tekapo, Twizel and Omarama outside the park. The West Coast is geared for people on the move, with campsites, holiday parks, backpackers, motels and hotels. A favourite region for Kiwi families, it's best to plan ahead in school holidays and around local events.

Resources

Visitor information centres Regional towns are tourist destinations in their own right, with i-SITE visitor centres or an equivalent.

Bike shops Gold mines of up-to-date info.

West Coast Wilderness Trail (*westcoastwildernesstrail.co.nz*)

Kaikōura Cycling Club (*kaikouracycling.co.nz*)

Alps 2 Ocean Cycle Trail (*alps2ocean.com*)

21

TRAVELLIGHT/SHUTTERSTOCK ©

Christchurch

Christchurch to the Beach

DURATION	DIFFICULTY	DISTANCE	START/END
3hr	Easy	30km return	Cathedral Sq

TERRAIN	Flat ride on streets and paved cycle path

Undoubtedly Christchurch is a city made for biking and the post-earthquake rebuild has enabled environmentally sustainable transport strategies. The result is 60km (and still counting) of cycle paths, plus shared cycleways and cycle lanes, which are getting people out of their cars and onto their bikes to commute and for exercise. The Port Hills have ample challenging mountain-biking trails and Adventure Park has downhill trails, but the city's flat topography is perfectly suited to gentle cycling. The user-friendly network links the city centre with many suburbs, part of which is the Christchurch to Sumner Coastal Pathway.

Bike Hire

Action Bicycle Club in the city centre and several suburban bike shops offer bike-hire services and will even deliver to your accommodation with advance bookings.

Starting Point

From directly behind the Christchurch Cathedral, follow Worcester St away from Cathedral Sq to join the signposted cycleway through quiet leafy suburbs, initially following signs for Ferrymead.

01 You'll start the ride, excitedly armed with your free Christchurch bike map, available from any library or council office, including from the Tūranga library at Cathedral Sq. Take care negotiating obstacles: the tram rails that run around the Cathedral Sq perimeter love to eat your front wheel and buck you off your bike!

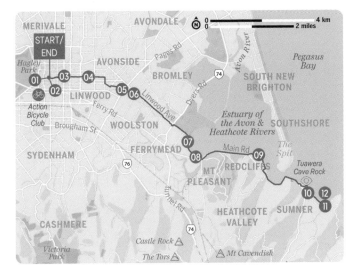

Elevation (m)

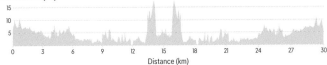

Distance (km)

02 The first section takes you behind the iconic cathedral that has been the hub of the city since its completion in 1904 after 40 years of construction. After its destruction in the earthquake of 2011, much debate ensued about what was to be done, and you can see that it is now being rebuilt in its original Gothic style to once again dominate the Square.

03 Your route on Worcester St will soon take you across Latimer Sq, where to your right the temporary stand-in city cathedral known as the Cardboard Cathedral is easily seen and well worth a quick stop for its innovative cardboard tubing, timber and steel design by Japanese architect Shigeru Ban.

04 The cycle path continues along Worcester St, now a quiet backstreet of weatherboard villas with traffic-calming speed bumps aplenty. Conveniently you can save your backside and go around the bump of the speed humps.

05 Following cycle signs for Ferrymead taking you onto England St, you will emerge onto the major thoroughfare of Aldwins Rd. At the road crossings make sure to cycle over the arrow to trip the cycle-priority sensor lights.

06 The path takes you through Linwood Park, past the playground and onto Linwood Ave. This is a busy road but made pleasant with a tree-lined cycleway down a wide

Bike-Friendly

The 2011 earthquake has given Christchurch a rare chance to redesign the transport system with options for walking, cycling, buses or using electric cars and scooters, aiming for net-zero carbon emissions by 2045. Cycle-centric features have been built into the network to keep you safe: bevelled kerbs, shared paths and cycle lanes that keep you separated from cars, cycle-designated signal lights that automatically detect your presence with convenient rails to lean on while you wait for the green light, cycle zones that are painted in green and signposts with distances on every corner.

avenue of green in the middle of the lanes.

07 This road gives way to a narrower path alongside Linwood Ave, and then through the recently replanted Charlesworth Reserve. This is an area of marshland, with re-created tidal pools and native wetland habitat that now attract native and migratory birds to nest, roost and feed. Look out for the bar-tailed godwits and other wading birds. They spend their summers here and other tidal areas on the estuary after their epic journeys south from Siberia each spring. The best time to spot them is around high tide when they are all squeezed up onto the few remaining bits of dry ground.

08 Crossing Humphreys Dr takes you onto the sea-wall. The cycle/pedestrian path is now on the water's edge as it skirts the southern edge of the Avon Heathcote Estuary, and with the tidal bay at your side it's pure waterfront cycling. With wind-surfing clubs and sea-facing cafes, restaurants and gyms, you have definitely left the city behind.

09 The path sidles around the cafes and shops of Red Cliffs – you will see why this coastal suburb was given this name. Here you are at the narrowest part of the estuary, with the tip of the northern sandbar at Southshore seemingly within a stone's throw.

10 Probably the best beach in Christchurch is at Sumner, and the western end is marked by the prominent natural rock stack of Rapanui Shag Rock. A home for cormorants, called shags, it was once an important navigational aid for seafarers entering the estuary. The earthquake has reduced its size, and the mess of fallen rocks has meant some locals now call it Shag Pile.

11 From here it's all ice creams and surfing vibes, or coffees and beers. This is a great place to watch, listen and meet the friendly locals, all at play in their favourite backyard. One beach suburb blends into the next with the eastern terminus of the cycle path along the Esplanade at the cliffs of Scarborough, with its own beachside cafe and clocktower.

12 Turn around and head back the same way or take a rest and use one of the frequent city buses equipped with bike racks to get you back to the Bus Exchange near Cathedral Sq where you started.

☕ Take a Break

Once you have made it to Sumner, give in to the call of the waves for a refreshing swim under the watchful eye of the lifeguards. The waves are also perfect for beginners to give surfing a try and you can attempt to emulate the antics of the local experts who have been coming here for years. Surfboard rentals, wet suits, boogie boards, lessons – it's all part of the surf scene. Or you can just get an ice cream and take it all in.

FILEDIMAGE/SHUTTERSTOCK ©

Tuawera Cave Rock

A Beach Landmark

Along with the eclectic beach-front architecture of Sumner, one of the other most recognisable features of the beach is Tuawera Cave Rock. Topped by a towered monument and flag mast in memory of Joseph Day, the Captain of the Sumner Lifeboat, this is a prominent eroded remnant of an ancient lava flow with a natural cave running through the base. At low tide it's possible to squeeze through the cave out onto the neighbouring beach, otherwise claw your way on top of the rock to find the plaque in remembrance to the hero who saved many lives.

Best for

MOUNTAIN SCENERY

Aoraki/ Mt Cook Explorer

DURATION	DIFFICULTY	DISTANCE	START/END
3hr	Easy	30km	Hermitage Hotel
TERRAIN	Gravel cycle paths interspersed with sealed road		

MATTHEW MICAH WRIGHT/GETTY IMAGES ©

Aoraki/Mt Cook National Park

The Alps to Ocean Trail from Aoraki/Mt Cook to Ōamaru is a four- to five-day adventure, passing glacially scoured lakes and following the downhill journey of that glacial water through the Waitaki Valley hydro lakes to sea level. The ride is surprisingly not all freewheeling. For those with less time, there are several stand-alone sections that are great for a day of riding and will get you fired up to come back. One of the highlights of the A2O is the start at Mt Cook village, and a day on a bike in this spectacular area is a treat.

Bike Hire

The Hermitage Hotel has an activity desk that will rent you a bike with a lock, and give you a map and important local information such as the weather forecast.

Starting Point

The small settlement of Mt Cook sits in an amphitheatre of glaciated mountains but the village is dominated by the Hermitage Hotel, plus the informative DOC Visitor Centre just below.

01 Cycle 100m down the path from the front of the hotel to the DOC Visitor Centre. With two floors of photographs, exhibits on the local natural and human history, along with expert information, this free exhibition is well worth a look around.

02 Back on your bike, follow the village loop road, past the picnic shelter at the entrance to the Governors Bush Walk, a one-hour forest loop with a lookout point.

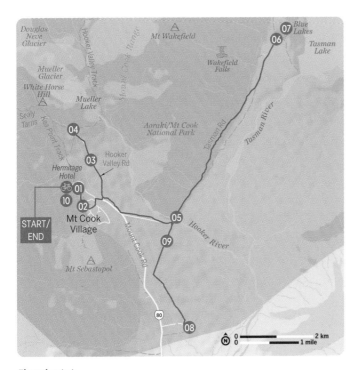

Global Warming

The Tasman Glacier is NZ's longest at 22km (reducing, on average, 180m per year), and its sudden retreat since the 1990s is now well documented. Its relatively easy access makes it popular for tourists and scientists alike, who wish to appreciate its grandeur and lament its slow demise. The Tasman Lake is testament to this retreat – it didn't exist until 1973 but within 30 years was already 7km in length. The glacier is still a mighty block of flowing ice, up to 600m thick in places, and the scale is appreciated when you realise the distant ice face you see is 50m high.

Elevation (m)

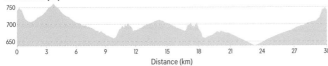

Distance (km)

03 The road then passes the local primary school and the YHA to bring you to the junction at the terminus of State Hwy 80. About 100m along the highway on the left you will see the signposted Hooker Valley Rd – alongside this road is the gravel A2O cycle path. Cross over to the cycle path and cycle the 2km to White Horse Hill campground. The glaciated face of Mt Sefton is in front of you as you savour the slow reveal of Aoraki/Mt Cook above a ridge of Mt Wakefield to your right.

04 The campground and car park is a hive of activity, with a shelter, toilets and multiple walking trails leading everywhere. Frequent avalanches and the audible groaning of ice movement on Mt Sefton add to the chaos of people and cars. Once you have decided on your plan, take a quick photo from here or nearby, and then turn around to retrace your tyre tracks 2km back towards the highway junction.

05 Staying on the gently undulating cycle path, 3km through the grassland, you emerge on to the Tasman Rd with a steel bridge over the Hooker River. Use this bridge to cross the river and then follow the flat sealed road for 6km through the Tasman Valley to a car-park area with a shelter and toilets.

06 You're now at the start of the stepped 20-minute climb to a viewpoint looking down onto the Tasman Lake. This is a relatively new lake created by the rapid retreat of the

Tasman Glacier, and often you will see large ice blocks that have broken away from the snout of the Tasman Glacier floating on the surface.

07 Head back down the steps to your bike, and decide whether to take side trips to the nearby not-so Blue Lakes and to the Tasman Lake that you spied from the viewpoint. The Blue Lakes are good swimming holes, with shallow and still waters that are warmer than any other body of water. Retrace your ride back down the road and immediately after the Hooker Bridge look for an A2O sign on your left. This gentle trail will take you the 3km to the airport.

08 If you want to understand the scale of the mountains and the park, you can't beat a scenic helicopter or aeroplane flight, complete with snow landing, but otherwise just watch the smiling faces of sightseers and mountaineers alike returning from their adventures up in the snow. The airport is a geographic break in the A2O. From here, a helicopter is required to get riders and their bikes over the unbridged and fast-flowing Tasman River to join the trail on the opposite side, down the eastern side of Lake Pukaki.

09 When ready to head back to the village, turn around to return up the trail. You are now doing a reverse O2A to the Tasman Valley Rd and the trail back to the start of the village loop road.

10 Returning to the Hermitage Hotel, take a seat on the balcony of the cafe with a drink and toast the mountain in front of you and the statue to your left. This is New Zealand's national hero, Sir Edmund Hillary. His statue stands outside the hotel's Sir Edmund Hillary Alpine Museum, looking towards the mountain where his exploits all started. The museum is dedicated to his life of adventure along with the long history that this fascinating hotel has witnessed.

☕ Take a Break

The mountains are the focus of any activity in this World Heritage Area, so it's all a case of how you want to set out to view them, and your budget. The Hooker Valley walk is indisputably NZ's most popular day walk, but if you want a more aerial vista of the surrounds, climb the steep staircase to the Sealy Tarns. Not into climbs? Then try a scenic helicopter flight for a snow landing or a guided walk on the Tasman Glacier.

STEVE TODD/SHUTTERSTOCK ©

Aoraki/Mt Cook National Park

Stay on the Trail

While you are within Aoraki/ Mt Cook National Park, keep in mind that bikes are welcome on some trails but not on others. The A2O is a dedicated bike trail so the gravel path from White Horse Hill campsite all the way to the airport is yours to ride. Taking your bike up any of the crowded hiking trails such as Kea Point, Hooker Valley, Tasman Lake, or the connector from the Hermitage Hotel to White Horse Hill, is definitely off limits. Stick to the A2O or the quiet sealed roads and there should be no conflict.

23

ALEX OMBAL/SHUTTERSTOCK ©

Hokitika to Treetops

DURATION	DIFFICULTY	DISTANCE	START/END
4hr	Intermediate	32km return	Hokitika

TERRAIN	Smooth gravel surface with some board-walk and road, and some short hill climbs

Bridge over the Hokitika River

This bite-size portion of the three-day West Coast Wilderness Trail gives a taste of the bigger picture with a fascinating treetop eco-activity to aim for. One of the many one-day possibilities, this ride is among forest giants and tranquil marshlands that thread their way through the coastal lowlands. It takes you over the river, across serene wetlands with boardwalks, and through treelined alleys to the Treetop Walkway attraction. Your West Coast experience will be completed from a unique perspective with a walk in the tree canopy of the ancient podocarp and hardwood rainforest.

Bike Hire

West Coast Cycle & Tours or Kiwi Journeys in Hokitika rent bikes and provide shuttle services to whisk you to other starting points along the West Coast Wilderness Trail.

Starting Point

Hokitika backs onto the beach and sits beside the river with the same name. The cycle trail starts at Gibson Quay and takes you over the river.

01 At the northern side of the Hokitika River bridge, follow the West Coast Wilderness signs that take you onto the dual-use path on the downstream side of the bridge. With the panorama of the Southern Alps and Aoraki/Mt Cook distracting your attention, try to stay aware of sudden wind gusts as you make your way over the 1km-long bridge.

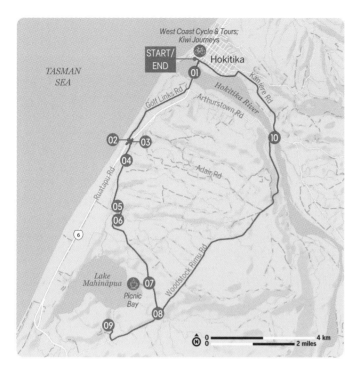

West Coast Cycle & Tours;
Kiwi Journeys

START/
END

Hokitika

TASMAN
SEA

Hokitika River

Kaniere Rd

Golf Links Rd

Arthurstown Rd

Adair Rd

Ruatapu Rd

6

Woodstock Rimu Rd

Lake
Mahināpua

Picnic
Bay

N 0   4 km
   0   2 miles

Sunset on the Beach

The summer evenings in Hokitika seem to stretch out with the observation of the sun's slow dip down to the horizon of the Tasman Sea, a ritual that draws a daily crowd. The beach sculptures built from the plentiful driftwood, plus the sunset, make it a photographer's playground. This is most spectacularly enjoyed during the Driftwood & Sand Festival in late January each year. Once it gets dark enough, round off the evening with a visit to enjoy the natural luminescence at the nearby free Glow-Worm Dell, just 1km from the beach.

Elevation (m)

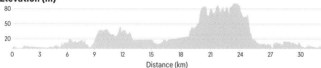

Distance (km)

02 Over the bridge, the trail follows a back road beside the meandering Mahināpua Creek, and then alongside the oceanfront Hokitika Golf Club on Golf Links Rd, to meet up with the main road at an information panel about Hokitika.

03 Cross the busy road here but don't be surprised when the trail takes you briefly back north in the direction you have come from. In 300m you will cross the old Mahināpua Creek Rail Bridge. After crossing

this impressive wooden structure the trail hooks back round to the south for a short steep climb up into the forest.

04 You are now on the historic Mahināpua Tramline, an old logging tramway that threads its way through old growth and regenerating native forest of rimu, kamahi and fern trees. The trams used to ply this tunnel-like avenue through the forest to haul the felled trees to the local sawmill. The gradient is gentle and the riding on the wide trail is easy.

05 After several kilometres and a couple of kinks in the otherwise straight trail you drop sharply down a zigzag and into the Mahināpua Wetland area. At the junction continue to the left, but before you do, take the opportunity to turn right. You will soon come across a photogenic suspension bridge over one of the many bodies of tea-coloured water. The waterways here were once used as the main route for early European settlers, explorers and gold diggers heading south. Now a nature reserve, it offers great opportunities for spotting birdlife and capturing mirror reflections of the surrounding mountains and flax-fringed water edges. The bridge actually takes walkers back out to the road and a car park, so turn back to the junction.

06 Continue along the trail to an open area of swampy wetland. This is crossed using a long section of boardwalk. Without any side barriers, you may feel slightly exposed on the boardwalk, but that's part of the charm. Just stop if you are unlucky enough to come across other cyclists or walkers.

07 Once safely across the wetland, the trail picks up the tramline again, running its line through the luxuriant West Coast forest. After just over 4km, look out for a sign showing the side trip to Picnic Bay.

08 From the Picnic Bay turn-off, continue for 2km of more tramline-riding until the trail meets Woodstock Rimu Rd, among farmland and exotic forest plantation. This is a rural sealed road around the inland side of the lake.

09 Turn right and follow the road for 3km. Just after a gradual downhill you should turn right into the West Coast Treetop Walkway visitor centre and cafe. This is a must-do activity, with enclosed walkways suspended between the trees, a cantilevered springboard platform and a lookout tower poking its head 47m above the ground for bird's-eye views of the tree canopy and Lake Mahināpua on the horizon. A new zip line also offers a 425m 60km/h adrenalin-filled flight through the trees.

10 Suitably fed and refreshed, it's back on your bike to head back to Hokitika along the same trail. For a marginally longer alternative, return using the back roads, continue on Woodstock Rimu Rd for 12km to the bridge over the Hokitika River at the small settlement of Kaniere. Here you will join the West Coast Wilderness Trail west to Hokitika for 5km along the true right of the river, taking you past the dairy factory and back to Gibson Quay after going under the Hokitika River bridge.

☕ Take a Break

Picnic Bay, as the name suggests, is a great spot to head down the shoreline of Lake Mahināpua. This 20-minute track is rough and slippery – leave the bikes behind – but gives the best view you will see of the lake. The lake was once a lagoon where the Hokitika River used to flow into the sea. It was left behind when the river changed to its present more-northerly course due to post–Ice Age sea levels rising and banking up coastal sand dunes.

DORADALTON/GETTY IMAGES ©

Hokitika oceanfront

Other Variations

The local bike-rental operators run shuttle services. Get dropped off at Hans Bay, beside Lake Kaniere, for a pleasant 22km ride back to town. You could even get dropped off at the Kawhaka Intake for the 50km ride back to Hokitika – it takes you over the lengthy climb of the Kawhaka Saddle, through Lake Kaniere and back to Hokitika. West Coast Scenic Waterways has an activities-based option on Lake Mahināpua. It offers nature-focused boat cruises through the wetlands, kayak hire for self-exploring the waterways, and bike hire, with or without shuttle services.

24

Greymouth to Kumara

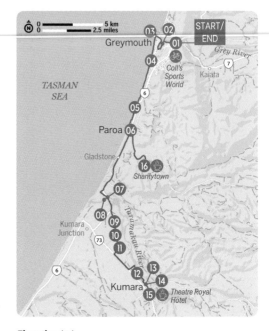

DURATION	DIFFICULTY	DISTANCE	START/END
6hr	Easy	62km return	Greymouth

TERRAIN	Flat gravel bike trail along beach and through forest

Elevation (m)

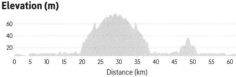

There is something magical about riding through avenues of towering trees among endless expanses of ancient native West Coast forest. The early European settlers created green corridors through the lush forests that have since been repurposed and stitched together into the West Coast Wilderness Trail, a 133km three-day ride showcasing the best of this area on a bike. This ride starts with a coastal trail within earshot of the surf pounding the shoreline nearby, then takes you to the goldrush town of Kumara.

Bike Hire

Coll's Sports World rent e-bikes and regular bikes, with trail transport options. There are other options in town too, all of which come with a friendly West Coast yarn.

Starting Point

The ride starts on the seawall overlooking the Grey River, opposite the railway station and i-SITE office. Parking is not an issue and everything is in walking distance.

01 After getting your selfie at the official starting gate of the trail, the path follows the Grey River floodwall past the Greymouth Clocktower towards the sea.

02 Signs take you along the raised walkway, flanked on your left by grand old buildings that echo of past trading days when this was a major port, with stately Victorian-style banks, courthouses and government buildings, now transformed into galleries, restaurants and cafes. If you

Best for

SEASIDE RIDES

LAKEVIEW IMAGES/SHUTTERSTOCK ©

Greymouth Clocktower

stop at the numerous fascinating interpretation panels with old photos of days gone by, it may take you some time to reach the basin where the present day fishing fleet unloads its catch.

03 Circumnavigating the basin brings you onto the Blaketown breakwater, protecting the harbour mouth. Before turning left to ride south along the coast, make sure you go out to the end of the breakwater to look along the beach or back inland to the town with its backdrop of forested hills. Envisage, if you can, that 44 ships have floundered on the notorious Greymouth Bar, a sandbar that

lurks under the waters where the Grey River meets the ocean. Many lives have been lost at the very point where those miners and prospectors keenly anticipated starting a prosperous life in a new country.

04 The flat trail takes you south, past the airfield and modern hospital building, across reclaimed estuarine lagoons that were once frequently inundated by the Grey River bursting its banks. There have been more than 20 severe floods in Greymouth in its short 170-year history, all with imaginative names such as the Jubilee Flood (1887), the Biggest Since

1887 (1936), the Biggest Since 1936 (1977) and the Big One (1988). The construction of the floodwall has protected the town since it was completed in 1990.

05 You will cross numerous access paths to the beach, and each one invites you to stop and take a peek at the frothing West Coast seas, admire the driftwood and perhaps come across blue penguin nesting boxes among the coastal vegetation.

06 After 11km, never straying far from the beach, the trail emerges at the roadside Paroa Hotel, opposite the road that takes you on the

☕ Take a Break

A worthwhile 3.5km side trip from the Paroa Hotel is the reimagination of an 1860s goldrush village at Shantytown, officially opened in 1971. It was the brainchild of a group of gold-panning locals with an interest in tourism, and then built by volunteers using donated materials. It's a fun place to visit, with steam train rides, gold-panning experiences, a sluice-gun demonstration and more, all set against a Wild West movie-set backdrop. Make sure you check the schedule of activities to be there at the best time.

side trip to Shantytown. The bike trail to Kumara, however, continues south, parallel to the road, snaking its way through glades of manuka and flax until, at the 18km mark, you approach the Taramakau River.

07 The upstream rail bridge, completed in 1893, was the last combined road-rail bridge to be used in the South Island. Until 2018 this was a single-lane bridge simultaneously used by road traffic and trains. With the train rails running down the middle of the bridge, car drivers had to commit to which side they would stick to. Trains were at the top of the pecking order, causing congestion and inevitably several crashes. With the new sharp-looking two-lane road bridge 30m downstream of the old one, the new road configuration takes walkers and riders under the road and up the other side on a cycle path. Trains now have the old bridge all to themselves and it is worth stopping to have a look at this well-known vestige of relatively recent history that many 'Coasters' have fond memories of.

08 During September and October look down the river to see hardy locals sitting on the riverbank tending their whitebait nets. A favourite New Zealand pastime and much-loved delicacy, whitebait are the juveniles of six varieties of fish, five of which are galaxiids, and four of which are now considered endangered. They fetch $100 to $160 per kilo, so sharing your catch can make you lots of friends.

09 After just one more kilometre, the trail bears to the left away from the busy State Hwy 6 on a road called Greymouth–Kumara Tramway. The last house on this side road is soon followed by a car park with a shelter and toilet for cyclists.

10 The trail then narrows as it enters a stand of regenerating native forest. The forest is rich in native birdlife, including tui and bellbirds, all singing away contentedly in their natural habitat in an unmistakable cacophony that was once the sound of New Zealand forests. Be careful not to run over any of the flightless weka that are often seen feeding in the trailside ditches and grassy verges.

11 From here the way is mostly straight, following the historic route of the freight and passenger tramway that connected the merchants of Greymouth with the rich goldfields of Kumara. The tramway rails through the

GREENS AND BLUES/SHUTTERSTOCK ©

Arahura River

Land Sales

This rugged region was one of the last to be explored by Europeans, but interest was mounting. In 1857, the local Māori *iwi* offered to sell the West Coast for £2500, with the proviso that they retained some traditional burial sites and the Arahura River, an important source of *pounamu*. A deal was finally signed at Māwhera, now Greymouth's CBD, selling the entire West Coast except for several scattered reserves for a mere £300, equating to $40,000 today. One such reserve is Māwhera, which is now worth $123 million, making the Māwhera Incorporation the biggest landlord in town.

forest were wooden to save construction costs and the tramcars were horse-drawn. The three-hour journey, which operated from 1877 to 1893, also involved a hair-raising cable winch in a cage across the often-raging Taramakau River. The tramway now makes a beautiful bike ride with many giant native podocarp, such as rimu, kahikatea and matai trees, towering above the trail on both sides.

12 After 3km on the tramway, the trail turns right and follows the highway along a fence line for a short distance before turning back towards the river and more tramway. This brings you to a suspension bridge which safely carries cyclists over the deep chasm of the Kumara Gully. In several places you get glimpses of the Taramakau River, which, along with the Arahura River, was an important source of *pounamu* (greenstone/jade) for the local *iwi* (tribe) Poutini Ngāi Tahu, residing at present-day Greymouth.

LAKEVIEW IMAGES/ALAMY STOCK PHOTO ©

Gold Nuggets

A reminder of the former significance of Kumara as a gold-rush town is the local racecourse with its impressive grandstand, where one of New Zealand's longest-running horse-racing events takes place each year in early January. Being one of the biggest social events on the West Coast calendar, this country-style race meeting, dating back to 1887, attracts a colourful crowd of thousands of revellers from all over New Zealand. The biggest race of the day is the Kumara Gold Nuggets, for which the winner appropriately receives a real gold nugget as well as the more traditional monetary prize.

13 Soon after this, the trail pops out of the forest into an opening to a scene that sets the tone for your visit to Kumara with a line of fenceposts all adorned with assorted rusty relics. The eclectic collection of bric-a-brac from the goldrush days includes saws, irons, sewing machines and the like. Soon after, at the 29km mark, the trail joins the main street of the quiet settlement of Kumara, whose importance to New Zealand's political history belies its present-day size.

14 Kumara has several carefully restored cottages and a whole outdoor area of interpretation panels with informative stories of its colourful history and characters, making it a great place to soak up the past. The fact that this town could once boast 50 drinking establishments speaks volumes.

15 Take some time to walk up and down the main street and perhaps stretch the legs with a 15-minute loop walk to Taylors Hill for a panoramic view of the area and the Taramakau River. Kumara is best known as the political starting point of Richard Seddon and the site of his home on the main street is marked. He was derisively nicknamed and still best remembered as King Dick. From a start in gold-mining, he became a store owner, then local mayor, and lastly a rather autocratic Prime Minister in 1893. He led the country for 13 years, making him New Zealand's longest serving PM, until he died onboard a ship returning from Australia while still in office.

TOP TIP:
Once you make your thirsty return to Greymouth, it would be hard to go past a visit to the iconic Monteith's Brewery, close to the town centre. They have been brewing here since 1868, using the resource the West Coast is most famous for – beautiful pure water.

16 The return to Greymouth is on the same trail. At the Paroa Hotel you have a second chance to take the recommended side trip along the sealed Rutherglen Rd to Shantytown. Follow the signposts under the railway and away from the sea towards the hills for a flattish 3.5km ride. Once you're done at Shantytown, return to the Paroa Hotel down the same route to pick up the coastal trail once again to the Greymouth town centre.

☕ Take a Break

The Theatre Royal Hotel is a sumptuously restored hotel from the halcyon gold-rush days of the 1860s, and the accommodation, bar and cafe is now an established destination for cyclists, many staying overnight and dining in the restaurant while on the two-night, three-day West Coast Wilderness Trail. In its heyday this was the home of a quirky theatrical establishment visited by travelling international troupes performing Shakespeare and the like in the centre of unruly and frenetic mining activity. It's a great spot to stop for a meal and refreshments.

Kumara Gold Nuggets

25

Best for

SEASIDE RIDES

Kaikōura Trail

DURATION	DIFFICULTY	DISTANCE	START/END
5hr	Intermediate	43km	Kaikōura i-SITE

TERRAIN	Gravel backcountry roads to challenging narrow single-track forest riding

RICHARD RYALL ©

Kaikōura Trail

Now that you've seen the whales, swum with the dolphins and walked around the seal colonies of the peninsula, it must be time to complete your total experience of this area of rich marine wildlife. This circuit ride takes in ocean views, beachside trails, native coastal forest and farmland populated by grazing sheep. All this with the impressive Kaikōura Range as the backdrop and the ocean as your horizon. With some challenging riding linking the country roads, this is a ride to take your time on. Make sure you pack your towel for frequent swimming breaks and save some snacks for a picnic.

Bike Hire

Coastal Sports in the town centre has a good range of bikes for hire, with a bike mechanic on-site to tweak your bike for action.

Starting Point

The ride begins, after a leisurely coffee, from the i-SITE and Museum on the main street, with a car park and toilets nearby. This is where you will finish, too.

01 Follow the Esplanade towards the peninsula, turning right up Yarmouth St beside the Encounter Kaikoura office, and right again up a short ascent along Killarney St, with a sharp hook to the left, to the main road entrance of the town centre on State Hwy 1.

02 Whether or not you take a side trip to the nearby lookout point, you'll soon see the cycle path down the left side of the main road SH1 to South Bay. You will be able to pick out the

Whale Trail

The Whale Trail is an inspirational new dual-use trail project, still under construction, connecting the ferry port of Picton with Kaikōura. It will create a 210km continuous stretch of cycling and walking trail along coast, across pastoral countryside and through vineyards. Once completed, it is sure to be a huge asset to the region's economy. The 7.8 magnitude 2016 earthquake that devastated much of the road and rail infrastructure has provided an opportunity to build a new multiday route for cyclists linking small settlements along the way, passing through areas rarely seen by visitors. Construction is now well underway.

Elevation (m)

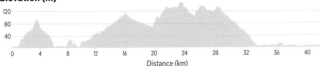

first of many of the trail markers that will show the way for the rest of the ride. Also look out for the convenient maps which show your progress along the trail.

03 The Kaikōura Racecourse on your left holds an annual two-day event in late October. Only separated from the beach by South Bay Pde, it's a spectacular location and a big local event. Most of the ocean-based activities, such as whale-watching, head out to sea from the marina at the end of this road. However, the

bike trail crosses South Bay Pde immediately, over into the Lions Club Reserve, where you will spot the trail disappearing south in a corner between some bushes.

04 Now on a single-track beachside trail that threads its way through coastal scrub and bush, you will see there are numerous picnic tables and tracks calling for you to explore the beach itself. The intertidal zone along the Kaikōura coast, where you might be standing, was lifted as much as 6m in the 2016 earthquake

that struck this northeast corner of the South Island. A species of bull-kelp seaweed was left high and dry above the sea itself and widely died off. This bay is also a favourite haunt for one of the stars of local tourism, the Dusky dolphins, that can often be seen playing, with frequent jumps, flips and even somersaults. If you see a boat shadowing something, it probably means they have found a pod that's ready to play.

05 The trail continues to a pine-forest section with some obstacles to

☕ Take a Break

While on the circuit, take your pick of a bracing swim in the South Pacific at any of a multitude of places at the start or end of the the loop, or a refreshing freshwater plunge in the Hapuka River, which is a local's favourite on a hot day and comes complete with a rope swing. About midway, the Kōura Golf Resort offers a full range of beverages and snacks, all served with panoramic views of the South Pacific.

negotiate, such as tree roots, pine cones and sandy patches that will stop you dead like quicksand. Now 5km from town, you are at the Kowhai River and the highway bridge over it, but the trail will take you under the bridge and away from any road crossings.

06 Around 50m after you have gone under the bridge, turn right at the marker to follow the trail, which is now between the boundary of the Kaikōura golf course and a flood bank of the Kowhai River. This is 7km of single-track riding on an almost imperceptible climb through mixed coastal forest, crossing some gravel roads along the way. The braided Kowhai River, flowing across a wide shingle bed with multiple channels, is the location of a program to control noxious weeds, allowing native plants to reestablish themselves on the riverbanks and subsequently provide nesting habitat for native birds. About midway, the climb to 'Mt Kowhai' is obviously a humorous exaggeration of a small mound. Approach it with a smile and descend to rejoin the trail that avoids this tongue-in-cheek mountain.

07 Eventually you will emerge from the dappled light of the forest trail to an open gravelled area among tidy fenced farmland at

Postmans Rd. You have climbed 100m. If you need some more exercise and adrenaline in your life, turn left here to the start of the intermediate-graded trails of the Kaiterau Bike Park. The 3km road climb takes you to 180m above sea level to the bike park and a further 7km climb to 570m, partway up the slopes of Mt Fyffe. The payback is a challenging 3km swoop back down to the bottom of the park and then a cruise to Postmans Rd. Otherwise follow the signs to the right that take you eventually onto a sealed road.

08 Enjoy this ride through Kiwi country life, with views of the imposing Seaward Kaikōura Range to your left and the blue ocean to your right. With a couple of signposted turns, left into McInnes Rd and right into Pooles Rd, you get off the roads and back into a single-track section across the (usually dry) bed of Luke Creek and through some pasture. Leave gates as you find them and give livestock a wide berth.

09 Continuing your eastern progress, follow Topline Rd, leading into a short single-track forest section across the unbridged Waimangarara Stream, which ultimately brings you to the Kōura Bay Golf Resort, for a well-earned break.

PALEOKASTRITSA/SHUTTERSTOCK ©

Sperm whale, Kaikōura

Seafood Pantry

The local marine mammals agree with us land-based mammals in the old adage about location being everything, as they have found nature's pantry on their doorstep in Kaikōura. Just 800m offshore from the coast, the shallow waters drop off into the Kaikōura Canyon, a 3km-deep trench stretching 60km out into the Pacific Ocean, with deep-water currents that support an incredible concentration of oceanic life rising to the surface. This sustains the rich food chain, from microscopic plankton right up to the giants of the seas, the mighty sperm whales that are resident here, along with other seasonal visitors.

10 Leaving the clubhouse down the main entrance driveway, you will pass new houses with enviable panoramic views of the coastline. At the junction with Bay Paddock Rd, turn left towards the mountains to climb to the high point of your circuit, at 140m above sea level, as you turn right along Grange Rd.

11 The sealed Grange Rd stretches off in a straight line ahead of you, but eventually gives way to a downhill gravel-road approach to the Hapuku River. At the first car-park area, look to your right towards the sea and find the start of the long single-track downhill towards the ocean – it's just near the swimming hole.

12 This 7km winding forest freewheel travels down the true right bank (south bank) of the Hapuku River and through the forest. It is only interrupted by a couple of short sharp climbs, and when it passes under the major road of SH1. The gradient is gentle, but caution is required as it has narrow rocky sections, tree roots aplenty and

the possibility of uphill bikers to contend with. Look out for some impressive stands of totara trees, a giant native evergreen podocarp that was once one of the trees that made up the dense native forest cover on these mountainsides.

13 Emerging onto Lovers Lane, bear left down to the ocean, crossing the barrier-free railway line to ride almost onto the popular surfing beach at the small settlement of Hapuku.

14 Recovering your senses after that long downhill, retrace your tyre tracks back from the ocean to turn left (or right after crossing the railway line without going to the beach) along Hapuku Rd, with peaceful rural houses and quaint gardens. A right turn takes you back across the same railway line, to join with Old Beach Rd, which leads away to the left. Be aware that trains, although infrequent, are always possible.

Point Kean, Peninsula Walkway

15 This sealed road will take you on a mostly flat ride parallel to the railway track and back towards town, with great views over the beach and along the coastline in both directions. Leaving the road on the left, at a signposted but easily missed bridge, and under the railway, the trail brings you to a single-track cruise on smooth trail through swaying coastal grassland parallel to North Beach.

TOP TIP:

If you turn left at the top of your climb out of Kaikōura town, you can take an optional 1.5km side trip along Scarborough St to the best lookout point of the town and its surrounds, a viewing platform atop one of the town water tanks.

16 With benches and more beach access, it's tempting to delay your return to town, but carrying on just a little further takes you to the Kaikōura train station on Whaleway Station Rd, within sight of the town centre and your starting point. The Coastal Pacific train stops here on its scenic journey between Christchurch and Picton. Watch out for pedestrians as you weave your way along the path beside the car park, over a boardwalk and down on the main street. With your ride done, make sure you consider a contribution to the maintenance of the trail through the Kaikōura Cycling Club, the local group that has created this great ride.

☕ Take a Break

While you have your bike on the road, why not ride down the Esplanade to the end of the road that leads to the Peninsula Walkway? This is a great spot to relax with the fur seals that hang out in the sun on the intriguingly shaped rocks and boulders, readying themselves for another nighttime foraging mission off the coast in the Southern Ocean. Once almost hunted to extinction, these protected marine mammals are a constant fascination to watch.

26

Omarama to Benmore Dam

Best for

OFF THE BEATEN TRACK

DURATION	DIFFICULTY	DISTANCE	START/END
6hr	Intermediate	58km return	Omarama

TERRAIN	Undulating lakeside gravel trail takes you into a narrow trail through a gorge on Lake Benmore

Lake Benmore (p164)

DMITRY PICHUGIN/SHUTTERSTOCK ©

This is an outstanding section of the Alps 2 Ocean trail, with something for everyone to enjoy. Starting with a gentle warm-up over the Chain Hills Saddle, it follows the Lake Benmore lakeshore trail. The autumn colours are at their peak in April, but at any time of year this is great riding with plenty of photo opportunities as you enter the challenging gorge section, where you are forced to decide how far you dare to continue if you haven't prearranged a shuttle service.

Bike Hire

Trail Adventures are the only bike hire in Omarama and they also offer shuttles to suit your plans. Otherwise the nearby town of Twizel has other operators.

Starting Point

Omarama is at the T-junction of State Hwy 8 and 83. Famous for gliding, fishing and the outdoor hot tubs, it has accommodation options plus a pub.

01 After a hearty breakfast and with your food ready for the day, start your ride on State Hwy 83, which is signposted for Ōamaru. You are following the A2O and it is clearly signposted, firstly on the left side of the road, then crossing the road to keep to a cycle path on the right side. The distances from your starting point at Omarama are marked along the trail.

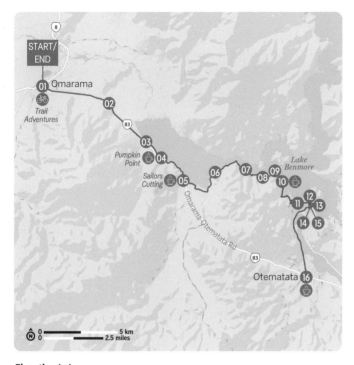

Hydropower

Lake Benmore and the massive dam that created it are both part of the much larger Waitaki Hydro Scheme, built between 1928 and 1985. With five lakes all connected by river, tunnel and 56km of canals, water is channelled downstream from the highest lake at Tekapo (altitude 710m), through the lakes and eight power stations, to finally pass through Waitaki Power Station near Kurow at 230m. On this journey from the Southern Alps, this elegant scheme uses the same water at each power station down the valley to supply enough electricity for almost one million households.

Elevation (m)

02 Past the livestock sale yards on the edge of town, a hub of local rural activity when an auction is on, is the start of a gentle ascent over the Chain Hills. Crossing the road again just before the high point, the trail bisects the chain of linked hills that gradually get smaller, running from your right to left, hence their name. Now 5km from Omarama, the view from the top affords a view of Lake Benmore stretching out ahead. This can be a tranquil sight, particularly in the morning, before the wind from the coast kicks in.

03 From the Chain Hills lookout point, it's a speedy cruise downhill to the lakeside trail, but be aware of squeeze barriers in your path that are successfully designed to slow you down and force you to get off your bike. There are several of these on this ride, some encouraging you to walk on the left of your bike, others on the right.

04 The ride along Lake Benmore is flat and full of interest, the trail making its way through willow trees and stands of poplar to the sheltered

swimming spot of Pumpkin Point at 10km.

05 The trail continues to hug the shoreline to bring you to the small harbour of Sailors Cutting at 13km, a scenic reserve with a boat ramp, a campground and public toilets. Fringed by willow trees, the autumn colours make this a popular photo stop, and summer can be busy with boating families all launching from here while camping. There is no water beyond here, so refill your bottle at the campground, as you are now about to enter a

☕ Take a Break

Looking over the lake, with numerous bays, islands and peninsulas to feast your eyes on, the viewpoint near the outdoor toilet at the 23km mark is a perfect place to have your picnic lunch. The jetty in the sheltered harbour of Sailors Cutting 13km from Omarama, along with the nearby grassy lakeshore at Pumpkin Point, are both perfect entry points for a swim on your way back to Omarama on a hot Mackenzie Country afternoon after a sweaty day of dusty riding.

bone-dry rocky gorge that can be swelteringly hot in summer.

06 You're now at the start of a new 16km section of the A2O to Benmore Dam, called the Lake Benmore Trail, opened in December 2020. Taking five months and $1.2 million to build, this trail takes cyclists along the Ahuriri Arm of Lake Benmore and into the hills, well hidden away from the old route along the main highway. The first 3km passes through the campground and continues as a wide, gentle and smooth gravel trail along the lakeside, but once you climb to a lookout point at Translator Saddle, you enter the remote but scenic narrow gorge.

07 Pace yourself for three decent climbs through the gorge, rewarded with long glides across sheer mountain faces. With numerous twists and corners, the zigzagging climbs and drops to reveal new vistas at every turn. Keep your eyes on the trail, though, as there are narrow bluffs to negotiate, and rocky sections with steep drop-offs and blind corners, meaning you have to constantly keep your wits about you.

08 Never forget this is a two-way trail used by bikers as a stand-alone return trip. In several places, there is particularly narrow bridging, a cantilevered platform or just a narrow section of trail, and simply getting off and walking enables you to look around to appreciate the incredible views that are constantly changing. Otherwise, make use of the picnic tables and viewpoints to take in where you have just come from and scope out the trail meandering across the hillsides in front of you.

09 Passing over the ornate A2O bridge and continuing on, the trail widens and the gorge starts to open out to reveal a bigger expanse of water. Two valleys were flooded to create the Ahuriri and Haldon arms of Lake Benmore, as part of the construction of the Benmore Dam, and this is where they join. With an area of 75 sq km and at 90m deep, this is NZ's biggest artificial lake, fed by the waters of the Ahuriri, Ohau, Pukaki and Tekapo rivers, but held back by the Benmore Dam.

10 Just after passing a view of the tiny Turnagain Island at the 23km mark, the trail comes to a photogenic rocky knob looking out to the lake. With tree-covered Junction Island in the foreground, and fingers of forested land poking into the lake in stark contrast to the dry tussock-covered hills in the background, this is a great spot to

Omarama

Omarama

Omarama, meaning the place of light, is paradoxically on the edge of the Mackenzie Country Dark Sky Reserve. The region received this designation for having a night sky devoid of light pollution, therefore providing excellent star-watching possibilities. Daytime activities in this small town of some 300 inhabitants include the world-famous airfield for gliders, the clay cliffs, fishing among the colourful lupins of the Ahuriri River, or a long soak of tired muscles (or perhaps saddle-sore buttocks) in the open-air wood-fired hot tubs, all enjoyed under the big skies of this open expanse of uninhabited high country.

take a breather. Nearby there is also a portable toilet.

11 With Junction Island on your left shoulder, the trail is now wider and less demanding on your concentration, and after one squeeze barrier and 3km, you have a steep 1km climb to another high point called Rostriever Saddle. This is the base of the Benmore Peninsula, which extends out into the main body of the lake.

12 Crossing over the saddle, you are greeted by a magnificent view of the impressive expanse of the Benmore Dam, the associated power plant at its base, and the water flowing away towards Lake Aviemore in the distance. At 118m high, this is NZ's largest earth-filled dam and second only in power production to the Manapouri Dam in Fiordland. To your right is the small township of Otematata. From the saddle, the narrowing trail runs across an exposed hillside down into an area of pine forest, forever descending towards more viewpoints over the dam.

FRANCESCA TAYLOR/SHUTTERSTOCK ©

13 Passing through another squeeze barrier in the trees, the steep descent continues. If you are riding back to Omarama, remember you will need to climb back up this hill, so you need to decide how far you want to keep going on this fun downhill. The trail passes through recently harvested pine forest, zigzagging its way past the start of the Benmore Peninsula Walking Track, a pleasant 4km hiking loop around the peninsula. The bike trail, however, finally emerges at a turning circle and car-park area looking down onto the road crossing the dam. A mobile ice-cream truck is sometimes here on a hot day.

14 This elevated car park marks the end of the Lake Benmore Trail and riders are now 29km from their starting point at Omarama. The A2O crosses the dam to continue down the side of Lake Aviemore.

15 Turn around to retrace your tyre tracks and savour the scenery once again from the opposite direction back through the Lake Benmore Trail through Sailors Cutting and onto Omarama.

16 Alternatively, with advance planning on how to get back to Omarama, consider cycling on a further 6km from the dam to Otematata. After a 2km super-fast descent off the top of the dam on a sealed road, the road flattens, passing picnic areas, campsites, a restored wetland area with a walkway and a golf course to join the main road at Otematata. Trail Journeys in Omarama runs a pre-book service back to Omarama for cyclists. The busy road between Otematata and Sailors Cutting is not recommended for cyclists, with only a narrow strip to keep to and a 230m climb. The stunning Lake Benmore Trail avoids the need for casual cyclists to venture onto this highway that was once part of the A2O.

TOP TIP:

Once you enter the remote gorge section of the trail there is no water and very limited mobile-phone coverage. Places where your provider may give coverage are signposted along the way. It is highly recommended that riders carry a Personal Locator Beacon in case of emergency.

Benmore Peninsula

☕ Take a Break

Otematata is the small town that once housed 4000 dam workers during construction of the Benmore and Aviemore Dams in the 1960s. With a country hotel, a coffee caravan and a small supermarket, it is an obvious place to rest at the end of your ride. With prior arrangement, the Omarama bike-hire shop does a shuttle service for cyclists, bikes or even just bags from Otematata back to their base each afternoon, giving lots of options for your adventure.

Also Try...

Cycling near Lake Tekapo

Little River Rail Trail

DURATION	DIFFICULTY	DISTANCE
5hr	Easy	46km

This ride follows a historic railway line that once linked Christchurch with the small settlement of Little River at the base of the hill climb into Akaroa. This is a flat dual-share trail starting in Prebbleton, connecting peaceful towns on the outskirts of the city, and snaking its way beside rivers through rural parks. The trail takes back roads to pick up the old railway line along the expansive shores of Lake Ellesmere. You can load your bike on the city bus to get to the start or extend the ride 14km by riding from the city centre and following the Little River Link cycle path to Prebbleton. The daily Akaroa French Connection bus service between Christchurch and Akaroa passes through Little River on its afternoon return and with prior notice they will pick you and your bike up at the trail end.

Tekapo Explore

DURATION	DIFFICULTY	DISTANCE
4hr	Easy	48km

The turquoise-blue waters of Lake Tekapo are one of the jewels in the crown of NZ tourism and the town on its shores makes a good base to rent a bike for a day and explore. This is actually an official alternative starting point for the Alps 2 Ocean for those who don't want to use the helicopter service over the Tasman River. It joins the main trail starting from Aoraki/Mt Cook at Lake Pukaki. The signposted trail takes riders through housing above town and along the mystifyingly blue canal that carries water from Lake Tekapo to Lake Pukaki. Turn around at the viewpoint of Lake Pukaki just after the salmon farm at 24km. In addition, there are flat trails along the lakefront that take you to the south corner of the lake to the Lake Tekapo Regional Park trails.

Paparoa Track

Homestead Run

DURATION	DIFFICULTY	DISTANCE
2hr	Intermediate	15km

Requiring transport from Hamner Springs, this gravel-road circuit has a short climb that is set within the bigger circuit of the challenging one- to two-day 59km St James Cycle Trail, all in a remote part of the St James Conservation Area. The trail starts 13km out of Hamner Springs, a hot-spring and biking destination, with bike-hire shops and a range of trails to suit everyone. The well-established network of trails around town is set among vineyards, forests and the alpine slopes nestled in the foothills of the Southern Alps, and it's only 90 minutes from Christchurch. With a long soak in the hot springs to relax after the ride, followed by great food, you will understand why bikers flock here. Grab a trail map from the local i-SITE and take your pick.

Paparoa Track

DURATION	DIFFICULTY	DISTANCE
2 days	Difficult	56km

This is NZ's newest Great Walk and is a year-round dual-use track for hikers and experienced bikers looking for a challenge among incredible scenery on the West Coast near Punakaiki. E-bikes are not permitted, so you will need to pedal your way 850m up the rough forest track to the high points near Ces Clark Hut and across the alpine section to Moonlight Tops Hut. This huge effort is rewarded with expansive views of the Southern Alps and the Tasman Sea. The next day is all downhill to the northern exit of the track. Bikers need to arrange transport, with the start and finish geographically distant from each other in remote country. The need to be experienced and prepared cannot be emphasised enough, but it is an adventure to remember.

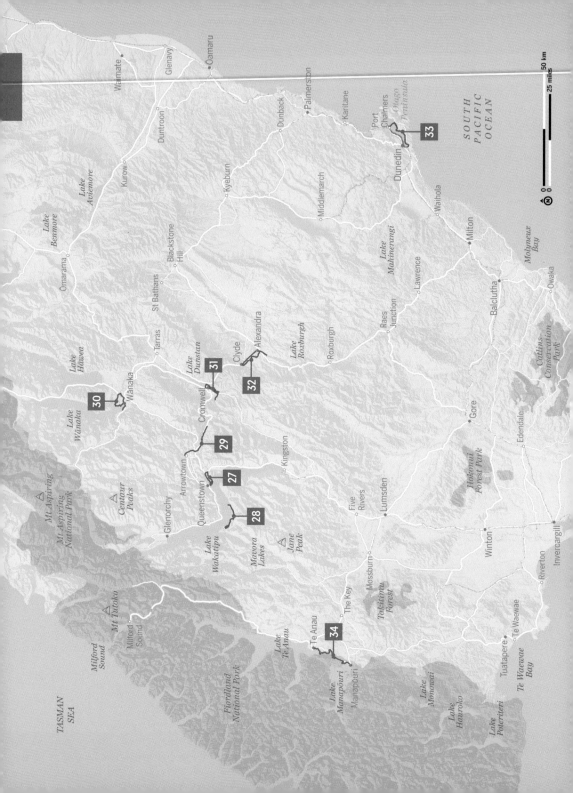

TASMAN
SEA

Milford Sound

Mt Tutoko ▲

Milford
Sound

Mt Aspiring ▲

Mt Aspiring
National Park

Centaur
Peaks ▲

Glenorchy

Lake
Wānaka

Wanaka

30

Lake
Hāwea

Arrowtown

29

Cromwell

Lake
Dunstan

31

Clyde

Alexandra

32

Lake
Roxburgh

Roxburgh

Tarras

St Bathans

Blackstone
Hill

Kyeburn

Middlemarch

Omarama

Kurow

Duntroon

Lake
Aviemore

Lake
Benmore

Waimate

Glenavy

Oamaru

Duntroon

Palmerston

Dunback

Karitane

Port
Chalmers

Otago
Peninsula

33

Dunedin

Waihola

Milton

Molyneux
Bay

Owaka

Balclutha

Lawrence

Lake
Mahinerangi

Raes
Junction

Catlins-
Conservation
Park

Gore

Edendale

Hokonui
Forest Park

Lumsden

Winton

Invercargill

Riverton

Te Waewae
Bay

Tuatapere

Lake
Poteriteri

Lake
Hauroko

Lake
Monowai

Manapōuri

Lake
Manapōuri

34

Lake
Te Anau

Te Anau

The Key

Takitimu
Forest

Mossburn

Five
Rivers

Jane
Peak ▲

Kingston

Mavora
Lakes

Lake
Wakatipu

Queenstown

27

28

Fiordland
National Park

SOUTH
PACIFIC
OCEAN

50 km

25 miles

N ⊙

0

0

JANICE CHEN/GETTY IMAGES ©

Lake Wānaka

Otago & the South

Explore

Otago & the South

There's brilliant biking down here in the south, with a myriad of off-road, purpose-built bike trails, especially in Central Otago and around the Southern Lakes resorts of Queenstown and Wānaka. And there are more trails being constructed. By the late 2020s, bikers should be able to ride off-road trails from both Queenstown and Wānaka all the way to Dunedin on the east coast. While the trails are superb, the scenery is unsurpassed and the region's resorts and towns provide excellent facilities, including numerous rental-bike outlets, hiring out both e-bikes and regular mountain bikes. This is New Zealand's premier biking hot spot.

Queenstown

There are good reasons why so many people flock to Queenstown – this is one of the premier alpine resorts on the planet, in an outstanding natural environment. The 'adventure capital of the world' may be known for its winter-sports playgrounds and as the birthplace of bungy jumping, but there are just so many other things to do, including biking around the Queenstown Trails network, which includes more than 130km of off-road bike trails. There's a cosmopolitan dining and arts scene, top vineyards, pulsating bars, plus a full range of places to stay.

Wānaka

Laid-back lakeside Wānaka has been well and truly discovered. The smaller of the Southern Lakes resorts, Wānaka is bristling with outdoor and adventure opportunities, including bike trails. Things get really busy at the height of the winter ski season and in midsummer. There's a growing number of good cafes, restaurants and bars, enticing visitors to base themselves here and stick around.

Cromwell & Clyde

These two small towns in Central Otago, only 20 minutes apart by car, have become a hub for keen bikers. There are a number of trails in 'Central', the best known being the 152km Otago Central Rail Trail. Both Cromwell and Clyde have 'old town' heritage precincts with buildings from the gold-rush days, options for bike hire, plus

WHEN TO GO

This is the deep south, home to alpine ski resorts in winter, and heaven for hikers and bikers in the warmer months of October to April. Things warm up and lambs will be frolicking on the farms in spring, the weather is generally settled from late December to March, and after that, autumn colours are an absolute showpiece.

boutique-style accommodation and eating establishments.

Te Anau

The gateway to Fiordland National Park, picturesque Te Anau is a bustling little lakeside town during the hiking season, from October to April. In the off-season...not so much. There are lots of places to stay, eat and drink, and visitors are spoilt for outdoor activities, especially in the national park on walking trails like the Milford, Routeburn and Kepler tracks.

Dunedin

Two words spring to mind when Kiwis think of Dunedin, the South's largest city: 'Scotland' and 'students'. The 'Edinburgh of the South' has a strong Scottish heritage, with hardy Scottish settlers arriving from 1848, while students at the University of Otago are renowned throughout the country for their partying and are known as 'scarfies'. There's lots of accommodation as Dunedin's

TRANSPORT

Queenstown International Airport, with direct flights from all the main centres and a slew of Australian cities, is the regional hub. Dunedin Airport serves the east coast of Otago. Buses crisscross the region linking all the main towns, while many visitors make use of the huge fleet of rental cars and campervans in Queenstown to explore the south.

indoor stadium hosts plenty of sports events and concerts, and cheap eats abound within cooee of the university.

WHAT'S ON

Queenstown & Wānaka have events throughout the year.

Cyclorama

(*cyclorama.co.nz*) New Zealand's first e-bike festival held in Arrowtown in October.

Arrowtown Autumn Festival

(*arrowtownautumnfestival.co.nz*) Six days of excitement in late April.

Wānaka A&P Show

(*wanakashow.co.nz*) Mid-March farm-related fun; going for 80+ years.

Dunedin Fringe Festival

(*dunedinfringe.nz*) The world's southernmost Fringe Festival in March.

Rhythm & Alps Festival

(*rhythmandalps.co.nz*) Three-day music festival in the Cardrona Valley.

WHERE TO STAY

Queenstown, in particular, has a huge range of accommodation to suit all budgets in all seasons. As a top resort, Wānaka also offers a good number and range of options, as does Te Anau, the gateway to Fiordland National Park. The Central Otago biking hot spots of Cromwell and Clyde have fewer places to stay, but are within an hour of both Queenstown and Wānaka by car. As a city of more than 100,000 people, Dunedin is a good place to base yourself on Otago's east coast. Bookings are essential in high seasons and New Zealand school-holiday periods.

Resources

Queenstown Trails (*queens towntrails.org.nz*)

Trail Hub (*trailhub.co.nz*) Tales from the Otago Bike Trails

Biking in Wānaka (*lakewanaka. co.nz*)

Central Otago Tracks & Trails (*centralotagonz.com*)

Dunedin Biking & Cycling (*dunedinnz.com*)

Southland Biking & Cycling (*southland nz.com*)

27

MOUNTAIN SCENERY

Around Frankton Arm

DURATION	DIFFICULTY	DISTANCE	START/END
4–5hr return	Easy	30km return	Queenstown beach

TERRAIN	Mostly unsealed compacted bike path

Lake Wakatipu

Head out around Lake Wakatipu's Frankton Arm from Queenstown on excellent trails with stunning alpine scenery the whole way. Viewpoints abound, as do historical nuggets of interest and places to stop for refreshments. There's even an impressive sculpture trail around Kelvin Peninsula. The track is both easy to follow and ride, taking in two of the extensive Queenstown Trails network. Shorten your ride if you wish, by putting your bike on Queenstown Ferries to Bayview on the Kelvin Peninsula, though riding the return trip is the recommended way to go.

Bike Hire

There are lots of options in downtown Queenstown. Reliable operator Outside Sports has mountain bikes (from $39) and e-bikes (from $89) available for four-hour online bookings.

Starting Point

Ride your bike to the War Memorial Gate at Queenstown Beach. It's easy to find by riding to the town waterfront on the lake, then heading towards the Remarkables.

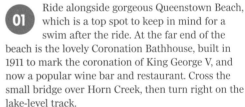

01 Ride alongside gorgeous Queenstown Beach, which is a top spot to keep in mind for a swim after the ride. At the far end of the beach is the lovely Coronation Bathhouse, built in 1911 to mark the coronation of King George V, and now a popular wine bar and restaurant. Cross the small bridge over Horn Creek, then turn right on the lake-level track.

02 You're in the magnificent Queenstown Gardens, first designated as a public park in the heady gold-rush days of 1867 and planted

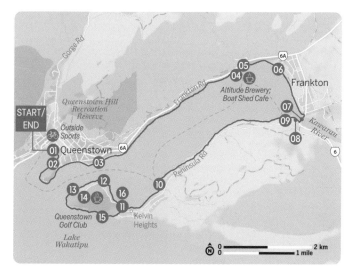

TOP TIP:

Keep your eyes open on Frankton Track, linking Queenstown and Frankton, and if you're on an e-bike, don't speed! All sorts use this track, including biking commuters, visiting bikers, dog-walkers, walking sightseers and runners. Let people heading in the same direction know that you'll be passing, and on which side.

Elevation (m)

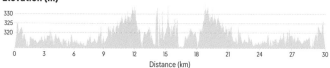

Distance (km)

with various tree and plant species from around the world. The trail heads out and around the Gardens, offering amazing views of Queenstown and Lake Wakatipu, and then of Kelvin Peninsula, your goal for the day, barely 500m away across the lake. Give thanks to the 'Friends of the Gardens', who on more than one occasion have had to save this peninsula park from zealous developers.

03 Leaving the Gardens, the track pops out onto Park St for about a kilometre, before reaching the start of the Frankton Track. From here, the trail is slightly rough in places and is shared with walkers and all sorts. Views of the lake and the Remarkables are mesmerising, but keep your eyes on the track as

you pass below some of Queenstown's top apartment complexes and real estate. Plenty of locals use this bike trail for their daily commute into town.

04 Things open up after about 5km on Frankton Track and you'll reach Boat Shed Cafe, in the restored New Zealand Railways Shipping Office, originally built in the 1870s. The building was moved from central Queenstown to its current spot in 1936. It went through a period of disrepair, was restored and reopened in 2013, and is now an excellent place for a break for coffee, breakfast, lunch or drinks by the lake. If you feel like you're just getting started on the ride, eye it up and save it for the return.

Kawarau River

Lake Wakatipu is a mighty lake at 80km long, 5km wide at its widest spot, and with a deepest point of 380m. With a lake level of 310m, that means the deepest point is 70m below sea level! Look at the lake on a map, and Frankton Arm, which this trail rides around, appears as an afterthought. The only river that drains from Lake Wakatipu is the Kawarau River, which you'll be crossing on the Kawarau Falls bridge. It flows east, boasts a famous bungy bridge, joins the Clutha River at Lake Dunstan, and its waters eventually flow into the Pacific Ocean.

☕ Take a Break

Kelvin Peninsula is halfway through your ride and home to the spectacularly located Queenstown Golf Club. Signage by the trail will point to the clubhouse at the top of the peninsula, a great spot for lunch, with good ready-to-go food and a reasonable menu. There are also toilets, a bar and a lovely terrace overlooking the 18th green where you can relax and gaze out towards Queenstown and the Skyline Gondola. On fine weather days, watch brightly coloured tandem paragliders as they soar high above Queenstown.

05 Another place to check out for the return ride is award-winning Altitude Brewing, barely 200m past the Boat Shed. Sit outside or in and try a Mischievous Kea IPA or a Powder Day Pilsener at one of Queenstown's top craft breweries. Food is available from the daily changing Food Truck. You're in the Frankton Marina complex here and on sealed road for a few hundred metres.

06 Back on the biking trail, there's a wide arc around Frankton Beach, an ideal place for a dip in the lake. The water is shallow here and relatively warm, something to keep in mind as Lake Wakatipu is chilly year-round, still fed by melting glaciers! Towards the far end of the beach, look up to your left. That long, low, brown building is Remarkables Primary School, in surely one of the greatest locations for a school on the planet. Lucky kids!

07 The trail climbs up to the historic Kawarau Falls bridge, first opened as a dam, with transport access over the top, in 1926. The historic one-lane bridge was in vehicle use until 2018, when the new State Hwy 6 curved bridge was opened just downstream and the old bridge became available for

walkers and bikers. Take your time, look down and see if you can spot a trout or two. Jetboats regularly race through below. Just over the bridge, the Kelvin Peninsula Trail drops down to the right.

08 Don't blink or you'll miss it, but almost immediately you'll come across tiny Rees Homestead Park. At the bottom of the Mall in Queenstown is a statue of the town's founding father, William Gilbert Rees, and a sheep. Rees first settled his farm in Queenstown Bay in 1861, but after gold was discovered in 1862, he was paid compensation for his land and his family moved out to Kawarau Falls. This small park marks the spot the family moved to, and by all accounts, the Rees family had a luxurious homestead here. There are information boards with old photos, plus two old buildings, the Meat Store and the Dairy.

09 Only 100m along the trail, you'll get to the Queenstown Hilton Resort & Spa, with its welcoming cafe right next to the trail. The Queenstown Ferries jetty is also here, with departures to Queenstown Bay.

10 Next is a nice 5km stretch of winding trail through to Bayview, with some short ascents and descents, never

KATACARV/SHUTTERSTOCK ©

TSS Earnslaw (p180), Lake Wakatipu

Queenstown Ferries

If the thought of this 30km ride sounds a bit daunting, consider putting your rental bike and yourself on a Queenstown Ferries departure from Queenstown Bay to the Bayview wharf in Kelvin Heights, thereby cutting nearly half the ride off your day. Get off at Bayview, ride to Kelvin Beach, then around Kelvin Peninsula and back to Queenstown as per the full ride. The small ferry prioritises people ahead of bikes. You've got a much better chance of getting a spot in the morning heading out of Queenstown than getting a ferry back into Queenstown in the afternoon.

more than 30m to 40m above lake level. You're below some of the region's most exclusive houses, and the Million Dollar Cruise boat putters by a few times a day on trips out of Queenstown Bay, pointing out whose house is which. Take your time and enjoy the views from one of the trailside benches. Bayview has a boat ramp, playground, reserve and

the Queenstown Ferries' jetty – you'll have hopped off here if you opted to bring your bike over on the ferry in the morning.

11 It's a short ride around to Kelvin Beach, an excellent swimming and picnic spot at the neck of the Kelvin Peninsula. The water here is shallow and relatively warm.

Your goal from here is to complete a 3.5km circumnavigation of the peninsula, which is home to the spectacular Queenstown Golf Club, surely one of the most picturesque golf courses in the world. Once around the peninsula, you're aiming to meet back up with the trail at Kelvin Beach and ride back to Queenstown.

GUAXINIM/SHUTTERSTOCK ©

12 Follow the trail through pine forest, just above lake level. You're on a bit of a treasure hunt, as you're now on the Kelvin Peninsula Sculpture Trail. First up is *Presence* by local artist Mark Hill, depicting a 'tree spirit'. It blends in with surrounding trees, so keep your eyes open.

13 Carry on past the Wakatipu Yacht Club and around to the Queenstown Golf Course jetty, which is used by golfers who arrive by water taxi. Directly opposite, over the lake, are the Queenstown Gardens, where you were biking earlier on.

14 If you're feeling peckish, follow the arrow on the 'Everyone Welcome' sign pointing up to the golf-course clubhouse and cafe. It's a short, sharp climb, well worth it for the views. The golf club was opened here in 1975 and effectively saved the peninsula from becoming a huge housing development. If you ride the gondola up to the Skyline lookout in Queenstown, fully 480m above the township, don't miss admiring this green peninsula and the Remarkables from up on high. The iconic view is seen on the resort town's marketing material and probably enticed you here in the first place.

15 Head back down to the trail for an after-lunch treat of more sculptures. First up, three distinctive corrugated-iron goats by Jeff Thomson overlook the trail, then around a few more corners, *Thru Link to Peak* by Shane Woolridge is made of 25 tonnes of schist and perfectly frames the view of Walter Peak on the far side of the lake. The trail heads onto the edge of the golf course, with signage warning bikers to watch out for golfers and flying balls. Last up for the sculptures is *Wakatipu Kuikui* by Mark Hill, an impressive figure of a woman with wild, blowing hair, facing south.

16 The trail then comes up onto the road beside the golf course. Follow it back to Kelvin Beach. Take a break here, before hopping on your bike for the return ride to Queenstown. It's difficult to overstate how amazing the views are on this ride and biking back in the other direction gives a totally different perspective to the ride out to the peninsula.

☕ Take a Break

Two excellent places to stop on the ride back into Queenstown are Altitude Brewery and Boat Shed Cafe, within a couple of hundred metres of each other at Frankton Marina. Take your pick. Altitude is for craft-beer aficionados, with a revolving tap-beer menu and a daily changing Food Truck out front. Boat Shed is more of a coffee spot with good cafe meals and cabinet food in a restored historic building just above the water. It's a 6km ride back into Queenstown from here.

Lake Wakatipu, near Queenstown

Best for

OFF THE BEATEN TRACK

Walter Peak Explorer

DURATION	DIFFICULTY	DISTANCE	START/END
4hr return	Easy	26km return	Walter Peak High Country Farm

TERRAIN	Compacted gravel road; reasonably maintained

WITTAWAT PAWPRASEART/SHUTTERSTOCK ©

Walter Peak

More than just a bike ride, this very satisfying mini-adventure is the first leg of the Around the Mountains Cycle Trail. From Queenstown, cross Lake Wakatipu to Walter Peak with your bike on the steamship *TSS Earnslaw*, ride the gravel road to Mt Nicholas High Country Farm, picnic lakeside on the beach, then ride back to Walter Peak in time to catch the *Earnslaw* back to Queenstown. You'll need to pre-book the *Earnslaw* for both directions and be prepared and self-sufficient, as there are no stores, no real back-up and you'll have limited mobile-phone coverage on this backcountry ride.

Bike Hire

You'll need to hire a bike in Queenstown and bring it with you. There are lots of options. Outside Sports on Shotover St rents both mountain bikes and e-bikes.

Starting Point

The *TSS Earnslaw* departs from Queenstown's Steamer Wharf. The ride starts on the western side of Lake Wakatipu at the Walter Peak High Country Farm wharf.

01 Ride your bike down to Steamer Wharf and check in for the 11am *TSS Earnslaw* departure, the first of the day, by 10.40am. Enjoy the 40-minute cruise across Lake Wakatipu on the 'Lady of the Lake'. The ship was launched in 1912, the same year as the *Titanic,* and until 1967, provided an essential link for isolated farming communities around the lake. Almost scrapped in 1968, it has been painstakingly restored and carrying tourists ever since. There are stupendous alpine views in all directions as you cross the lake.

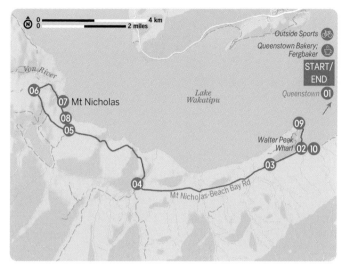

Elevation (m)

02 Hop off at the Walter Peak wharf in Beach Bay, but don't just head straight up the road on the ride. The gardens at Walter Peak are well worth a stroll and there are sheep, donkeys, *kunekune* pigs, alpacas, horses and other animals to view in the tourist-accessible part of this working high-country farm.

03 The ride itself is fairly straightforward. There's only one way to go, a wide, well-maintained gravel road for 12km to Mt Nicholas High Country Farm. You'll be riding west through farm country on a narrow plain between towering gnarled, rocky cliffs, jagged peaks and pinnacles inland on your left, and sprawling Lake Wakatipu on your right.

The mountains on the far side of the lake are just as impressive as those on your left, only further away.

04 The road drops to cross a creek on a one-lane bridge, then heads out towards the lake. After 8km, you'll pass over a cattle stop at the Walter Peak and Mt Nicholas farm boundary. Mt Nicholas itself is the high, rounded mountain above to the left. Views north of the head of Lake Wakatipu and distant mountains just get better and better, including 2819m Mt Earnslaw, with glaciers clinging to its upper sides. The mountain and the steamship were both named after a village in Berwickshire, Scotland.

Be Prepared!

You need to book the *TSS Earnslaw* with RealNZ. Do this in person at their Steamer Wharf office or by email. Tourists ride this historic steamship to Walter Peak for the farm show and it gets extremely busy, especially during summer and NZ holidays. Book the 11am departure from Queenstown and the 3.45pm return from Walter Peak ($60 each way, including your bike). Take everything you're going to need with you, including food, drink and warm clothing. There's no accommodation on the western side of the lake, so ensure you make your return-cruise departure time to get back to Queenstown.

05 Carry on to where there's a split in the road with a 'Honey for Sale' sign, on what looks like a beehive. Open the top to find bottles of Nic's Gold, mountain wildflower honey produced at Mt Nicholas farm. From this point you'll be riding a loop around Von Rd and things will be easier if you head left first.

06 Continue up the road for 2km to the next intersection and turn right. If you were to go straight, you'd be on the Around the Mountains Cycle Trail, with 40km up the Von Valley to Mavora Lakes. Passing farm sheds, you'll soon get a great view of the Von River below to your left, flowing into Lake Wakatipu.

07 The road descends down to lake level where there's a marvellous pebbly beach, a perfect spot for a picnic. Mt Nicholas is a working farm, and while the road that runs through it is a public road, accessible to all, the farm is private property and bikers need to be mindful that all buildings are off limits. Be careful of farm machinery and stock on the road, and light no fires.

08 Ready for the return ride, carry on along the lakefront, then up the gentle climb back to the 'Honey for Sale' corner, to complete the loop. From here, it's a 10km ride back to Walter Peak, with the jagged mountains now on your right and views down the lake to Queenstown and the Remarkables ahead and to the left.

09 Back at Walter Peak wharf, take the clearly marked track to Beach Point, passing through two farm gates (leave them how you found them) out to the secluded camping and picnic area, only 900m away. There are superb views from this lovely spot.

10 Keep an eye on the time and make sure to be back at Walter Peak by 3.30pm. Check in for your return trip at the gift-shop ticket office. Back on the *TSS Earnslaw,* enjoy a cold, local Canyon Brewing beer on the trip back across the lake to Queenstown, arriving around 4.30pm.

☕ Take a Break

Once you've passed the Walter Peak gift shop, that's it for stores, and they only have cold drinks and ice creams. Before you hop on the *TSS Earnslaw* in Queenstown, visit a supermarket or bakery and prepare a picnic lunch and drinks for the day. On opposite sides of Shotover St, not far from Steamer Wharf, are Queenstown Bakery and Fergbaker, of the legendary Fergburger group. There are refreshments on the *Earnslaw* for the ride home, including local craft beer on tap by Canyon Brewery.

BOYLOSO/SHUTTERSTOCK ©

William Rees statue, Queenstown

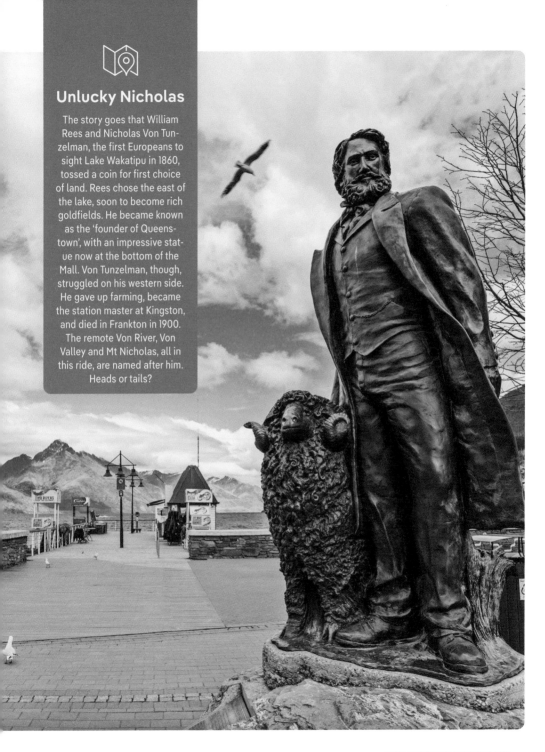

Unlucky Nicholas

The story goes that William Rees and Nicholas Von Tunzelman, the first Europeans to sight Lake Wakatipu in 1860, tossed a coin for first choice of land. Rees chose the east of the lake, soon to become rich goldfields. He became known as the 'founder of Queenstown', with an impressive statue now at the bottom of the Mall. Von Tunzelman, though, struggled on his western side. He gave up farming, became the station master at Kingston, and died in Frankton in 1900. The remote Von River, Von Valley and Mt Nicholas, all in this ride, are named after him. Heads or tails?

29

Arrow River & Gibbston Wineries

DURATION	DIFFICULTY	DISTANCE	START/END
3–4hr	Easy	23km one way	Arrowtown/ Gibbston Valley

TERRAIN	Unpaved bike trail, mostly flat

DAVID WALL/ALAMY STOCK PHOTO ©

Kawarau Suspension Bridge (p186)

Part of the Queenstown Trails network, this ride gives a couple of excellent options. Consider riding from Arrowtown out to the Kawarau Suspension Bridge (often called the Bungy Bridge) and back for a 28km return ride on the Arrow River Bridges Trail. Alternatively, continue on from the Bungy Bridge on the Gibbston River Trail for another 9km to visit a slew of wineries and points of interest. The latter will give you a 23km one-way ride and the bike-hire company will pick you up and bring you and your bike back to Arrowtown for $30 per person.

Bike Hire

There are a few options. Better By Bike, based on Butler's Green in Arrowtown, has e-bikes for $135 for the day; pickup in Gibbston is $30 per person.

Starting Point

Butler's Green is the reserve at the western end of Arrowtown, next to the Chinese Settlement, just up from the Arrow River. There is a sizeable car park here.

01 You're at Butler's Green in Arrowtown, so check out the intriguing Chinese Settlement, a partially restored set of buildings from the gold-rush days of the 1880s, before heading out. When you're ready, ride out through the willows and bike downstream alongside the Arrow River. The trail runs below the busy little township and you'll have to keep an eye open for walkers as it's a shared trail. Ignore the first small bridge over the river and carry on along the delightful winding trail until you have no choice but to cross on the second bridge.

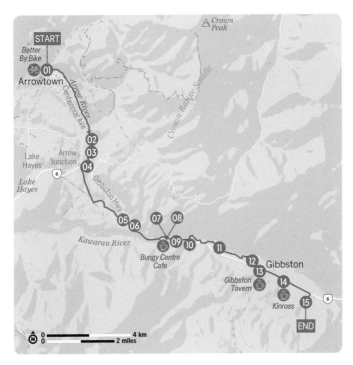

Gold in the Arrow

When gold was discovered in the Arrow River in 1862, all sorts turned up to seek their fortune, including prospectors who had previously been in the California (from 1849) and Australian (from 1851) gold rushes. Chinese prospectors lived in the settlement at the start of this bike trail. There are still many who pan in the Arrow River, though locals joke that while people used to come to town to grab the gold and take it away, these days, most bring their gold with them and drop it in Arrowtown's shops and restaurants before returning home!

Elevation (m)

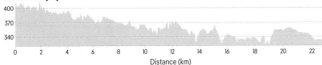

Distance (km)

02 The river is now on your right, and the trail straightens as it heads south, with Arrowtown Golf Course visible on the far side of the river. The trail from Arrowtown to Gibbston is known as the Arrow River Bridges Trail, and from here, you'll be crossing five sizable bridges. The first and smallest is the wooden Swain Bridge, after a quick zigzag descent to the river, followed shortly after by the impressive Southern Discoveries suspension bridge, purpose-built as part of the Queenstown Trails project. This is a popular photo stop.

03 The track climbs up to sealed Whitechapel Rd, a quiet rural lane, and runs along it for about 500m. The farmer here raises alpacas and there's a friendly group that live in the paddock on the right who have seen more than their fair share of cyclists. Just where the trail heads right, off the road, you'll find Bee the Change apiary. This operation is trying to facilitate the ongoing cultivation of healthy bee colonies in the Wakatipu Basin, and this is one of their three public apiaries.

04 The trail now heads down and crosses the Arrow River again, this time on the Knight Family Bridge, which has been built directly under the State Hwy 6 road bridge for the use of cyclists and walkers. It's a strange feeling to hear vehicles roaring over the bridge on the road above you! The trail then climbs alongside the main road for about 200m, before turning left onto quiet Arrow Junction Rd. Don't miss saying hello to the friendly goats on the far side of this peaceful lane as you cruise past.

05 The trail forks off Arrow Junction Rd, before approaching the extremely impressive Edgar Suspension Bridge, a purpose-built 80m swing bridge that crosses high

☕ Take a Break

You'll have ridden 14km from Arrowtown to the Kawarau Suspension Bridge and there's no better place for a break for refreshments than the Bungy Centre cafe. Grab a bite or a coffee and enjoy the thrill of watching bungy jumpers dive off the 43m-high bridge, much to the excitement of throngs of watchers. There are zipline rides here too and the panorama from the viewing platform, which overhangs the Kawarau River, is absolutely enthralling. Jump if you get the urge!

above the Arrow River gorge. This is a real thrill for many, but not much fun for those who suffer from a fear of heights. On the far side is a Wall of Recognition, acknowledging local groups and individuals who have made the Queenstown Trails a reality.

06 Bike across the flat plain above the gorge, then under State Hwy 6 again through an underpass. Climb above the main road as it curls around to where the Arrow River flows into the much larger Kawarau River, which has flowed down from Queenstown's Lake Wakatipu. It's tough to see the river junction from the bike trail, but if you look across the main road and river gorge, you'll see the immaculate vineyards of Chard Farm Winery sitting below the high rounded mountains. Take a side trip to Chard Farm later, should you wish.

07 The Kawarau Suspension Bridge, a highlight for the day, is just around a few more corners. Opened in 1880 with much celebration, this magnificent bridge was the main route to Queenstown until the new road bridge that is in use today was opened in 1963. The old bridge fell into disrepair, only to be saved by the development of one of the most innovative

tourism activities the world has ever seen – the bungy jump! In 1988, AJ Hackett Bungy was born and while looking for a permanent location for the world's first commercial bungy-jumping operation, an extensive bridge restoration was undertaken with the Department of Conservation. Nowadays, there's a huge bungy complex. Cyclists need to push their bikes over the bridge. Take your time here to enjoy views of tourists jumping off a perfectly good bridge with a rubber band tied to their ankles.

08 At this point, you will have biked 14km to get to the Kawarau Suspension Bridge. If your plan is to complete a 28km return trip of the Arrowtown River Bridges Trail, this is the turnaround point. Take a break for refreshments, jump off the bridge (if you get the urge), then return to Arrowtown along the same trail you came on. Otherwise, keep cycling down the valley on the Gibbston River Trail (9km one way). If you've rented your bike from Better By Bike in Arrowtown, they'll pick up you and your bike at the end of the Gibbston River Trail for $30 per person.

09 Ride up through the bungy car park and meet the bike trail at the

Chard Farm Winery (p188)

Gibbston Valley Frost Fans

Until the 1980s, most of the Gibbston Valley was taken up with sheep farms, a very different look to the one you'll see today. Gibbston is now the coolest and highest of the Central Otago wine regions, with the land gently sloping to the north, helping vineyards to grow excellent grapes with increased sunlight and the reduced possibility of frost. Frost is still a significant threat to the grapes, though. Those propellers you see among the vines are 'frost fans', switched on to create a wind to draw warmer air down into the vineyard when a frost threatens.

entrance to the Winehouse, a popular wedding venue. In 200m, a turn-off to the right gives you the option to bike to Chard Farm Winery, the vineyards you saw across the river earlier, as you approached the Bungy Bridge. It's an enjoyable 4km return ride to Chard Farm along a winding, unsealed road.

10 This is the start of wine country and the Gibbston Valley is full of vines. Carry on down the bike trail. Soon there will be another option to take a short side trip to Gibbston Valley Winery, established in 1990 as the first winery in the valley. There are tastings, a restaurant and tours of the largest wine cave in the country,

home to more than 400 barrels of pinot noir and chardonnay, which line its rocky schist-wall interior.

11 Back on the main trail, it winds around high above the Kawarau River with a number of spectacular lookout spots, some with enticing picnic tables. The river is far below,

BEEHAPPY28/SHUTTERSTOCK ©

while on the far side, rocky peaks tower high above. There's not much rainfall out here and the mountains and hills are rocky, dry and brown.

12 When the trail splits, just before Peregrine Wines, make sure to climb up right on the trail that soon arrives out at the main road. Turn left,

and you'll soon reach Peregrine, where the eye-catching winery building was designed to evoke the rotation of a falcon's wing in flight.

13 You're now in the heart of the valley and it's only a short ride to Gibbston Tavern, with a rich history dating to the 1860s, though the present building is new. Another good place to stop for refreshments, this spot has become popular with cyclists for its wood-fired pizza menu.

14 Another kilometre down the road is welcoming Kinross, with its popular outdoor bistro and wine garden. The cellar door here not only showcases Kinross wine, but also the labels of four neighbouring vineyards who don't have their own cellar doors.

15 The end of the bike trail is nigh, though it will only be a few years until the Kawarau Gorge Trail will be open for bikers to ride through to Bannockburn and connect up with the Lake Dunstan Trail.

TOP TIP:

If you're looking to do some tasting at some of the excellent wineries in the Gibbston Valley while on your ride, arrange a pickup with Better by Bike ($30 per person), either when you leave Arrowtown or by calling from any of the wineries.

Eventually riders will be able to bike all the way to Dunedin, on the east coast, on off-road, purpose-built bike trails. As it is, carry on down on the Gibbston River Trail to the Gibbston Back Rd, turn right, then bike up the road 400m to Mt Rosa Wines. Brennan Wines is another 600m up the road. Both offer tastings and a winery restaurant. When you're ready, make the call to Better By Bike for a pickup.

Kawarau Suspension Bridge (p186)

☕ Take a Break

About 5km down the Gibbston River Trail from the Bungy Bridge, signage will take you across the main road and down to the Gibbston Tavern. While this is a new building, the old Gibbston Hotel was here in the gold-rush days of the 1860s. Fuel up on wood-fired pizzas and try the Rockburn Wines next door. Another click down the road is Kinross, with a cellar door featuring the wines of five local vineyards and a popular bistro with outdoor seating.

30

MOUNTAIN SCENERY

SHERYL WILLIAMS - APSNZ/SHUTTERSTOCK ©

Lake Wānaka

Wānaka Loop Trail

DURATION	DIFFICULTY	DISTANCE	START/END
3–4hr	Easy	22km	Wānaka waterfront

TERRAIN	Mostly unpaved, level bike trail

The mountain resort of Wānaka is one of the most admired places on the globe. Start this ride by getting a feel for its sheer alpine beauty by riding west around its lake foreshore to Waterfall Creek and back on an easy, flat trail. Back at the township, head out on a big loop, initially north along the foreshore to Beacon Point, then east along the banks of the turquoise Clutha River, from the Outlet down to the Albert Town bridge, before heading back around the southern side of rocky Mt Iron to the township.

Bike Hire

There are a few options in Wānaka. Bike It Now! is based in the Three Parks development along the loop trail in this ride. It has bikes/e-bikes for $60/120 per day.

Starting Point

Start at the big, black *Hand that Nurtures* sculpture of an open hand, at the eastern end of the Lake Wānaka foreshore, next to the car park and children's playground.

01 *The Hand that Nurtures* sculpture is said to symbolise notions of safety, protection, friendship, openness and honesty, and is a lovely spot to start this ride, looking out on Lake Wānaka and the surrounding mountains. You'll start with a friendly 7km return ride west around the lake's waterfront to Waterfall Creek.

02 Head out along the foreshore. There are likely to be people sunbathing, swimming, kayaking, paddle boarding and making the most of this pristine alpine environment. At the western

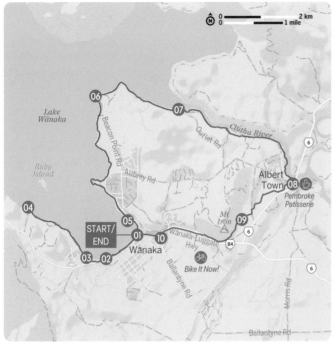

Southern Crested Grebe

Extinct in the North Island and close to it in the South, this weird and wonderful bird has issues as it breeds on floating nests. In Wānaka, though, a retired zoologist and the local primary school have taken them under their wing, so to speak. In a roaring success story, Wānaka's southern crested grebes, down to one breeding pair in 2012, now breed on handmade floating platforms that are attached to the floating marina and rise and fall with the lake level. The kids build and decorate the platforms, help check nests and write grebe diaries. Spot the colourful nests as you ride past the marina.

Elevation (m)

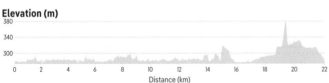

Distance (km)

end of the foreshore there are lots of willows and poplars that turn spectacular shades of gold and yellow in autumn.

03 Cross the small bridge just past the Wānaka Watersports building and carry on around the corner. Watch out for sightseers going to view #ThatWanakaTree, a small willow growing out in the lake that has become an Instagram phenom, as supposedly the most photographed tree in the country. Locals just shake their heads in disbelief.

04 The trail carries on past enticing Edgewater Resort, a popular spot for riders to stop for coffee and scones, past Rippon Winery's vineyards, then through native kanuka woodlands to Waterfall Creek. It's not as romantic as it sounds, as it's hard to find a waterfall or a creek, but a very pleasant, large lakeside picnic area looks across to nearby Ruby Island, out in the lake.

05 The bike trail continues from Waterfall Creek for 15km around to Glendhu

Bay, but is considered suitable for experienced and confident bikers only. Jump back on your bike and enjoy the gentle, scenic ride back around to *The Hand that Nurtures*. Be a good biker and obey signage by pushing your bike through the children's playground, before carrying on lakeside across Bullock Creek and past Wānaka Marina, home of the famous Southern Crested Grebe. There are excellent information boards on the metal boardwalk.

06 The off-road bike trail carries on lakefront, past Wānaka Yacht Club, rounds wooded Eely Point Reserve, then heads north past some of Wānaka's most expensive real estate to Beacon Point. Views out west over the lake to the mountains of Mt Aspiring National Park are captivating.

07 The trail curves around to the east, towards the lake's only outlet, the mighty Clutha River. The lake gradually narrows until there is clearly flow in the water at the outlet. Stay beside the water to get to the start of the 3km Outlet Track to Albert Town, a narrow, winding trail that is shared with walkers. Control your speed and check ahead as both hikers and bikers can be just around the next corner and may be coming straight at you. It's a superb ride next to the fast-flowing turquoise waters all the way down to the Albert Town Bridge, on this trail renowned for its autumn colours.

08 Just before the bridge, head up and ride the bike trail next to State Hwy 6 for about 400m, before taking the first right, on Alison Ave. A biker's haven, the Pembroke Patisserie,

with bike racks outside, is about 100m up the road on the right.

09 Directly opposite Pembroke Patisserie is Frye Cres. It's an easy jaunt through Albert Town suburbia on sealed roads to get up to the rocky base of Mt Iron. Follow Frye Cres to Sherwin Ave and turn left. Sherwin climbs up the hill to Aubrey Rd, where you turn left again, then right onto Old Racecourse Rd. The bike trail is then clearly signposted, about 300m down on the right.

10 Follow the relatively flat bike trail around the base of Mt Iron, then take the sealed path down through the underpass under State Hwy 84. The trail is now sealed all the way into Wānaka township along the side of SH84. Pass Wānaka Golf Course, drop into the Tititea/Mt Aspiring National Park Visitor Centre, then ride carefully down through busy Wānaka township to the lake at *The Hand that Nurtures* statue.

☕ Take a Break

A bike-rider favourite, Pembroke Patisserie in Albert Town is a top spot to stop for lunch or refreshments. There's a big bike-rack area right out front on the road, beside large-table outside seating. These guys claim to be a 'classic French patisserie with a modern Kiwi twist'. They are famous in Wānaka for their custard squares, doughnuts, pies and almond croissants. Head inside for a huge selection of cabinet food, baked daily. Virtually next door is Albert Town's Four Square supermarket.

Clutha River, near Albert Town

Clutha River

The longest river in the South Island, the Clutha flows 338km from Lake Wānaka all the way out to the east coast and the Pacific Ocean, near Balclutha, south of Dunedin. The turquoise colour of the river is derived from cloudy glacier-melt and snow-melt waters that flow into Lake Wānaka from the high mountains. The lake then acts as a settling pond, taking out the heavier elements in the water, leaving the Clutha an exquisite turquoise colour as it flows out of the lake, a highlight of the ride down the side of this swift-flowing river.

31

Cromwell & Bannockburn

DURATION	DIFFICULTY	DISTANCE	START/END
4–5hr	Easy	33km	Cromwell giant fruit sculpture

TERRAIN	Mostly unpaved bike trail

Felton Rd

Enjoy a variety of scenery and trailside spots of interest on this easy ride around human-made Lake Dunstan. From Cromwell's giant fruit sculpture, visit the historic Cromwell Heritage Precinct, ride the lakeside trail out to Bannockburn Bridge, then enjoy three ride options heading out in various directions. The bike trail along Felton Rd passes top-notch wineries such as Mt Difficulty, tiny Bannockburn village has a couple of good spots for refreshments, while the lovely scenery out to Cornish Point and back makes an excellent cruisy ride.

Bike Hire

There are a few options. Bike It Now! in Cromwell township, near the giant fruit sculpture, rents bikes/e-bikes for $60/120 per day and offers excellent advice.

Starting Point

Start at the unmissable 8m-high giant fruit sculpture that sits alongside State Hwy 8 and Cromwell Mall, made up of an apple, pear, nectarine and apricot.

 As Cromwell is renowned for its stone fruit, it's only right that this ride should start at the giant fruit sculpture that has stood at the entrance to town since 1989. As one local official said: 'New York may be nicknamed the "big apple" but Cromwell has the real thing.' It's been suggested of late that a cherry and a grape need to be added to the bunch, but don't hold your breath.

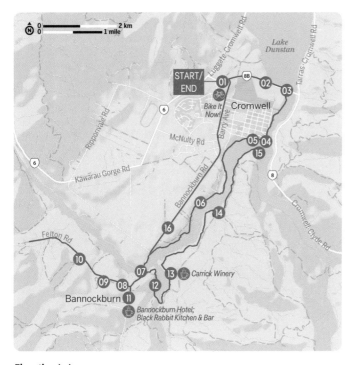

Lake Dunstan Trail

This 41km bike trail that connects Cromwell and Clyde has become extremely popular since its opening in 2021. It is one of the 23 Ngā Haerenga New Zealand Cycle Trails and features clip-on boardwalks, an 86m suspension bridge and impressive rock walls. The first section, from Cromwell through to Cornish Point, is easy and included in the ride we recommend here. Past Cornish Point, however, it is remote, with some challenging grade-three sections, only recommended for confident and experienced bike-riders. If that's you, take it on. If not, don't go. There are regular rescues of those who overestimate their ability.

Elevation (m)

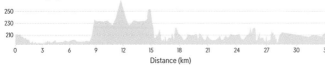

02 Ride east and pick up the trail on the far side of Barry Ave. It runs down the side of SH8 as far as Freeway Orchard, where you may like to drop in and try some of the local fruit. A couple of wineries, Misha's Vineyard and Pisa Range Estate, are also based here, offering tastings and sales.

03 Carefully cross the road to the 'Dunstan View' sign and move out to the bike trail, with its magnificent views north of the Clutha Arm of Lake Dunstan. It may be hard to believe, but until the Clyde Dam was completed in 1992, more than 20km to the southeast, this was a dusty, dry valley with the Clutha River, which flows from Lake Wānaka, running through it. It's a 2.7km ride from here, around the shore of the lake to Cromwell's Heritage Precinct. You'll pass under the SH8 road bridge and past what is now some of Cromwell's most exclusive waterfront real estate on the way to Junction Point.

04 At the Junction Lookout it all becomes a bit easier to picture. Below the lookout is where the Clutha River, flowing south from Lake Wānaka, and the Kawarau River, flowing east from Queenstown's Lake Wakatipu, used to come together. Cromwell township was at the junction. The river then flowed southeast through the Cromwell Gorge to Clyde, Alexandra and eventually out to the east coast near Balclutha, south of Dunedin. When the Clyde Dam was completed and the lake filled, the somewhat bizarrely shaped Lake Dunstan was formed. Junction Point is where the three arms of the lake now meet. The Clutha arm, which you've just

☕ Take a Break

Bannockburn village, a 700m ride up the hill from the Bannockburn Bridge, has a couple of great options for lunch or refreshments. The Bannockburn Hotel is no longer a country pub offering beer and pies, but a refurbished, upmarket restaurant with inside and outside seating, requiring bookings. A tad further up the road, Black Rabbit Kitchen & Bar is a much more casual cafe with a good selection of cabinet food and coffees, plus room to park bikes out front.

ridden down, is to the north; the Kawarau arm, which you'll shortly be riding around, is to the west; and the Dunstan arm is to the southeast. Looking across the lake, directly east, you'll see cars whizzing along the road towards Clyde. Looking south, you'll see Cornish Point, where you'll be riding to later.

05 Ride the bike trail around to the Cromwell Heritage Precinct. When the Clyde Dam was back-filled, it not only formed Lake Dunstan, it also flooded old Cromwell town. In 1985, before the original business area at the junction of the Clutha and Kawarau rivers was flooded, enterprising locals moved many of the buildings to higher ground to form what is now the lakeside Heritage Precinct. So, while it isn't the original, the precinct's buildings are historic, now housing cafes, art galleries and homeware shops.

06 The bike trail runs lakeside from here for 6km along the Kawarau arm of the lake to the Bannockburn Bridge. It's an easy ride, past boat ramps, tree plantings and lakeside willows, always with views of vineyards on the far side of the arm, and higher up, dry brown hills. There's a constant whiff of pine and thyme. Just before the bridge, there are lovely views of

the Bannockburn Inlet on the far side of the lake, which you'll be riding around later.

07 A bridge for cyclists and walkers has been attached to the upstream side of the Bannockburn Bridge, so there's no need to battle traffic. There is, however, a need to make a decision once you've ridden over it. There are three options, and if you're enjoying the ride, it's recommended to bike all three.

08 For option one, after crossing the bridge, turn right and ride up the bike trail for 500m to where it turns right at Felton Rd. This road heads west for about 5km and is lined with some of the best vineyards and wineries in the Central Otago region. First up on the right, though, are major plantings of cherries, the trees protected from hungry birdlife by black netting. Cherries are a major industry for the area and are in abundance in the summer months, particularly December and January. If your timing is good, the Cherry Hut roadside stall will have delicious cherries on offer.

09 High above the road on the left is the Mt Difficulty Winery Cellar Door & Restaurant. It's a short, sharp ride up, but worth it for

DAVID WALL/ALAMY STOCK PHOTO ©

Felton Rd, near Bannockburn

Connection to Queenstown

After crossing the Bannockburn Bridge, as you ride west along Felton Rd, looking ahead and slightly right, you'll see the rugged Kawarau Gorge, through which the mighty Kawarau River flows from Queenstown and Lake Wakatipu. There is an ambitious plan to connect Queenstown to Dunedin by off-road bike trails by the mid-2020s. It involves a trail being built from the end of the Gibbston River Trail (see p189) through to the trail you're riding beside Felton Rd. It's going to be no easy job, though. Mt Difficulty, after which the winery was named, is up that gorge!

the views looking north over the valley. The terrace restaurant here is incredibly popular, so book before you go. Otherwise, enjoy tasting some of Central Otago's best before heading back down to Felton Rd and continuing west. You'll pass Te Kano Estate, Gate 20 Two, Calvert, Desert Heart, Domain Rd, Terra Sancta and, at the end of the road, requiring bookings, Felton Rd Winery. All offer tastings and some have small restaurants. Check out your options online before you go.

10 A couple of kilometres along Felton Rd from the turn-off, on the left, you'll find Bannockburn Sluicings Historic Reserve. This scarred landscape looks like something out of the wild west, with the remains of dams, water races, rock tailings and caves, left virtually untouched since the gold-miners went through. There are walking tracks, plus mountain-bike trails for hard-core riders. Just opposite is the bright yellow Little Cup of Happy food and coffee truck, should you be in need of refreshments.

DAVID WALL/ALAMY STOCK PHOTO ©

11 Back at the Felton Rd turn-off, option two is to bike uphill for 200m on the road to get to tiny Bannockburn village, named after the battlefield in Scotland where the Scots beat the English in 1314. This small gold-mining village of the 1860s is now a world-renowned wine-producing village. The Bannockburn Hotel is

an upmarket restaurant requiring bookings, while a bit further up the road, Black Rabbit Kitchen & Bar is a more casual cafe.

12 Cruise back down to the Bannockburn Bridge and, for option three, follow the signage pointing east saying 'Cornish Point 7.3km'. You'll be riding this extremely enjoyable trail there and back. Shortly, you'll get to Bannockburn Inlet, for a fun ride down by the water. If you're planning to take a swim, pick a good spot around the inlet.

13 The trail ducks and dives down by the water, then climbs with a zigzag up to Carrick Winery, with a cellar door and restaurant, a large backyard lawn, bike parking and, especially for cyclists, a wine, pizza and coffee trailer.

14 The trail continues, now alongside vineyards on your right, the Kawarau arm of Lake Dunstan on your left, with gorgeous views. It twists and turns, sometimes coming out to the road, then returning to the lake. When you see olive trees on your left, look right to spot alpacas in a farm over the road.

15 Eventually you'll get to the turnaround spot of Cornish Point, marked

TOP TIP:

Once you ride over the Bannockburn Bridge, ride all three options, in any order. Head along Felton Rd for wineries and unique landscapes, up to Bannockburn village for lunch, and out to Cornish Point for a great ride and magnificent views.

by an information board and a bench, almost directly opposite the Junction. The bike trail heads around the corner and continues to Clyde as the not-for-novices Lake Dunstan Trail.

16 Turn around and ride back to the Bannockburn Bridge. Once across it, either follow the picturesque lakeside path you rode out on back to the Cromwell Heritage Precinct, or ride the less picturesque trail alongside Bannockburn Rd that is a shortcut directly back to Cromwell Mall and the giant fruit sculpture.

☕ Take a Break

On the eastern side of Bannockburn Inlet, you'll climb a couple of zigzags and arrive at Carrick Winery. You can't miss it as the bike trail goes right through the back garden. Producing certified organic wine, this enticing place is great for a stop. Park your bike under the trailside willow, then head across the lawn to the wine, coffee and pizza trailer set up for cyclists, with outdoor tables, seating and beanbags, plus a buzzing vibe. You're unlikely to be the only bike-rider here.

Bannockburn Bridge

32

Clyde Rail & River Loop

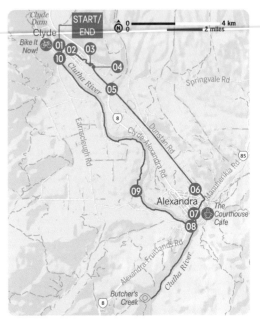

DURATION	DIFFICULTY	DISTANCE	START/END
3–4hr	Easy	22km	Old Town Clyde

TERRAIN	Mostly level, unsealed bike trail

Elevation (m)

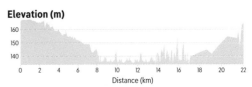

There's great variety on this easy loop ride, which sets out from historic 'old town' Clyde. Get a taste of the Otago Central Rail Trail on the surprisingly straight 8km stretch from the Clyde railhead to Alexandra, then explore this Central Otago township, before heading back to Clyde along the lovely, winding Clutha River Trail. There's an option to add to your day's enjoyment by venturing into the badlands of the Roxburgh Gorge after crossing the Clutha River at Alexandra.

Bike Hire

There are a number of bike-rental options in Clyde. Bike It Now! is an excellent operator in the hub of 'old town' Clyde. They have bikes/e-bikes per day $60/120.

Starting Point

'Old town' Clyde is a top place to start, with a cruise around town checking out the gold-rush-era buildings and the vibes of excited visitors.

01 Cruise around Clyde's lovely 'old town' and check out iconic historical buildings from the gold-rush days, especially along Sunderland St. The Masonic Lodge (1869), Benjamin Naylor's Store (1870; now Olivers) and Dunstan Hotel (1903) are very impressive.

02 When you're ready to go, head up Naylor St and follow the paved path through to Clyde Railway Station, opened with great fanfare in 1907 when the railway reached Clyde. After the Central Otago rail line closed in 1990, the building

Clyde Bridge (p203)

Otago Central
Rail Trail

Most allow three days for this 152km ride from the Clyde railhead to Middlemarch, from where you can get transport either on to Dunedin or back to Clyde. It's an easy ride, great for families, as it's along what was formerly the route of the Otago Central Railway, which was closed in 1990. Opened in 2000 to cyclists and walkers, there are plenty of places to stay and eat along the trail, plus exciting old viaducts, tunnels and station sites to be explored. Enjoy the unique landscapes and rich local history of the trail.

fell into disrepair, but was later restored. Ride along the old station platform!

03 Continue on the paved trail through suburban Clyde, following clear 'Rail Trail' signage down Albert Dr, then left and through the underpass under State Hwy 8. The underpass is marked 'Caution: Mural' with good reason. Take your time going through – the inside has been painted on both sides with fascinating pictorial renditions of the region's history, such as old steam trains, tunnels, stations and modern mountain bikers.

04 Almost immediately, you're at the Clyde Railhead, the start of the 152km Otago Central Rail Trail, the trail that opened in 2000 and inspired the creation of the NZ Cycle Trails network. Our ride takes in the first 8km of the Rail Trail. Steam trains used to run along here, so after the rail lines and sleepers were pulled up, bikers were left with a straight, flat trail to ride.

05 Enjoy some gems, such as the trailside Clyde Turntable, used in days past to rotate and turn locomotives around. A tad further on, the 110m Muttontown Viaduct,

constructed in 1907, has 18 spans. The information board shows a photo of a steam train crossing the rickety-looking bridge in 1962. The trail continues, lined with farmland, a couple of wineries, Alexandra Golf Club, then Alexandra's community sports facilities.

06 Coming into Alexandra township, the Industry Lane Eatery is right on the trail and boasts tasty cabinet food and coffees, and inside and outside seating. Just over Chicago St, Hinton Fruit & Wine Sales features a trailside refrigerator, dressed up to look like a steam locomotive, selling seasonal fruit. Next is the site of the former Alexandra Station, with only a rail siding left.

07 Follow signage at Tarbert St to turn right to Alexandra Town Centre. It's only 700m to the middle of town on a cycle lane. Central Stories Museum & Art Gallery is a free community-funded and built facility in Pioneer Park that is worth a stop. Next to the towering War Memorial is Courthouse Cafe, in the town's original courthouse, which was built in 1876. This is a popular place for lunch.

08 Carrying on through town, cross the Clutha River on the Alexandra

Bridge (opened 1958), but be sure to look downstream to see the adjacent piers, abutments and towers of the historic old bridge, which was in use from 1882 to 1958. On the southern side of the bridge, consider adding an 8km return ride to Butcher's Creek in the Roxburgh Gorge.

09 Our main trail now heads northwest, upstream alongside the Clutha

Roxburgh Gorge

☕ Take a Break

The Courthouse Cafe, next to Alexandra's War Memorial, is an excellent spot for lunch. It has seating both inside and out. The cafe is in the town's original courthouse building, which dates from the gold-rush times of the 1870s. It was the courthouse until 1972 and became a classified historic building later that decade. There's a tasty collection of sandwiches and salads, cakes and slices, macaroons and doughnuts, plus coffees, milkshakes and smoothies. Don't overdo it as there's still riding to do!

River, much of the time shaded by trees, for 12km. It's an enjoyable, easy, winding ride. To the right is the Clutha River, flow controlled by the Clyde Dam, and to the left, remnants of the gold-mining days in the form of tailings, mounds of ground-up rock that were crushed as the miners searched for gold, first by hand, then later with steam dredges to drive bucket chains.

Roxburgh Gorge Option

After crossing the Alexandra Bridge, consider adding an 8km return ride to Butcher's Creek in the Roxburgh Gorge to your day. Follow signage, and as you ride south along this well-maintained riverside trail, enjoy the turquoise colours of the river and look up into the rocky, dry badlands that tower above on both sides of the gorge. This trail will eventually lead all the way to Dunedin, but for today's ride, going as far as Butcher's Creek and back will give a good taste of the gorge and add a lot of enjoyment to your day.

10 Eventually the steel-arched Clyde Bridge, opened in 1934, comes into view. As you cross it, look upriver to see the 100m-high Clyde Dam, opened in 1992, which controversially flooded old Cromwell, created Lake Dunstan and became the country's third-largest hydroelectric dam. Bike up the hill and consider a stop at the the Post Office Cafe & Bar, in a magnificent 1865 stone building, before or after returning your bike in 'old town' Clyde.

33

Otago Harbour Loop

DURATION	DIFFICULTY	DISTANCE	START/END
4hr	Easy	33km	Dunedin city

TERRAIN	Paved bike path; mostly flat

DAVID WALL/ALAMY STOCK PHOTO ©

St Leonards cycleway (p206)

This newly developed loop trail around the inner harbour from central Dunedin is mostly on a built-for-purpose paved cycleway. You will ride up the western side of the inner harbour to Port Chalmers, make a ferry crossing to Portobello, then ride back down the eastern side of the harbour to the city. It's a fun ride with plenty to see along the way, including wildlife, painted bus shelters and boat sheds, quirky and controversial sculptures and historical hot spots. Expect magnificent views both of Otago Peninsula and the inland hills to the west of the harbour.

Bike Hire

Dunedin eBike Hire rents e-bikes for $50/75 for four/eight hours from their self-service kiosk at 14 Harrow St; book online. The pickup and drop-off system works fairly seamlessly.

Starting Point

This ride is a loop from Dunedin city; it doesn't matter which way you go around. Make your decision on direction after booking the Port to Port ferry.

01 There is really only one bike-hire option, so this ride starts at Dunedin eBike Hire at 14 Harrow St, riding around the harbour clockwise. There's no reason not to ride anti-clockwise, however. In terms of navigation for the day, the trickiest bit is actually getting out of the city and onto the cycleway. Leaving the rental-bike kiosk, turn left on Anzac Ave, then at the third intersection, with Hocken Library on the corner, turn left to stay on what is still Anzac Ave. Go straight, and before crossing the small bridge, turn right on Minerva St, following the

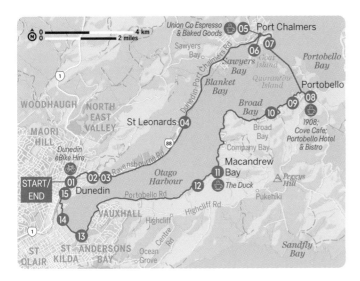

TOP TIP:

Make sure to book the Port to Port Ferry that runs between Port Chalmers and Portobello, as there are limited spaces for bikes (12) and passengers (20). This is a small, friendly operation, but don't just turn up expecting it to run to the published schedule.

Elevation (m)

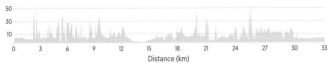

Distance (km)

sign that says 'Harbour Cycleway'. Ride to the end of Minerva St, pass under the road bridge, then take the cycleway bridge over the Water of Leith. There will be no navigation issues from here.

02 The name Dunedin is the anglicised form of *Dùn Èideann,* the Scottish Gaelic name for Edinburgh; the city was famously settled by hardy Scots from 1848. Dunedin's somewhat murky Water of Leith, which flows out into Otago Harbour, is named after the river that runs through the Scottish capital. It is unlikely to grab your attention as much as the massive 30,000-seat indoor Forsyth Barr Stadium, which was opened in time for the 2011 Rugby World Cup. A game-changer for Dune-

din, it has brought international sporting events and concerts to the city, thanks to its roof, which guarantees decent weather indoors, even if there's a howling Antarctic southerly pummelling Dunedin outdoors.

03 Over the bridge, there's a small marina, the Otago Yacht Club, rowing clubs and outrigger canoes. Don't miss the Kuri sculpture of a dog on a railway track to nowhere, with wheels for feet, looking out over the harbour. The cycleway is alongside the railway line that connects Port Chalmers and Dunedin and becomes the West Harbour Recreation Trail. As you pedal, you'll pass trailside outdoor gym equipment, picnic tables and BBQs for public use.

Artsy Bus Stops

Highlights along the cycleway on the eastern harbour include a large number of painted bus shelters, the brainchild of Broad Bay artist John Noakes. After seeing a group of school-children huddled in a dark, graffiti-covered shelter, he decided to make the bus stops more appealing and enjoyable, eventually painting 65 Dunedin bus shelters before his death in 2006. His murals have been restored ever since and his face is immortalised on the first bus stop he painted in Company Bay. Don't miss the bus shelter in Oyster Bay, which features crabs, seabirds and flying pigs.

☕ Take a Break

Union Co Espresso & Baked Goods, at the bottom of the main street in Port Chalmers, almost directly in front of the port entrance, is the place to stop for refreshments before catching the ferry to Portobello. The cabinet offerings include filos and pastries, cinnamon scrolls and muffins, plus tasty coffees and teas. There's also a good cafe menu. Allow 10 minutes from here for the ride around to Back Beach to catch the Port to Port Ferry.

Views out over to the far side of the harbour, to Otago Peninsula, are impressive and they'll be with you all the way to Port Chalmers.

04 The cycleway is in excellent shape, fully paved, and continues up the western side of the harbour, past the small suburbs of Ravensbourne, Burkes and St Leonards. Just before St Leonards, the cycleway sticks with the railway out on a couple of short causeways, while the road has followed the inland curve of the coast. This has created shallow inlets that are good for spotting various seabirds. Keep an eye outwards too, at the shallows of the inner harbour, for shark fins. Seven-gill sharks, which can grow up to 3m long but generally pose no threat to humans, are often spotted in summer as they come into the harbour to give birth in shallow water.

05 The stretch of purpose-built cycleway from St Leonards was the last to be completed in early 2023 and includes a boardwalk section out over the water. The trail passes Sawyers Bay, then up a slight rise into Port Chalmers. You'll have ridden 14km from central Dunedin to get here. Port Chalmers became the main port for Dunedin as the inner harbour was too shallow for large ships.

The town was surveyed in 1846 and is named after Dr Thomas Chalmers, the leader of the Free Church movement in Scotland. While efforts were later made to dredge a channel through the inner harbour to Dunedin city itself, Port Chalmers became accepted as the deep-water port for big ships, and a railway connection with Dunedin city was completed in 1873.

06 Port Chalmers has become a vibrant little place with a slightly quirky vibe, home to artists and alternative lifestylers. Drop into Atelier Royale for handmade hats, 2Gypsies for unique art and homeware, Barking Fish for jewellery and the Flying Whale for the artwork of children's writer and local resident, David Elliot. Union Co Espresso & Baked Goods is great for refreshments. Don't miss your ferry time around at Back Beach, a short ride around past mountains of logs being exported overseas.

07 The Port to Port ferry at Back Beach is a friendly one-person operation that can carry 20 people and 12 bikes. On the 10-minute trip across to Portobello, you'll pass Quarantine Island/Kamau Taurua, the largest island in Otago Harbour, used as the quarantine station for Otago from 1863 until 1924.

RAMUNAS BRUZAS/SHUTTERSTOCK ©

Port Chalmers

Cruise Ship Days

Visiting cruise ships have become an important part of the Dunedin economy, docking at the deep-water port of Port Chalmers, mostly over the summer season from October to April. Both Port Chalmers and Dunedin get extremely busy on 'cruise ship days', with a sudden influx of thousands of visitors. Usually quiet Port Chalmers can become a bustling hot spot, with international visitors jostling in lines at cafes and often, much to the chagrin of locals, at the public bus stop. Book ahead online if you want a bike on these days. Check the cruise-ship schedule on the Port Otago website.

08 Named after a coastal suburb of Edinburgh, Portobello is a pleasant little community on the east coast of the inner harbour. In days past, residents caught a ferry into the city, before Portobello Rd, along the foreshore of the harbour, was constructed. The new boat jetty, where the ferry comes in, is just short of Portobello, so make sure to ride into the village before heading back towards Dunedin. It's a 19km ride along the cycleway, shared with walkers, to get back to Dunedin city, so if you didn't have time in Port Chalmers, fuel up here at one of a number of restaurant and cafe options.

09 The cycleway is waterside, wide and flat virtually the whole way into Dunedin. There are plantings of native flora, benches with views, and all sorts of interesting this and that. There are, however, few guardrails, so don't gaze at the outstanding panorama too much or you may tumble into the

harbour. Highlights along the way include painted bus shelters, boat sheds and walls.

10 Just before Broad Bay, keep an eye out for Fletcher House, the country's only authentically restored and refurbished Edwardian villa. Built in 1909

Otago Harbour, near Dunedin

by Sir James Fletcher, it was a family home until 1990 and has been furnished in the style of the period by the Otago Early Settlers Museum. Its gardens were designed by a team from the Dunedin Botanical Gardens.

11 Macandrew Bay boasts the Duck Cafe, a cute little Lilliput library, plus the only white sandy beach in the inner harbour. If it's a hot day and you want to swim, this is the place.

12 Around a few more bends in the road, Glenfalloch Woodland Gardens sits above the road. Glenfalloch is Gaelic for 'hidden valley' and the gardens feature lovely walks about the 12-hectare property. There are both native trees and exotic imports that thrive here, such as rhododendrons, azaleas, fuchsias and magnolias. There is also a popular garden cafe and restaurant.

13 Almost at the head of the harbour, ride over the Andersons Bay causeway, built in the 1870s, which created the Anderson Bay inlet on your left. The cycleway curves around

to the right, and on the far side of the road, spot the Rongo Stone Memorial, which commemorates 211 Māori prisoners transported from Taranaki in the North Island to Dunedin between 1869 and 1879. The men worked on projects such as the Andersons Bay causeway and building retaining walls around the harbour, many never making it back to Taranaki.

14 Carry on around the harbour-front on the cycleway, next to Portsmouth Dr. The final highlight is the Harbour Mouth Molars, a set of six 2.6m-high wisdom teeth, constructed from concrete and soft Oamaru stone, designed to break down over time, and highly controversial (thanks to their quirkiness and price tag!) when unveiled in 2010. Apart from the pun associated with being at the harbour mouth, they are a tad ironic as the country's only School of Dentistry is just down the road at the University of Otago.

15 From the molars, follow the cycle trail, and then cycle lanes on the road back into central Dunedin.

☕ Take a Break

On the eastern inner harbour, there are a number of good options for refreshments and fuelling up. In Portobello, 1908 is a popular sit-down restaurant, with inside and outside seating, in a historic building. Cove Cafe is a more relaxed place with bagels, cakes and coffees, while the Portobello Hotel & Bistro, first opened in 1874, offers hearty meals and cold beer. In Macandrew Bay, the Duck serves top light meals, coffees and views.

34

Te Anau Lake2Lake

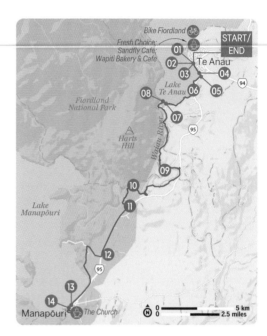

DURATION	DIFFICULTY	DISTANCE	START/END
3–4hr	Easy	28km one way	Te Anau main street

TERRAIN	Mainly compacted cycle trail

Elevation (m)

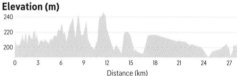

This most enjoyable ride, connecting lakes Te Anau and Manapōuri, is full of local stories, history and intrigue. See one of Aotearoa's most vulnerable birds, the takahe, thought extinct for 50 years, ride through native beech forest alongside the Waiau River. See also the site of the country's first major environmental campaign, visiting the Save Manapōuri Memorial. While a relatively easy ride, there are a few hills where cyclists will enjoy the power provided by an e-bike. The mountains of Fiordland National Park loom large to the west.

Bike Hire

Bike Fiordland is in Te Anau's main street and is an excellent operator, offering a one-way 'Lake2Lake' option with shuttle return from Manapōuri.

Starting Point

The large takahe statue at the roundabout, at the lake end of Te Anau's main street, is a local landmark and a great story in itself.

01 The takahe statue commemorates the 1948 rediscovery of the takahe, a flightless bird that had been thought extinct for 50 years. An Invercargill doctor, believing there must be a live takahe out there somewhere in Fiordland, found a small population in what was to become Takahē Valley, high in the Murchison mountains on the far side of the lake. You're going to see live takahe, much smaller than the statue, on the ride.

PHOTO ECCLES/SHUTTERSTOCK ©

Lake Te Anau

02 On the lake side of the roundabout is the RealNZ office and wharf. The big boat there heads across the lake on tours to the Te Anau Caves, coincidentally, directly below Takahē Valley. Te Anau means 'the Cave of Swirling Waters', and Māori legends had long been told of mystical glowing caves somewhere around the lake, but nobody knew where. Coincidentally, also in 1948, the caves were rediscovered by local explorer Lawson Burrows and are now a highlight of Te Anau. Head across the lake during your visit to see the caves and their spectacular glowworms.

03 Turn south, along the waterfront. The pub on your left, the Moose, is named after another local legend. A small number of moose were brought from Canada and released in Fiordland in the early 1900s. The last photographic evidence of a moose was taken in 1952, but every now and then someone pops up claiming to have seen a moose. The takahe was thought extinct for 50 years and then 're-discovered', so why not a moose? While some claim it's a publicity stunt, others believe there are moose out there somewhere, and motion-sensor cameras have been set up in remote Fiordland valleys. Don't hold your breath!

04 Pass the overwater helipad and the float-plane jetty and ride down towards the end of the lake. Keep an eye out for the Quintin MacKinnon statue. A Scottish-born explorer, MacKinnon is credited with finding the MacKinnon Pass in 1888 and establishing the Milford Track. MacKinnon went missing on Lake Te Anau in 1892, presumed drowned. The statue was unveiled in 1988, on the 100th anniversary of his find.

05 You'll soon arrive at the Fiordland National Park Visitor Centre. This is the main hub for Aotearoa's largest national park, which covers virtually

☕ Take a Break

Once you've started riding, there's nowhere to get refreshments before Manapōuri, so head out well-prepared. This is a great ride for taking a picnic lunch and there are plenty of places to take a break. There are picnic tables at Queens Reach Recreation Area, but also lots of attractive, informal riverside spots with excellent views. In Te Anau, Fresh Choice is the big supermarket on the main street. Just opposite is Sandfly Cafe, and next to that, Wapiti Bakery & Cafe.

all of the southwest corner of the South Island. Inside, there are informative displays and information on everything to do in the region, considered the top hiking hot spot in the country.

06 Ride around the corner of the lake to Punanga Manu o Te Anau/Te Anau Bird Sanctuary. This is the place to stop and try to spot a takahe. The sanctuary is a laid-back operation run by the Department of Conservation. It's free, but a gold-coin donation is requested. The takahe can be hard to spot in their enclosure, but it's worth persevering. DOC has a Takahe Recovery Program and numbers in the country are up to around 400 in total – not bad, since the takahe was considered extinct from 1898 until 1948. Other birds to see are kākā, a native parrot, whio (the blue duck) and Antipodes Island parakeets, an 'insurance' population should the wild population on those remote islands somehow disappear.

07 The trail continues around the waterfront, below Te Anau's golf course, to the Kepler Track car park and entrance. The Kepler is a 60km, three- to four-day loop hiking track around the mountains of Fiordland and one of Aotearoa's 10 Great Walks. The season is October to April. One

of Te Anau's most popular events is the Kepler Challenge, held annually in early December since 1988, involving mountain runners racing around the 60km trail.

08 The Kepler Track effectively starts when hikers pass over the Lake Te Anau Control Gates. These gates, opened in 1974, regulate water flow on the Waiau River, between lakes Te Anau and Manapōuri, for the West Arm hydroelectric power station, and maintain the natural lake levels of both lakes. Walk out on top of the gates and take in the views both to the north of Lake Te Anau and of the Waiau River to the south. The Waiau flows for 10km from this point until it enters Laka Manapōuri.

09 Just before the Control Gates, the bike trail is easy to spot heading down the side of the river. It's a great ride, sometimes right beside the river, sometimes high above it, most of the time on compacted gravel bike track through native beech forest, but occasionally popping out onto both sealed and gravel roads beside farmland. The national park with its dense forest is spectacular on the far side of the river. Eventually you'll get to the large open Queens Reach Recreation Area, with a boat ramp and picnic tables.

Lake Te Anau

Lake Te Anau

Look at a map of Lake Te Anau and you'll see that the South Island's largest lake is a most unusual shape. Formed by glacial action, it is 66km long and has three major arms known as North Fiord, Middle Fiord and South Fiord entering it from the west. These are the country's only 'inland fiords', the other 14 being out on the coast and misnamed by early European explorers as 'sounds'. The lake level is controlled at around 210m above sea level at the Control Gates, at its only outlet, the Waiau River, which you'll pass on this ride.

10 Follow the bike trail downriver to an intersection, with signage pointing right to Rainbow Reach. It's well worth the side trip, riding through the car park and walking across the Rainbow Reach swing bridge to check out both the Waiau River and bits of the Kepler Track on the far side. The Upper Waiau, between the lakes, was the fictional River Anduin at the end of the first film of *The Lord of the Rings* film trilogy.

11 Back on your bike, Balloon Loop will eventually deposit you out onto SH95, the Manapōuri–Te Anau Hwy. Turn right and you have 4km of riding on this sealed main road. Take care, as cars race along here with a 100km/h speed limit! It may seem like they're going faster.

12 Eventually, on the left, you'll spot Te Anau Manapōuri Airport. Aviation buffs will no doubt be surprised by the lengthy sealed runway here. It's a leftover of the 1970s West Arm hydroelectric power-station construction, when equipment

Waiau River Trout

As you ride the trail along the upper Waiau between the lakes, keep your eyes open for trout. According to nzfishing.com, this is one of the most populated rivers in the country, with as many as 600 trout per kilometre of river, and extremely popular with fishers. You'll see both rainbow and brown trout, more if you have polarised sunglasses. Both are introduced species for sportfishing, the browns from Europe in the 1860s, and the rainbows from North America in the 1880s. You're most likely to see local fishers out there on summer evenings.

and materials were flown in. The local council has maintained the airport, even building an impressive terminal building, in hopes of enticing an airline such as Air New Zealand to schedule regular departures. So far, no cigar! Just past the airport, turn right down gravel Supply Bay Rd, then left when the dedicated bike trail appears as you hit the forest.

Waiau River

13 A gentle ride will bring you out at Lake Manapōuri and eventually at the Save Manapōuri Memorial, overlooking the lake. Between 1969 and 1972, Manapōuri was the site of the country's first major environmental campaign, a landmark event in Aotearoa's history. Original plans for the Manapōuri Power Station involved raising Lake Manapōuri by 30m. In 1970, a staggering 265,000 Kiwis, 17% of the voting-age population at the time, signed a Save Manapōuri petition, only to be ignored by the government of the day. Manapōuri became a major issue in the 1972 election, won by the Labour Party. New Prime Minister Norman Kirk honoured his election pledge, guaranteeing that existing lake levels would be maintained. The words on the rock monument are profound: 'This monument is a tribute to the campaigners, their love and respect for natural beauty, their fortitude and tenacity triumphed over political and official interference.'

14 You've arrived in the small township of Manapōuri, and if you've arranged a pickup here with

TOP TIP:

For a 28km one-way ride on the Lake 2 Lake Trail, arrange with Bike Fiordland for a shuttle return from Manapōuri to Te Anau. Alternatively, it's a flat 21km ride along State Hwy 95, the Manapōuri–Te Anau Hwy, if you feel like an easy ride home.

Bike Fiordland, it will be at the Church, a very merry pub and restaurant, right on the main road. Before you settle in with a cold one, however, pedal around Waiau St to the Waiau River and Pearl Harbour, the departure point for trips across the lake that eventually take visitors to Doubtful Sound. The Waiau River exits Lake Manapōuri here and flows south for 70km to the Foveaux Strait on the South Island's southern coast.

☕ **Take a Break**

A top spot in Manapōuri is the Church, a 1898-built former Presbyterian church that was moved here in 2002 from its former home in the Catlins and converted into a bar and restaurant. Nothing fancy, but the Church is a merry locals' pub with welcoming staff, cold beer and a decent choice of bar snacks and meals. There's even a tiny dog called 'Mouse' (as in church mouse!). Park yourself in the cute little armchair nook, known as 'the confessional', and savour your day.

Also Try...

Manuherikia Bridge

Queenstown to Arrowtown

DURATION	DIFFICULTY	DISTANCE
1 day	Intermediate	33km one way

Take a look at the Queenstown Trails website, as there are a couple of excellent off-road bike-trail options between Queenstown and Arrowtown. This 33km one links the Frankton Track, Twin Rivers Trail and the Arrow River Bridges Trail to create a wonderful day out on two wheels. A number of companies offer bike rental and shuttle options for this ride from Queenstown, meaning that you only have to bike one way to Arrowtown. If you're feeling enthused, however, you may want to bike back to Queenstown via the Countryside Trail and Lake Hayes. You'll feel happy about renting an e-bike for these trails.

Rail Tunnels & Viaducts

DURATION	DIFFICULTY	DISTANCE
1 day	Easy	55km

Rent a bike in Clyde and take a one-way bike shuttle to Auripo in the quiet Ida Valley on the Otago Central Rail Trail. You then have a 55km ride back to Clyde on the most fascinating part of the rail trail, riding through the stunning Poolburn Gorge, which cuts through the Raggedy Range and into the Manuherikia Valley. Pass through two tunnels and across viaducts, before exploring small townships such as Lauder, Omakau, Chatto Creek and Alexandra on the way back to Clyde. The trail is compacted gravel and never steep, as steam trains could only manage a minimal gradient.

Hāwea River Track

Duntroon to Ōamaru

DURATION	DIFFICULTY	DISTANCE
1 day	Intermediate	54km

This is the last stage of the 315km Alps 2 Ocean Cycle Trail that stretches from Mt Cook to Ōamaru. Arrange a bike and a shuttle transfer to Duntroon with Alps 2 Ocean Cycles, based in Weston, near Ōamaru. Around 7km into the ride from Duntroon, you'll get to Elephant Rocks, huge limestone boulders in a farm paddock that featured in the *Chronicles of Narnia* movie. After more limestone oddities and the Rakis Railway Tunnel, the trail jumps on and off the railway line through Windsor, Enfield and Weston, and on to Ōamaru. Ride through Ōamaru's Victorian Precinct, then to the end of the trail at Friendly Bay.

Hāwea River Track

DURATION	DIFFICULTY	DISTANCE
1–2hr one way	Easy	12km one way

This easy riverside trail links Lake Hāwea township to Albert Town and is popular with bikers and walkers. Rent a bike in Wānaka and organise a one-way shuttle back from Lake Hāwea for later. Bike from Wānaka via Beacon Point and the Outlet Track to Albert Town (7km), cross the Clutha River on the Albert Town bridge, then ride the Hāwea River Track for 12km to Lake Hāwea township. On the way, you'll pass the Hāwea Whitewater Park, a 'standing wave' playground for kayak, white-water bodyboarding and surfing enthusiasts. Head into Hāwea Store & Kitchen at the end of your ride for refreshments.

Arriving

Almost all international visitors arrive by aircraft. Most long-haul flights from Asia and North America fly into Auckland, and a few into Christchurch. Queenstown and Wellington airports have direct links with Australia. Only Auckland Airport has a bus/train link into the city centre; the others have efficient bus systems, with shuttles, taxis and ride-shares available. Rental-car outlets are at major airports.

Travelling With a Bike

Only hardcore cyclists turn up in Aotearoa from overseas with their own bike. Preparing a bike for an international or domestic flight requires plenty of commitment. For domestic flights, Air New Zealand requires bikes to be correctly packed in a bike box or bag, subject to oversized items rules.

Kiwis travel around Aotearoa with bike racks on their cars, either off a towbar on the back, or on the roof. If you're spending some time in the country, investing in a bike rack may be a good option. Some rental-car and campervan companies offer a 'Bike Carrier' option, usually on specific vehicles. Each company has different options, so enquire when booking your rental vehicle.

Many city buses have bike racks to carry two or three bikes on the front of the bus, on a first-come, first-served basis. Fullers360 carries bikes for free on its ferries, such as from Auckland to Waiheke Island.

	Auckland	Christchurch	Queenstown
BUS	40 mins $17	30 mins $40	15 mins $10
TAXI	30 mins $40	20 mins $40	15 mins $40
SHUTTLE	30 mins $20	30 mins $20	15 mins $12

CUSTOMS

Be extremely careful filling in your Passenger Arrival Card. New Zealand Customs is very strict, particularly when it comes to food; make a mistake and you'll face an instant $400 fine.

FLIGHTS

The high season for flights into NZ is summer. Flights in December get busy, with Kiwis living overseas heading home to spend the Christmas and New Year holiday period with family and friends.

CASH OR CARD?

It's always good to have a bit of cash, and ATMs are everywhere, but you can pay for virtually anything in Aotearoa by card. Visa and MasterCard are the most widely accepted.

INSURANCE

Accident Compensation Corporation covers everyone, including visitors, who are injured in an accident in Aotearoa; visitors need travel insurance for issues such as illness, baggage and disrupted travel.

Getting Around

BIKING BOOM

Who would have thought that a pandemic would help fuel a cycling boom? When heading overseas was out of the question, many Kiwis who hadn't been on a bike for 10 or 20 years purchased an e-bike to explore their own backyard. Luckily, Aotearoa had been constructing purpose-built, off-road bike trails for the previous decade, believing them to be a good investment for the future. So it proved, and more new bike trails are now under construction.

Air

Kiwis are big on flying around the country. Air New Zealand is the main operator, with Jetstar competing on the main routes connecting Auckland, Wellington, Christchurch and Queenstown. Book early for decent fares. Smaller operators fly regional routes that Air New Zealand doesn't.

Rental Vehicle

This is a country to be explored with rental wheels, be that a car or campervan. One-way rentals are common; many international visitors arrive and pick up a vehicle in Auckland, then return it in Queenstown. Book ahead for peak periods.

Bus

An extensive bus network covers Aotearoa. The biggest operator is InterCity, which has a number of bus-pass options. InterCity and a few other operators also run day tours to popular destinations such as Milford Sound. Smaller operators fill the voids.

Train

Regional passenger-train links are limited. KiwiRail runs the Interislander ferry between the North and South Islands, plus three scenic train journeys: Northern Explorer between Auckland and Wellington, Coastal Pacific between Picton and Christchurch and TranzAlpine (pictured) between Christchurch and Greymouth.

Accommodation

FREEDOM CAMPING

Responsible freedom camping, staying on public land in a tent, campervan or vehicle, with no facilities like toilets or showers, is a popular choice for some visitors to Aotearoa. While it is free of charge, it is not free of responsibility. Campers need to follow basic rules designed to keep the country clean and protect the environment. There are over 500 'responsible freedom camping' locations around Aotearoa. Some cities and towns have banned freedom camping within city limits; obey signage. Check out newzealand.com for details of where you can 'freedom camp'.

HOW MUCH FOR A NIGHT IN...

Room at a country pub
$100

Motel room
$100 to $200

Bunk in a hostel dorm
$40

Cyclist Accommodation

The construction of bike trails around the country, such as the 23 Great Rides (Ngā Haerenga Cycle Trails), has revitalised a number of small communities, bringing in hungry, thirsty, tired bikers in need of a room. Think tired town pubs and hotels that have been upgraded, old school buildings converted to accommodation, farmstays and B&Bs alongside bike trails.

Motels

Even small towns have a motel or two, as many Kiwis travel around their country by car and like to have full kitchen facilities and parking virtually right outside their room. Expect free wi-fi and clean rooms. Bookings can be made via accommodation search engines. Book early for the cheapest rates and for school-holiday periods, when motels fill up fast.

Holiday Parks

An excellent choice if you're camping or touring in a campervan, with options from unpowered tent sites to dorm rooms to family-sized cabins. Most have a communal kitchen, dining room, TV and games room, plus bathroom facilities and plenty of parking. It's good budget accommodation, usually in top locations; prices depend on the option you choose.

Hostels & Backpackers

Budget places with dorm rooms, pods and some private rooms are all over Aotearoa, ranging from YHA Youth Hostels to privately run backpacker operations, some belonging to chains. It's a competitive market out there for the budget traveller, though like everywhere now, prices fluctuate with demand. Book early for busy holiday periods.

AIRBNB & HOME RENTALS

A huge number of Kiwis offer rooms, apartments and homes for short-term rental. They're available all over the country and listed on websites such as airbnb.com, bookabach.co.nz and holidayhouses. co.nz. Prices depend on location, size of rental and facilities, from budget places to luxurious houses in top resorts accommodating multiple families.

Bikes

HOW
MUCH
FOR A
BIKE...

Mountain-bike rental

$60 per day

E-bike rental

$120 per day

One-day bike tour

$150

Bike Rental & Day Tours

The number of bike-rental outlets in Aotearoa is on the rise, thanks to the biking boom. In resort towns like Queenstown and Wānaka, there are a number of stand-alone bike-rental businesses, while in other towns they're often part of a bike shop or a bike-tour operation.

A large number of bike-tour businesses have set up of late, offering rental bikes and one-way or two-way shuttle transport to or from trails for bikers. An example is Better By Bike, based in Arrowtown. They'll rent you a bike, then pick you and

your bike up from any of the wineries at the end of the Gibbston River Trail and transport you back to Arrowtown.

E-Bikes

To many Kiwis, the 'e' stands for 'easy'. Rental e-bikes are everywhere, catering to all sorts, including the 'middle-aged', many of whom haven't been on a bike for years. One issue is...speeding! Those with rental e-bikes, who don't really know how to ride them properly, need to stay in control and follow bike-trail etiquette, especially on shared-use trails.

Rental e-bikes generally come with a charge that will last 60km to 80km when used at prudent boost levels, so more than enough for any of the rides in this book. For multiday hires, the rental outlet will provide you with charging equipment. Accommodation providers on bike trails generally provide e-bike charging facilities for their guests, some at a small cost.

OTHER GEAR

A cycle helmet is compulsory in Aotearoa and is usually included with your bike rental. Depending on where you're going, the bike-rental place may also include spares and tools such as tubes, bike pump and tyre levers. Take a torch, headlamp or bike lights if your ride features any tunnels.

Health & Safe Travel

Biking Safety

Riders should know how to use their bike, know their ability, and prepare for the ride by doing some homework. Stay in control and anticipate other trail users around corners or in blind spots. Most negative feedback from walkers on shared-use tracks relates to being surprised by bikers approaching without warning. Stay left and give way to walkers, runners and horse riders.

Lock It or Lose It

Aotearoa is a relatively safe country, but leaving valuables in a car at a remote biking or hiking trailhead is inviting problems, especially if the valuables are visible. Take passports, wallets, keys and such in your daypack on the ride and if you have to leave anything in your vehicle, try to place it out of sight.

Be Prepared

Aotearoa's weather is extremely changeable, especially in the mountains and at altitude. Check weather forecasts, make sure to take appropriate clothing and use your common sense. Temperatures can plummet in a blink and hypothermia can be a major issue for hikers and bikers, especially if a chilly southerly blows up.

Slip, Slop, Slap

A safety issue that can sneak up on you in Aotearoa is unhealthy sun exposure. Slip, Slop, Slap, as in slipping on a shirt, slopping on sunblock, and slapping on a sunhat, originated as a public-service television jingle in the 1980s, but it's still relevant today. Wear a cap under your bike helmet, and use sunglasses.

BIKE BREAKDOWN

In general, rental-bike outlets will come and help you out if you have trouble with their bike on the trail. Of course, that only works when you are somewhere contactable and accessible. Mobile-phone coverage can be patchy, so you might need to get into a coverage area just to contact them. Ask about phone coverage for your planned route.

Responsible Travel

Climate Change

It's impossible to ignore the impact we have when travelling, and the importance of making changes where we can. Lonely Planet urges all travellers to engage with their travel carbon footprint. There are many carbon calculators online that allow travellers to estimate the carbon emissions generated by their journey; try resurgence.org/resources/carbon-calculator.html. Many airlines and booking sites offer travellers the option of offsetting the impact of greenhouse gas emissions by contributing to climate-friendly initiatives around the world. We continue to offset the carbon footprint of all Lonely Planet staff travel, while recognising this is a mitigation more than a solution.

Department of Conservation

doc.govt.nz
Conserves Aotearoa's natural and historic heritage.

Ministry for the Environment

environment.govt.nz
Help support the environment.

Farmers Markets New Zealand

farmersmarkets.org.nz
Find a market.

REDUCING EMISSIONS

Emissions from cars, buses and other vehicles affect air quality and contribute to climate change. Spend more time on your bike, enjoy an active visit to Aotearoa and reduce emissions, all at the same time!

HELPING WILDLIFE

Take part in wildlife experiences where your participation benefits the wildlife, such as at the Ōamaru Blue Penguin Colony, the National Kiwi Hatchery in Rotorua or Otago Peninsula's Royal Albatross Centre.

SUPPORTING LOCALS

Support and meet locals by going to farmers markets all over Aotearoa; as well as fruit and vegetables, you'll find ready-to-eat local delicacies, arts and handicrafts, coffee trailers and locals 'keen for a yarn'.

Nuts & Bolts

CURRENCY: NEW ZEALAND DOLLAR ($)

Paywave

Kiwis generally pay for everyday purchases by contactless payment, known as PayWave. If your card has a 'wave' symbol, you can use it to 'tap and pay' at most merchants, even for minor purchases such as a cup of coffee. Check the amount shown on the machine before you tap!

Cash

While few Kiwis carry around much cash these days, you can still pay for pretty much everything with cash. ATMs are everywhere, so getting cash should not be a problem. Changing foreign cash is not as easy as it used to be and some banks do not exchange foreign currencies.

ELECTRICITY 230V/50HZ

Type I
230V/50Hz

Tipping Etiquette

Tipping is totally optional in Aotearoa and not required. That said, Kiwis will often tip good service, usually by rounding up a bill. Some restaurants or bars may charge a public-holiday surcharge of 10% to 15% to cover extra wages paid to staff on public holidays.

Tips

Tap Water

Generally good throughout Aotearoa. Bottled water is available, but surprisingly expensive for a country that is not short of water. Do not drink untreated water from streams, rivers or lakes.

Smoking

Not allowed indoors in bars, restaurants, casinos or clubs, on public transport or in indoor workplaces. The government's Smokefree goal is that by 2025 less than 5% of Kiwis will be smokers.

Internet Access

Around 95% of Kiwis are active internet users. Access is good across Aotearoa, except in remote areas. Most accommodation, plus some restaurants, cafes and bars, offer free internet usage to customers.

By Difficulty

Index

Bike Rides 000
Map Pages 000, 000

THE AUTHORS

Craig McLachlan
A keen outdoors guy, Craig has been exploring the world and writing for Lonely Planet since the late 1990s. @yuricraig

Brett Atkinson
From his home in Auckland, Brett writes about craft beer, street food and travelling in emerging destinations. @travelwriternz

Rosie Fea
Rosie is a writer and content creator turned 'corporate-gypsy', and the author of Then, Now, Maybe - a book about mid-20's life lived in the chokehold of perpetual nostalgia. @rosiefea http://rosiefea.com/

Richard Ryall
Richard is a writer on New Zealand's flora and birdlife, working as a guide for cycling, hiking and skiing tours. @richardryall

Eileen Schwab
Eileen takes photos and occasionally writes, mostly about a love of two-wheeled escapades in the mountains @eileenschwabnz

BEHIND THE SCENES

This book was researched and written by Craig McLachlan, Brett Atkinson, Rosie Fea, Richard Ryall and Eileen Schwab. It was produced by the following:

Commissioning Editor Darren O'Connell

Product Editor Joel Cotterell

Book Designer Megan Cassidy

Cartographers Corey Hutchison, Katerina Pavkova, Vojtech Bartos

Cover Design & Researcher Marc Backwell

Assisting Editors Kellie Langdon, Kate Mathews, Anne Mulvaney, Maja Vatrić

Product Development Amy Lynch, Marc Backwell, Katerina Pavkova, Fergal Condon, Ania Bartoszek

Thanks to Karen Henderson, Alison Killilea

ACKNOWLEDGMENTS

Digital Model Elevation Data Contains public sector information licensed under the Open Government Licence v3.0 website http://www.nationalarchives.gov.uk/doc/open-government-licence/version/3/

Cover photograph Cycling along Lake Pukaki, near Aoraki/Mt Cook, TDway/Shutterstock ©